The Great English Short-Story Writers

William J. Dawson
Coningsby W. Dawson

CONTENTS

The Evolution of the Short-Story

I

The short-story commenced its career as a verbal utterance, or, as Robert Louis Stevenson puts it, with "the first men who told their stories round the savage camp-fire."

It bears the mark of its origin, for even to-day it is true that the more it creates the illusion of the speaking-voice, causing the reader to listen and to see, so that he forgets the printed page, the better does it accomplish its literary purpose. It is probably an instinctive appreciation of this fact which has led so many latter-day writers to narrate their short-stories in dialect. In a story which is communicated by the living voice our attention is held primarily not by the excellent deposition of adjectives and poise of style, but by the striding progress of the plot; it is the plot, and action in the plot, alone which we remember when the combination of words which conveyed and made the story real to us has been lost to mind. "Crusoe recoiling from the foot-print, Achilles shouting over against the Trojans, Ulysses bending the great bow, Christian running with his fingers in his ears; these are each culminating moments, and each has been printed on the mind's eye for ever."[1]

The secondary importance of the detailed language in which an incident is narrated, when compared with the total impression made by the naked action contained in the incident, is seen in the case of ballad poetry, where a man may retain a vivid mental picture of the localities, atmosphere, and dramatic moments created by Coleridge's Ancient Mariner, or Rossetti's White Ship, and yet be quite incapable of repeating two consecutive lines of the verse. In literature of narration, whether prose or verse, the dramatic worth of the action related must be the first consideration.

In earlier days, when much of the current fiction was not written down, but travelled from mouth to mouth, as it does in the Orient to-day, this fact must have been realized—that, in the short-story, plot is superior to style. Among modern writers, however, there has been a growing tendency to make up for scantiness of plot by high literary workmanship; the result has been in reality not a short-story, but a descriptive sketch or vignette, dealing chiefly with

---

[1] A Gossip on Romance, from Memories and Portraits, by R.L. Stevenson.

moods and landscapes. So much has this been the case that the writer of a recent Practical Treatise on the Art of the Short-Story has found it necessary to make the bald statement that "the first requisite of a short-story is that the writer have a story to tell."[2]

However lacking the stories which have come down to us from ancient times may be in technique, they invariably narrate action—they have something to tell. If they had not done so, they would not have been interesting to the men who first heard them, and, had they not been interesting, they would not have survived. Their paramount worth in this respect of action is proved by the constant borrowings which modern writers have made from them. Take one case in illustration. In the twenty-eighth chapter of Aristotle's Secretum Secretorum appears a story in which "a queen of India is said to have treacherously sent to Alexander, among other costly presents, the pretended testimonies of friendship, a girl of exquisite beauty, who, having been fed with serpents from her infancy, partook of their nature." It comes to light again, in an altered and expanded form, in the Gesta Romanorum, as the eleventh tale, being entitled Of the Poison of Sin.

"Alexander was a prince of great power, and a disciple of Aristotle, who instructed him in every branch of learning. The Queen of the North, having heard of his proficiency, nourished her daughter from the cradle upon a certain kind of deadly poison; and when she grew up, she was considered so beautiful, that the sight of her alone affected many to madness. The queen sent her to Alexander to espouse. He had no sooner beheld her than he became violently enamoured, and with much eagerness desired to possess her; but Aristotle, observing his weakness, said: 'Do not touch her, for if you do, you will certainly perish. She has been nurtured upon the most deleterious food, which I will prove to you immediately. Here is a malefactor who is already condemned to death. He shall be united to her, and you shall soon see the truth of what I advance.'

"Accordingly the culprit was brought without delay to the girl; and scarcely had he touched her lips, before his whole frame was impregnated with poison, and he expired. Alexander, glad at his escape from such imminent destruction, bestowed all thanks on his instructor, and returned the girl to her mother."

After which follows the monkish application of the moral, as long as the entire story: Alexander being made to stand for a good Christian; the Queen of the North for "a superfluity of the things of life, which sometimes destroys the spirit, and generally the body"; the Poison Maid for luxury and gluttony, "which feed men with

<hr>

[2] Short-Story Writing, by Charles Raymond Barrett.

delicacies that are poison to the soul"; Aristotle for conscience and reason, which reprove and oppose any union which would undo the soul; and the malefactor for the evil man, disobedient unto his God.

There have been at least three writers of English fiction who, borrowing this germ-plot from the Gesta Romanorum, have handled it with distinction and originality. Nathaniel Hawthorne, having changed its period and given it an Italian setting, wove about it one of the finest and most imaginative of his short-stories, Rappaccini's Daughter. Oliver Wendell Holmes, with a freshness and vigor all his own, developed out of it his fictional biography of Elsie Venner. And so recent a writer as Mr. Richard Garnett, attracted by the subtle and magic possibilities of the conception, has given us yet another rendering, restoring to the story its classic setting, in The Poison Maid.[3] Thus, within the space of a hundred years, three master-craftsmen have found their inspiration in the slender anecdote which Aristotle, in the opulence of his genius, was content to hurry into a few sentences and bury beneath the mass of his material.

II

Probably the first stories of mankind were true stories, but the true story is rarely good art. It is perhaps for this reason that few true stories of early times have come down to us. Mr. Cable, in his Strange True Stories of Louisiana, explains the difference between the fabricated tale and the incident as it occurs in life. "The relations and experiences of real men and women," he writes, "rarely fall in such symmetrical order as to make an artistic whole. Until they have had such treatment as we give stone in the quarry or gems in the rough, they seldom group themselves with that harmony of values and brilliant unity of interest that result when art comes in—not so much to transcend nature as to make nature transcend herself." In other words, it is not until the true story has been converted into fiction by the suppression of whatever is discursive or ungainly, and the addition of a stroke of fantasy, that it becomes integral, balanced in all its parts, and worthy of literary remembrance.

In the fragments of fiction which have come down to us from

---

[3] Vide The Twilight of the Gods and Other Tales, published by John Lane, 1903.

3

the days when books were not, odd chapters from the Fieldings and Smollets of the age of Noah, remnants of the verbal libraries which men repeated one to the other, squatting round "the savage camp-fire," when the hunt was over and night had gathered, the stroke of fantasy predominates and tends to comprise the whole. Men spun their fictions from the materials with which their minds were stored, much as we do to-day, and the result was a cycle of beast-fables—an Odyssey of the brute creation. Of these the tales of Aesop are the best examples. The beast-fable has never quite gone out of fashion, and never will so long as men retain their world-wonder, and childishness of mind. A large part of Gulliver's adventures belong to this class of literature. It was only the other day that Mr. Kipling gave us his Just-so Stories, and his Jungle-Book, each of which found an immediate and secure place in the popular memory.

Mr. Chandler Harris, in his introduction to Uncle Remus, warns us that however humorous his book may appear, "its intention is perfectly serious." He goes on to insist on its historic value, as a revelation of primitive modes of thought. At the outset, when he wrote his stories serially for publication in The Atlanta Constitution, he believed that he was narrating plantation legends peculiar to the South. He was quickly undeceived. Prof. J.W. Powell, who was engaged in an investigation of the mythology of the North American Indians, informed him that some of Uncle Remus's stories appear "in a number of different languages, and in various modified forms among the Indians." Mr. Herbert H. Smith had "met with some of these stories among tribes of South American Indians, and one in particular he had traced to India, and as far east as Siam." "When did the negro or North American Indian ever come in contact with the tribes of South America?" Mr. Harris asks. And he quotes Mr. Smith's reply in answer to the question: "I am not prepared to form a theory about these stories. There can be no doubt that some of them, found among the negroes and the Indians, had a common origin. The most natural solution would be to suppose that they originated in Africa, and were carried to South America by the negro slaves. They are certainly found among the Red Negroes; but, unfortunately for the African theory, it is equally certain that they are told by savage Indians of the Amazon's Valley, away up on the Tapajos, Red Negro, and Tapura. These Indians hardly ever see a negro.... It is interesting to find a story from Upper Egypt (that of the fox who pretended to be dead) identical with an Amazonian story, and strongly resembling one found by you among the negroes.... One thing is certain. The animal stories told by the negroes in our Southern States and in Brazil were brought by them from Africa. Whether they originated there, or with the Arabs, or

Egyptians, or with yet more ancient nations, must still be an open question. Whether the Indians got them from the negroes or from some earlier source is equally uncertain." Whatever be the final solution to this problem, enough has been said to show that the beast-fable is, in all probability, the most primitive form of short-story which we possess.

III

For our purpose, that of tracing the evolution of the English short-story, its history commences with the Gesta Romanorum. At the authorship of this collection of mediaeval tales, many guesses have been made. Nothing is known with certainty; it seems probable, however, judging from the idioms which occur, that it took its present form in England, about the end of the thirteenth or the beginning of the fourteenth century, and thence passed to the Continent. The work is written in Latin, and was evidently compiled by a man in holy orders, for its guiding purpose is to edify. In this we can trace the influence of Aesop's beast-fables, which were moral lessons drawn from the animal creation for the instruction of mankind. Every chapter of the Gesta Romanorum consists of a moral tale; so much so that in many cases the application of the moral is as long as the tale itself.

The title of the collection, The Deeds of the Romans, is scarcely justified; in the main it is a garnering of all the deathless plots and dramatic motives which we find scattered up and down the ages, in the legend and folklore of whatsoever nation. The themes of many of its stories were being told, their characters passing under other names, when Romulus and Remus were suckled by their wolf-mother, before there was a Roman nation or a city named Rome.

In the Bible we have many admirable specimens of the short-story. Jotham's parable of the trees of the wood choosing a king is as good an instance of the nature-fable, touched with fine irony and humor, as could be found. The Hebrew prophet himself was often a story-teller. Thus, when Nathan would bring home the nature of his guilt to David, he does it by a story of the most dramatic character, which loses nothing, and indeed gains all its terrific impact, by being strongly impregnated with moral passion. Many such instances will occur to the student of the Bible. In the absence of a written or printed literature the story-teller had a distinct vocation, as he still has among the peoples of the East. Every visitor to

Tangier has seen in the market-place the professional story-teller, surrounded from morn till night with his groups of attentive listeners, whose kindling eyes, whose faces moved by every emotion of wonder, anger, tenderness, and sympathy, whose murmured applause and absorbed silence, are the witnesses and the reward of his art. Through such a scene we recover the atmosphere of the Arabian Nights, and indeed look back into almost limitless antiquity. Possibly, could we follow the story which is thus related, we might discover that this also drew its elemental incidents from sources as old as the times of Jotham and Nathan.

The most that can be said for the Latin origin of the Gesta Romanorum is that the nucleus is made up of extracts, frequently of glaring inaccuracy, from Roman writers and historians. The Cologne edition comprises one hundred and eighty-one chapters, each consisting of a tale or anecdote followed by a moral application, commencing formally with the words, "My beloved, the prince is intended to represent any good Christian," or, "My beloved, the emperor is Christ; the soldier is any sinner." They are not so much short-stories as illustrated homilies. In the literary armory of the lazy parish priest of the fourteenth century, the Gesta Romanorum must have held the place which volumes of sermon-outlines occupy upon the book-shelves of certain of his brethren to-day.

"The method of instructing by fables is a practice of remote antiquity; and has always been attended with very considerable benefit. Its great popularity encouraged the monks to adopt this medium, not only for the sake of illustrating their discourses, but of making a more durable impression upon the minds of their illiterate auditors. An abstract argument, or logical deduction (had they been capable of supplying it), would operate but faintly upon intellects rendered even more obtuse by the rude nature of their customary employments; while, on the other hand, an apposite story would arouse attention and stimulate that blind and unenquiring devotion which is so remarkably characteristic of the Middle Ages."[4]

---

4 Introduction to Gesta Romanorum, translated by the Rev. Charles Swan, revised and corrected by Wynnard Hooper, B.A.

IV

The influence of the Gesta Romanorum is most conspicuously to be traced in the work of Gower, Chaucer, and Lydgate; but it has served as a source of inspiration to the flagging ingenuity of each succeeding generation. It would be tedious to enter on an enumeration of the various indebtednesses of English literature to these early tales. A few instances will serve as illustration.

It seems a far cry from the The Ingoldsby Legends to The Deeds of the Romans, nevertheless The Leech of Folk-stone was directly taken from the hundred and second tale, Of the Transgressions and Wounds of the Soul. Shakespeare himself was a frequent borrower, and planned his entire play of Pericles, Prince of Tyre, upon the hundred and fifty-third tale, Of Temporal Tribulation. In some cases the language is almost identical, as for instance in the fifth tale, where the king warns his son, saying, "Son, I tell thee that thou canst not confide in her, and consequently ought not to espouse her. She deceived her own father when she liberated thee from prison; for this did her father lose the price of thy ransom." Compare with this:

> "Look to her, Moor; have a quick eye to see; She has deceived her
> father, and may thee."[5]

But the ethical treatment of the short-story, as exemplified in these monkish fables, handicapped its progress and circumscribed its field of endeavor. Morality necessitated the twisting of incidents, so that they might harmonize with the sermonic summing-up that was in view. Life is not always moral; it is more often perplexing, boisterous, unjust, and flippant. The wicked dwell in prosperity. "There are no pangs in their death; their strength is firm. They are not in trouble as other men; neither are they plagued as other men. They have more than heart could wish." But the art of the teller of tales "is occupied, and bound to be occupied not so much in making stories true as in making them typical."[6]

The ethical method of handling fiction falls between two stools; it not only fails in portraying that which is true for the individual, but it incurs the graver error of ceasing to be true to the race, i.e., typical.

---

[5] Othello, act I, scene III.

[6] From a Humble Remonstrance, in Memories and Portraits, by R.L. Stevenson.

It would be interesting, had we space, to follow Shakespeare in his borrowings, noticing what he adopts and incorporates in his work as artistically true, and what he rejects. Like a water-color landscape-painter, he pauses above the box of crude materials which others have made, takes a dab here and a dab there with his brush, rarely takes all of one color, blends them, eyes the result judicially, and flashes in the combination with swiftness and certainty of touch.

For instance, from the lengthy story which appears as the hundred and first tale in Mr. Douce's edition of the Gesta, he selects but one scene of action, yet it is the making of Macbeth—one would almost suppose that this was the germ-thought which kindled his furious fancy, preceding his discovery of the Macbeth tradition as related in Holinshed's Chronicle.[7]

The Emperor Manelay has set forth to the Holy Land, leaving his empress and kingdom in his brother's care. No sooner has he gone than the regent commences to make love to his brother's wife. She rejects him scornfully. Angered by her indignation, he leads her into a forest and hangs her by the hair upon a tree, leaving her there to starve. As good-fortune will have it, on the third day a noble earl comes by, and, finding her in that condition, releases her, takes her home with him, and makes her governess to his only daughter. A feeling of shame causes her to conceal her noble rank, and so it comes about that the earl's steward aspires to her affection. Her steadfast refusal of all his advances turns his love to hatred, so that he plans to bring about her downfall. Then comes the passage which Shakespeare seized upon as vital: "It befell upon a night that the earl's chamber door was forgotten and left unshut, which the steward had anon perceived; and when they were all asleep he went and espied the light of the lamp where the empress and the young maid lay together, and with that he drew out his knife and cut the throat of the earl's daughter and put the knife into the empress's hand, she being asleep, and nothing knowing thereof, to the intent that when the earl awakened he should think that she had cut his daughter's throat, and so would she be put to a shameful death for his mischievous deed."

The laws of immediateness and concentration, which govern the short-story, are common also to the drama; by reason of their brevity both demand a directness of approach which leads up, without break of sequence or any waste of words, through a dependent series of actions to a climax which is final. It will usually be found in studying the borrowings which the masters have made

---

⁷ The Chronicle of England and Scotland, first published in 1577.

from such sources as the Gesta Romanorum that the portions which they have discriminated as worth taking from any one tale have been the only artistically essential elements which the narrative contains; the remainder, which they have rejected, is either untrue to art or unnecessary to the plot's development.

These tales, as told by their monkish compiler, lack "that harmony of values and brilliant unity of interest that results when art comes in"—they are splendid jewels badly cut.

V

As has been already stated, a short-story theme, however fine, can only be converted into good art by the suppression of whatever is discursive or ungainly, so that it becomes integral and balanced in all its parts; and by the addition of a stroke of fantasy, so that it becomes vast, despite its brevity, implying a wider horizon than it actually describes; but, in excess of these qualities, there is a last of still greater importance, without which it fails—the power to create the impression of having been possible.

Now the beast-fable, as handled by Aesop, falls short of being high art by reason of its overwhelming fantasy, which annihilates all chance of its possibility. The best short-stories represent a struggle between fantasy and fact. And the mediaeval monkish tale fails by reason of the discursiveness and huddling together of incidents, without regard to their dramatic values, which the moral application necessitates. In a word, both are deficient in technique— the concealed art which, when it has combined its materials so that they may accomplish their most impressive effect, causes the total result to command our credulity because it seems typical of human experience.

The technique of the English prose short-story had a tardy evolution. That there were any definite laws, such as obtain in poetry, by which it must abide was not generally realized until Edgar Allan Poe formulated them in his criticism of Nathaniel Hawthorne.

As he states them, they are five in number, as follows: Firstly, that the short-story must be short, i.e., capable of being read at one sitting, in order that it may gain "the immense force derivable from totality." Secondly, that the short-story must possess immediateness; it should aim at a single or unique effect—"if the very initial sentence tend not to the outbringing of this effect, then it

9

has failed in its first step." Thirdly, that the short-story must be subjected to compression; "in the whole composition there should not be one word written of which the tendency, direct or indirect, is not to the one pre-established design." Fourthly, that it must assume the aspect of verisimilitude; "truth is often, and in very great degree, the aim of the tale—some of the finest tales are tales of ratiocination." Fifthly, that it must give the impression of finality; the story, and the interest in the characters which it introduces, must begin with the opening sentence and end with the last.

These laws, and the technique which they formulate, were first discovered and worked out for the short-story in the medium of poetry.[8] The ballad and narrative poem must be, by reason of their highly artificial form, comparatively short, possessing totality, immediateness, compression, verisimilitude, and finality. The old ballad which commemorates the battle of Otterbourne, fought on August 10, 1388, is a fine example of the short-story method. Its opening stanza speaks the last word in immediateness of narration:

> "It felle abowght the Lamasse tyde,
> When husbands wynn ther haye,
> The dowghtye Dowglasse bowynd hym to ryde
> In England to take a praye."

Thomas Hood's poem of The Dream of Eugene Aram, written at a time when the prose short-story, under the guidance of Hawthorne and Poe, was just beginning to take its place as a separate species of literary art, has never been surpassed for short-story technique by any of the practitioners of prose. Prof. Brander Matthews has pointed out that "there were nine muses in Greece of

---

[8] Poe himself implies this when he says, in an earlier passage of his essay on Hawthorne: "The Tale Proper" (i.e., short-story), "in my opinion, affords unquestionably the fairest field for the exercise of the loftiest talent which can be afforded by the wide domains of mere prose. Were I bidden to say how the highest genius could be most advantageously employed for the best display of its own powers, I should answer, without hesitation, in the composition of a rhymed poem, not to exceed in length what might be perused in an hour. Within this limit alone can the highest order of true poetry exist. I need only here say, upon this topic, that in almost all classes of composition the unity of effect or impression is a point of the greatest importance. It is clear, moreover, that this unity cannot be thoroughly preserved in productions whose perusal cannot be completed at one sitting."

old, and no one of these daughters of Apollo was expected to inspire the writer of prose-fiction."[9]

He argues from this that "prose seemed to the Greeks, and even to the Latins who followed in their footsteps, as fit only for pedestrian purposes." It is more probable that, as regards prose-fiction, they did not realize that they were called upon to explain the omission of the tenth muse. Her exclusion was based on no reasoned principle, but was due to a sensuous art-instinct: the Greeks felt that the unnatural limitations of the poetic medium were more in keeping with the unnatural[10] brevity of a story which must be short. The exquisite prose tales which have been handed down to us belong to the age of their decadence as a nation; in their great period their tellers of brief tales unconsciously cast their rendering in the poetic mould.[11] In natures of the highest genius the most arduous is instinctively the favorite task.

Chaucer, by reason of his intimate acquaintance with both the poetry and prose-fiction of Boccaccio, had the opportunity to choose between these two mediums of short-story narration; and he chose the former. He was as familiar with Boccaccio's poetic method, as exemplified in the Teseide, as with his prose, as exemplified at much greater length in the Decameron, for he borrowed from them both. Yet in only two instances in the Canterbury Tales does he relapse into prose.

The Teseide in Chaucer's hands, retaining its poetic medium, is converted into the Knight's Tale; while the Reeve's Tale, the Franklin's, and the Shipman's, each borrowed from the prose version of the Decameron, are given by him a poetic setting. This preference for poetry over prose as a medium for short-story narration cannot have been accidental or unreasoned on his part; nor can it be altogether accounted for by the explanation that "he was by nature a poet," for he did experiment with the prose medium to the extent of using it twice. He had the brilliant and innovating

---

[9] In his introduction to Materials and Methods of Fiction, by Clayton Hamilton, published by the Baker & Taylor Co., New York.

[10] "The short-story is artificial, and to a considerable degree unnatural. It could hardly be otherwise, for it takes out of our complex lives a single person or a single incident and treats that as if it were complete in itself. Such isolation is not known to nature."—Page 22 of Short-Story Writing, by Charles Raymond Barrett, published by the Baker & Taylor Co., New York.

[11] For example, the story told by Demodocus of The Illicit Love of Ares for Aphrodite, and the Revenge which Hephaestus Planned—Odyssey, Bk. VIII.

precedent of the Decameron, and yet, while adopting some of its materials, he abandoned its medium. He was given the opportunity of ante-dating the introduction of technique into the English prose short-story by four hundred and fifty years, and he disregarded it almost cavalierly. How is such wilful neglect to be accounted for? Only by his instinctive feeling that the technique, which Boccaccio had applied in the Decameron, belonged by right to the realm of poetry, had been learned in the practising of the poetic art, and could arrive at its highest level of achievement only in that medium.

That in Chaucer's case this choice was justified cannot be disputed; the inferiority of the short-story technique contained in his two prose efforts, when compared with that displayed in the remainder of the Canterbury Tales, is very marked. Take, for instance, the Prioress' Tale and apply to it the five short-story tests established by Poe, as a personal discovery, four and a half centuries later; it survives them all. It attains, in addition, the crowning glory, coveted by Stevenson, of appearing typical. There may never have been a Christian child who was martyred by the Jews in the particularly gruesome way described—probably there never was; but, in listening to the Prioress, it does not enter into our heads to doubt her word—the picture which she leaves with us of how the Christian regarded the Jew in the Middle Ages is too vivid to allow any breathing-space for incredulity. No knowledge of mediaeval anti-Jewish legislation, however scholarly, can bring us to realize the fury of race-hatred which then existed more keenly than this story of a little over two thousand words. By its perusal we gain an illuminating insight into that ill-directed religious enthusiasm which led men on frenzied quests for the destruction of the heretic in their own land and of the Saracen abroad, causing them to become at one and the same time unjust and heroic. In a word, within the compass of three hundred lines of verse, Chaucer contrives to body forth his age—to give us something which is typical.

The Morte D'Arthur of Malory is again a collection of traditional stories, as is the Gesta Romanorum, and not the creative work of a single intellect. As might be expected, it straggles, and overlays its climax with a too-lavish abundance of incidents; it lacks the harmony of values which results from the introduction of a unifying purpose—i.e., of art. Imaginative and full of action though the books of the Morte D'Arthur are, it remained for the latter-day artist to exhaust their individual incidents of their full dramatic possibilities. From the eyes of the majority of modern men the brilliant quality of their magic was concealed, until it had been disciplined and refashioned by the severe technique of the short-story.

By the eighteenth century the influence of Malory was scarcely felt at all; but his imaginativeness, as interpreted by Tennyson, in The Idylls of the King, and by William Morris, in his Defence of Guinevere, has given to the Anglo-Saxon world a new romantic background for its thoughts. The Idylls of the King are not Tennyson's most successful interpretation. The finest example of his superior short-story craftsmanship is seen in the triumphant use which he makes of the theme contained in The Book of Elaine, in his poem of The Lady of Shalott. Not only has he remodelled and added fantasy to the story, but he has threaded it through with atmosphere—an entirely modern attribute, of which more must be said hereafter.

So much for our contention that the laws and technique of the prose short-story, as formulated by Poe, were first instinctively discovered and worked out in the medium of poetry.

VI

"The Golden Ass of Apuleius is, so to say, a beginning of modern literature. From this brilliant medley of reality and romance, of wit and pathos, of fantasy and observation, was born that new art, complex in thought, various in expression, which gives a semblance of frigidity to perfection itself. An indefatigable youthfulness is its distinction."[12]

An indefatigable youthfulness was also the prime distinction of the Elizabethan era's writings and doings; it was fitting that such a period should have witnessed the first translation into the English language of this Benjamin of a classic literature's old age.

Apuleius was an unconventional cosmopolitan in that ancient world which he so vividly portrays; he was a barbarian by birth, a Greek by education, and wrote his book in the Romans' language. In his use of luminous slang for literary purposes he was Rudyard Kipling's prototype.

---

[12] From the introduction, by Charles Whibley, to the Tudor Translations' edition by W.E. Henley, of The Golden Ass of Apuleius, published by David Nutt, London, 1893. All other quotations bearing upon Apuleius are taken from the same source.

"He would twist the vulgar words of every-day into quaint unheard-of meanings, nor did he deny shelter to those loafers and footpads of speech which inspire the grammarian with horror. On every page you encounter a proverb, a catchword, a literary allusion, a flagrant redundancy. One quality only was distasteful to him—the commonplace."

There are other respects in which we can trace Mr. Kipling's likeness: in his youthful precocity—he was twenty-five when he wrote his Metamorphoses; in his daring as an innovator; in his manly stalwartness in dealing with the calamities of life; in his adventurous note of world-wideness and realistic method of handling the improbable and uncanny.

Like all great artists, he was a skilful borrower from the literary achievements of a bygone age; and so successfully does he borrow that we prefer his copy to the original. The germ-idea of Kipling's Finest Story in the World is to be found in Poe's Tale of the Ragged Mountains; Apuleius's germ-plot, of the man who was changed by enchantment into an ass, and could only recover his human shape by eating rose-leaves, was taken either from Lucian or from Lucius of Patrae. In at least three of his interpolations he remarkably foreshadows the prose short-story method, upon which we are wont to pride ourselves as being a unique discovery of the past eight decades: these are Bellepheron's Story; The Story of Cupid and Psyche, one of the most exquisite both in form and matter in any language or age; and the story of The Deceitful Woman and the Tub, which Boccaccio made use of in his Decameron as the second novel for the seventh day.

In the intense and visual quality of the atmosphere with which he pervades his narrative he has no equal among the writers of English prose-fiction until Sir Walter Scott appears. "Apuleius has enveloped his world of marvels in a heavy air of witchery and romance. You wander with Lucius across the hills and through the dales of Thessaly. With all the delight of a fresh curiosity you approach its far-seen towns. You journey at midnight under the stars, listening in terror for the howling of the wolves or the stealthy ambush. At other whiles you sit in the robbers' cave and hear the ancient legends of Greece retold. The spring comes on, and 'the little birds chirp and sing their steven melodiously.' Secret raids, ravished brides, valiant rescues, the gayest intrigues—these are the diverse matters of this many-colored book."

But as a short-story writer he shares the failing of all his English brothers in that art, until James Hogg, the Ettrick Shepherd, penned his tales—namely, that his short-stories do not stand apart, as things total in themselves, but are woven into a larger narrative by whose proportions they are dwarfed, so that their true completeness is disguised. "He cares not how he loiters by the way; he is always ready to beguile his reader with a Milesian story—one of those quaint and witty interludes which have travelled the world over and become part, not merely of every literature, but of every life." It is to three of these chance loiterings of this Kipling of Rome in its decadence that we owe the famous stories alluded to above.

To the Elizabethan period belong the most masterly translations of which the English language is possessed; and this not by virtue of their accuracy and scholarship, but because, to use Doctor Johnson's words, the translator "exhibits his author's thoughts in such a dress as the author would have given them had his language been English." That same "indefatigable youthfulness" which converted courtiers into sailors and despatched them into unknown seas to ransack new worlds, urged men of the pen to seek out and to pillage, with an equal ardor of adventure, the intellectual wealth of their contemporaries in other lands and the buried and forgotten stores of the ancients upon their own neighboring book-shelves. A universal and contagious curiosity was abroad. To this age belong William Paynter's version of the Decameron, entitled The Palace of Pleasure, 1566, from which Shakespeare borrowed; Geoffrey Fenton's translation of Bandello's Tragical Discourses, 1567; Sir Thomas North's rendering of Plutarch's Lives, 1579; Thomas Underdowne's Heliodorus, 1587; Thomas Shelton's Don Quixote, 1612; and others too numerous to mention. It seems extraordinary at first sight that when such models of advanced technique were set before them, Englishmen were so slow to follow; for though Professor Baldwin is probably correct in his analysis of the Decameron when he states that, of the hundred tales, over fifty are not much more than anecdotes, about forty are but outlined plots, three follow the modern short-story method only part way, and, of the hundred, two[13] alone are perfect examples, yet those two perfect examples remained and were capable of imitation. The explanation of this neglect is, perhaps, that the Elizabethans were too busy originating to find time for copying; they were very willing to borrow ideas, but must be allowed to develop them in their own way—usually along dramatic lines for stage purposes, because this was at that time the most financially profitable.

---

[13] The second novel of the second day, and the sixth of the ninth day.

VII

The blighting influence of constitutional strife and intestine war which followed in the Stuarts' reigns turned the serious artist's thoughts aside to grave and prophetic forms of literary utterance, while writers of the frivolous sort devoted their talent to a lighter and less sincere art than that of the short-story—namely, court-poetry. It was an age of extremes which bred despair and religious fervor in men of the Puritan party, as represented by Bunyan and Milton, and conscious artificiality and mock heroics in those of the Cavalier faction, as represented by Herrick and the Earl of Rochester.

The examples of semi-fictional prose which can be gathered from this period serve only to illustrate how the short-story instinct, though stifled, was still present. Isaak Walton as a diarist had it; Thomas Fuller as an historian had it; John Bunyan as an ethical writer had it. Each one was possessed of the short-story faculty, but only manifested it, as it were, by accident. Not until Daniel Defoe and the rise of the newspaper do we note any advance in technique. Defoe's main contribution was the short-story essay, which stands midway between the anecdote, or germ-plot, buried in a mass of extraneous material, and the short-story proper. The growth of this form, as developed by Swift, Steel, Addison, Goldsmith, and Lamb, has been traced and criticised elsewhere.[14] It had this one great advantage that, whatever its departures from the strict technique of the modern short-story, it was capable of being read at one sitting, stood by itself, and gained "the immense force derivable from totality."

In the True Revelation of the Apparition of One Mrs. Veal, Defoe is again strangely in advance of his time, as he is in so many other ways. Here is an almost perfect example of the most modern method of handling a ghost-tale. Surely, in whatever department of literature we seek, we shall find nothing to surpass it in the quality of verisimilitude. The way in which Drelincourt's Book on Death is introduced and subsequently twice referred to is a master-stroke of genius. In days gone by, before they were parted, we are told, Mrs. Veal and Mrs. Bargrave "would often console each other's adverse fortunes, and read together Drelincourt On Death and other good books." At the time when the story opens Mrs. Bargrave has gone to live in Canterbury, and Mrs. Veal is in Dover. To Mrs. Bargrave in

---

[14] In the third chapter of The Great English Essayists, vol. iii of The Reader's Library, published by Messrs. Harper & Brothers, 1909.

Canterbury the apparition appears, though she does not know that it is an apparition, for there is nothing to denote that it is not her old friend still alive. One of the first things the apparition does is "to remind Mrs. Bargrave of the many friendly offices she did her in former days, and much of the conversation they had with each other in the times of their adversity; what books they read, and what comfort in particular they received from Drelincourt's Book on Death. Drelincourt, she said, had the clearest notions of death and of the future state of any who had handled that subject. Then she asked Mrs. Bargrave whether she had Drelincourt. She said, 'Yes,' Says Mrs. Veal, 'Fetch it.' Some days after, when Mrs. Bargrave, having discovered that the visitor was a ghost, has gone about telling her neighbors, Defoe observes, 'Drelincourt's Book on Death is, since this happened, bought up strangely,'"

This masterpiece of Defoe is before its time by a hundred years; nothing can be found in the realm of the English prose short-story to approach it in symmetry until the Ettrick Shepherd commenced to write.

Of all the models of prose-fiction which the Tudor translations had given to English literature, the first to be copied was that of Cervantes's Don Quixote, rendered into English by Thomas Shelton in 1612. Swift must have had the rambling method of Cervantes well in mind when he wrote his Gulliver; and Smollett confessedly took it as his pattern and set out to imitate. The most that was required by such a method in the way of initial construction was to select a hero, give some account of his early history, from the day of his birth up to the point where the true narrative commences, and then send him upon his travels. Usually it was thought necessary to have a Sancho to act as background to Don Quixote; thus Crusoe is given his Man Friday, Tom Jones his Mr. Partridge, and Roderick Random his Strap; but this was not always done, for both Gulliver and the hero of the Sentimental Journey set out on their journeyings unaccompanied. The story which grew out of such a method usually consisted of a series of plots, anecdotes, and incidents linked together only by the characters, and governed by no unifying purpose which made each one a necessary and ascending step toward a prearranged climax. These early novels are often books of descriptive travel rather than novels in the modern sense; the sole connection between their first incident and their last being the long road which lies between them, and has been traversed in the continual company of the same leading characters. Many of the chapters, taken apart from their context, are short-story themes badly handled. Some of them are mere interpolations introduced on the flimsiest of excuses, which arrest the progress of the main narrative—i.e., the travel—and give the author an opportunity to use up some spare material which he does not know what to do with. Such are "The Man of the Hill," in Tom Jones; "The History of Melopoyn the Playwright" in Roderick Random; the "Memoirs of a Lady of Quality," occupying fifty-three thousand words, in Peregrine Pickle; "The Philosophic Vagabond," in the Vicar of Wakefield; and "Wandering Willie's Tale," in Redgauntlet. The reason why the eighteenth-century novelist did not know what to do with these materials was, in certain cases, that he had discovered a true short-story theme and was perplexed by it. He knew that it was good—his artist's instinct made him aware of that; but somehow, to his great bewilderment and annoyance, it refused to be expanded. So, in order that it might not be entirely lost to him, he tied the little boat on behind the great schooner of his main narration, and set them afloat together.

By the modern reader, whether of the short-story or the novel, the lack of atmosphere and of immediateness in eighteenth-century prose-fiction is particularly felt. There is no use made of landscapes, moods, and the phenomena of nature; the story happens at almost any season of the year. Of these things and their use the modern short-story writer is meticulously careful. By how much would the worth of Hardy's The Three Strangers be diminished if the description of the March rain driving across the Wessex moorland were left out? Before he commences the story contained in A Lodging for the Night, Stevenson occupies three hundred words in painting the picture of Paris under snow. In the same way, in his story of The Man Who Would Be King, Kipling is at great pains to make us burn with the scorching heat which, in the popular mind, is associated with India. For such effects you will search the prose-fiction of the eighteenth century in vain; whereas the use of atmosphere has been carried to such extremes to-day by certain writers that the short-story in their hands is in danger of becoming all atmosphere and no story.

The impression created by the old technique, such as it was, when contrasted with the new, when legitimately handled, is the difference between reading a play and seeing it staged.

As regards immediateness of narration, Laurence Sterne may, perhaps, be pointed out as an example. But he is not immediate in the true sense; he is abrupt, and this too frequently for his own sly purposes—which have nothing to do with either technique or the short-story.

Most of the English short-stories, previous to those written by James Hogg, are either prefaced with a biography of their main characters or else the biography is made to do service as though it were a plot—nothing is left to the imagination. Even in the next century, when the short-story had come to be recognized in America, through the example set by Hawthorne and Poe, as a distinct species of literary art, the productions of British writers were too often nothing more than compressed novels. In fact, it is true to say that there is more of short-story technique in the short-story essays of Goldsmith and Lamb than can be found in many of the brief tales of Dickens and Anthony Trollope, which in their day passed muster unchallenged as short-stories.

VIII

But between the irrelevant brief story, interpolated in a larger narrative, and the perfect short-story, which could not be expanded and is total in itself, of Hawthorne and Poe, there stands the work of a man who is little known in America, and by no means popular in England, that of the Ettrick Shepherd, James Hogg. He was born in Scotland, among the mountains of Ettrick and Yarrow, the son of a shepherd. When he was but six years old he commenced to earn his living as a cowherd, and by his seventh year had received all the schooling which he was destined to have—two separate periods of three months. Matthew Arnold, when accounting for the sterility of Gray as a poet, says that throughout the first nine decades of the eighteenth century, until the French Revolution roused men to generosity, "a spiritual east wind was blowing." Hogg's early ignorance of letters had at least this advantage, that it saved him from the blighting intellectual influences of his age—left him unsophisticated, free to find in all things matter for wonder, and to work out his mental processes unprejudiced by a restraining knowledge of other men's past achievements. In his eighteenth year he taught himself to read, choosing as his text-books Henry the Minstrel's Life and Adventures of Sir William Wallace and the Gentle Shepherd of Allan Ramsay. Not until his twenty-sixth year did he acquire the art of penmanship, which he learned "upon the hillside by copying the Italian alphabet, using his knee as his desk, and having the ink-bottle suspended from his button." During the next fourteen years he followed his shepherd's calling, making it romantic with sundry more or less successful attempts at authorship. He had reached his fortieth year before he abandoned sheep-raising and journeyed to Edinburgh, there definitely to adopt the literary career. He was by this time firm in his philosophy of life and established in his modes of thought; whatever else he might not be, among townsmen and persons of artificial training, his very simplicity was sure to make him original. In his forty-seventh year, having so far cast his most important work into the poetic form, he contributed to Blackwood's Magazine his Shepherd's Calendar, followed in the same year by the publishing of The Brownie of Bodsbeck; these were his first two serious excursions into the realm of prose-fiction. From then on until his death, in 1835, he continued his efforts in this direction, pouring out a mass of country-side tradition and fairy-folklore, amazing in its fantasy and wealth of drama.

For the imparting of atmosphere to his stories, a talent so conspicuously lacking not only in his predecessors, but also in many of his contemporaries, he had a native faculty. The author of Bonny Kilmeny could scarcely fail in this respect, when he turned his attention from poetry to prose. He had lived too close to nature to be able ever to keep the green and silver of woods and rivers far from his thoughts; they were the mirrors in which his fancy saw itself. Professor Wilson, who had known him as a friend, writing of him in Blackwood's after his death, says: "Living for years in solitude, he unconsciously formed friendships with the springs, the brooks, the caves, the hills, and with all the more fleeting and faithless pageantry of the sky, that to him came in place of those human affections from whose indulgence he was debarred by the necessities that kept him aloof from the cottage fire and up among the mists of the mountain-top. The still green beauty of the pastoral hills and vales where he passed his youth inspired him with ever-brooding visions of fairyland, till, as he lay musing in his lonely shieling, the world of fantasy seemed, in the clear depths of his imagination, a lovelier reflection of that of nature, like the hills and heavens more softly shining in the water of his native lake."

His taste is often defective, as is that of Burns on occasions. This is a fault which might be expected in a man of his training; but the vigor and essential worth of the matters which he relates are beyond all question. He did not always know where to begin his short-story, or where to terminate. Some of his tales, if edited with blue-pencil erasures, would be found to contain a nucleus-technique which, though far from perfect, is more than equal to that of Washington Irving, who, like Apuleius, "cared not how he loitered by the way," and very superior to that of most of his immediate successors in the art. His story here included, of The Mysterious

Bride,[15] could scarcely be bettered in its method. To tell it in fewer words would be to obscure it; to tell it at greater length would be to rob it of its mystery and to make it obvious. Moreover, by employing atmosphere he tells it in such a way as to leave the reader with the impression that this occurrence, for all its magic, might not only be possible, but even probable—which achievement is the greatest triumph of the short-story writer's art.

As this history of the evolution of the English short-story commenced with a poet, Chaucer,[16] who wrote all save two of his short-stories in poetry, so it fittingly closes with a poet, the Ettrick Shepherd, who wrote most of his short-stories in prose. It remained for yet another poet, Edgar Allan Poe, who may never have heard the name or have read a line from the writings of James Hogg, to bring to perfection the task on which he had spent his labor.

---

[15] Compare with Kipling's treatment of a similar theme in The Brushwood Boy.

[16] The Gesta Romanorum was written in Latin.

THE APPARITION OF MRS. VEAL

Daniel Defoe (1661-1731)

This thing is so rare in all its circumstances, and on so good authority, that my reading and conversation have not given me anything like it. It is fit to gratify the most ingenious and serious inquirer. Mrs. Bargrave is the person to whom Mrs. Veal appeared after her death; she is my intimate friend, and I can avouch for her reputation for these fifteen or sixteen years, on my own knowledge; and I can confirm the good character she had from her youth to the time of my acquaintance. Though, since this relation, she is calumniated by some people that are friends to the brother of Mrs. Veal who appeared, who think the relation of this appearance to be a reflection, and endeavor what they can to blast Mrs. Bargrave's reputation and to laugh the story out of countenance. But by the circumstances thereof, and the cheerful disposition of Mrs. Bargrave, notwithstanding the ill usage of a very wicked husband, there is not yet the least sign of dejection in her face; nor did I ever hear her let fall a desponding or murmuring expression; nay, not when actually under her husband's barbarity, which I have been a witness to, and several other persons of undoubted reputation.

Now you must know Mrs. Veal was a maiden gentlewoman of about thirty years of age, and for some years past had been troubled with fits, which were perceived coming on her by her going off from her discourse very abruptly to some impertinence. She was maintained by an only brother, and kept his house in Dover. She was a very pious woman, and her brother a very sober man to all appearance; but now he does all he can to null and quash the story. Mrs. Veal was intimately acquainted with Mrs. Bargrave from her childhood. Mrs. Veal's circumstances were then mean; her father did not take care of his children as he ought, so that they were exposed to hardships. And Mrs. Bargrave in those days had as unkind a father, though she wanted neither for food nor clothing; while Mrs. Veal wanted for both, insomuch that she would often say, "Mrs. Bargrave, you are not only the best, but the only friend I have in the world; and no circumstance of life shall ever dissolve my friendship." They would often condole each other's adverse fortunes, and read together Drelincourt upon Death, and other good books; and so, like two Christian friends, they comforted each other under their sorrow.

Some time after, Mr. Veal's friends got him a place in the custom-house at Dover, which occasioned Mrs. Veal, by little and little, to fall off from her intimacy with Mrs. Bargrave, though there was never any such thing as a quarrel; but an indifferency came on by degrees, till at last Mrs. Bargrave had not seen her in two years and a half, though above a twelvemonth of the time Mrs. Bargrave hath been absent from Dover, and this last half-year has been in Canterbury about two months of the time, dwelling in a house of her own.

In this house, on the eighth of September, one thousand seven hundred and five, she was sitting alone in the forenoon, thinking over her unfortunate life, and arguing herself into a due resignation to Providence, though her condition seemed hard: "And," said she, "I have been provided for hitherto, and doubt not but I shall be still, and am well satisfied that my afflictions shall end when it is most fit for me." And then took up her sewing work, which she had no sooner done but she hears a knocking at the door; she went to see who was there, and this proved to be Mrs. Veal, her old friend, who was in a riding-habit. At that moment of time the clock struck twelve at noon.

"Madam," says Mrs. Bargrave, "I am surprised to see you, you have been so long a stranger"; but told her she was glad to see her, and offered to salute her, which Mrs. Veal complied with, till their lips almost touched, and then Mrs. Veal drew her hand across her own eyes, and said, "I am not very well," and so waived it. She told Mrs. Bargrave she was going a journey, and had a great mind to see her first. "But," says Mrs. Bargrave, "how can you take a journey alone? I am amazed at it, because I know you have a fond brother." "Oh," says Mrs. Veal, "I gave my brother the slip, and came away, because I had so great a desire to see you before I took my journey." So Mrs. Bargrave went in with her into another room within the first, and Mrs. Veal sat her down in an elbow-chair, in which Mrs. Bargrave was sitting when she heard Mrs. Veal knock. "Then," says Mrs. Veal, "my dear friend, I am come to renew our old friendship again, and beg your pardon for my breach of it; and if you can forgive me, you are the best of women." "Oh," says Mrs. Bargrave, "do not mention such a thing; I have not had an uneasy thought about it." "What did you think of me?" says Mrs. Veal. Says Mrs. Bargrave, "I thought you were like the rest of the world, and that prosperity had made you forget yourself and me." Then Mrs. Veal reminded Mrs. Bargrave of the many friendly offices she did her in former days, and much of the conversation they had with each other in the times of their adversity; what books they read, and what comfort in particular they received from Drelincourt's Book of Death, which was the best, she said, on the subject ever wrote. She also mentioned Doctor Sherlock, and two Dutch books, which were translated, wrote upon death, and several others. But Drelincourt, she said, had the clearest notions of death and of the future state of any who had handled that subject. Then she asked Mrs. Bargrave whether she had Drelincourt. She said, "Yes." Says Mrs. Veal, "Fetch it." And so Mrs. Bargrave goes up-stairs and brings it down. Says Mrs. Veal, "Dear Mrs. Bargrave, if the eyes of our faith were as open as the eyes of our body, we should see numbers of angels about us for our guard. The notions we have of Heaven now are nothing like what it is, as Drelincourt says; therefore be comforted under your afflictions, and believe that the Almighty has a particular regard to you, and that your afflictions are marks of God's favor; and when they have done the business they are sent for, they shall be removed from you. And believe me, my dear friend, believe what I say to you, one minute of future happiness will infinitely reward you for all your sufferings. For I can never believe" (and claps her hand upon her knee with great earnestness, which, indeed, ran through most of her discourse) "that ever God will suffer you to spend all your days in this afflicted state. But be assured that your afflictions shall leave you, or you them, in a short time." She spake in that pathetical and heavenly manner that Mrs. Bargrave wept several times, she was so deeply affected with it.

Then Mrs. Veal mentioned Doctor Kendrick's Ascetic, at the end of which he gives an account of the lives of the primitive Christians. Their pattern she recommended to our imitation, and said, "Their conversation was not like this of our age. For now," says she, "there is nothing but vain, frothy discourse, which is far different from theirs. Theirs was to edification, and to build one another up in faith, so that they were not as we are, nor are we as they were. But," said she, "we ought to do as they did; there was a hearty friendship among them; but where is it now to be found?" Says Mrs. Bargrave, "It is hard indeed to find a true friend in these days." Says Mrs. Veal, "Mr. Norris has a fine copy of verses, called Friendship in Perfection, which I wonderfully admire. Have you seen the book?" says Mrs. Veal. "No," says Mrs. Bargrave, "but I have the verses of my own writing out." "Have you?" says Mrs. Veal; "then fetch them"; which she did from above stairs, and offered them to Mrs. Veal to read, who refused, and waived the thing, saying, "holding down her head would make it ache"; and then desiring Mrs. Bargrave to read them to her, which she did. As they were admiring Friendship, Mrs. Veal said, "Dear Mrs. Bargrave, I shall love you forever." In these verses there is twice used the word "Elysian." "Ah!" says Mrs. Veal, "these poets have such names for Heaven." She would often draw her hand across her own eyes, and say, "Mrs. Bargrave, do not you think I am mightily impaired by my fits?" "No," says Mrs. Bargrave; "I think you look as well as ever I knew you."

After this discourse, which the apparition put in much finer words than Mrs. Bargrave said she could pretend to, and as much more than she can remember—for it cannot be thought that an hour and three quarters' conversation could all be retained, though the main of it she thinks she does—she said to Mrs. Bargrave she would have her write a letter to her brother, and tell him she would have him give rings to such and such; and that there was a purse of gold in her cabinet, and that she would have two broad pieces given to her cousin Watson.

Talking at this rate, Mrs. Bargrave thought that a fit was coming upon her, and so placed herself on a chair just before her knees, to keep her from falling to the ground, if her fits should occasion it; for the elbow-chair, she thought, would keep her from falling on either side. And to divert Mrs. Veal, as she thought, took hold of her gown-sleeve several times, and commended it. Mrs. Veal told her it was a scoured silk, and newly made up. But, for all this, Mrs. Veal persisted in her request, and told Mrs. Bargrave she must not deny her. And she would have her tell her brother all their conversation when she had the opportunity. "Dear Mrs. Veal," says Mrs. Bargrave, "this seems so impertinent that I cannot tell how to comply with it; and what a mortifying story will our conversation be to a young gentleman. Why," says Mrs. Bargrave, "it is much better, methinks, to do it yourself." "No," says Mrs. Veal; "though it seems impertinent to you now, you will see more reasons for it hereafter." Mrs. Bargrave, then, to satisfy her importunity, was going to fetch a pen and ink, but Mrs. Veal said, "Let it alone now, but do it when I am gone; but you must be sure to do it"; which was one of the last things she enjoined her at parting, and so she promised her.

Then Mrs. Veal asked for Mrs. Bargrave's daughter. She said she was not at home. "But if you have a mind to see her," says Mrs. Bargrave, "I'll send for her." "Do," says Mrs. Veal; on which she left her, and went to a neighbor's to see her; and by the time Mrs. Bargrave was returning, Mrs. Veal was got without the door in the street, in the face of the beast-market, on a Saturday (which is market-day), and stood ready to part as soon as Mrs. Bargrave came to her. She asked her why she was in such haste. She said she must be going, though perhaps she might not go her journey till Monday; and told Mrs. Bargrave she hoped she should see her again at her cousin Watson's before she went whither she was going. Then she said she would take her leave of her, and walked from Mrs. Bargrave, in her view, till a turning interrupted the sight of her, which was three-quarters after one in the afternoon.

Mrs. Veal died the seventh of September, at twelve o'clock at noon, of her fits, and had not above four hours' senses before her death, in which time she received the sacrament. The next day after Mrs. Veal's appearance, being Sunday, Mrs. Bargrave was mightily indisposed with a cold and sore throat, that she could not go out that day; but on Monday morning she sends a person to Captain Watson's to know if Mrs. Veal was there. They wondered at Mrs. Bargrave's inquiry, and sent her word she was not there, nor was expected. At this answer, Mrs. Bargrave told the maid she had certainly mistook the name or made some blunder. And though she was ill, she put on her hood and went herself to Captain Watson's, though she knew none of the family, to see if Mrs. Veal was there or not. They said they wondered at her asking, for that she had not been in town; they were sure, if she had, she would have been there. Says Mrs. Bargrave, "I am sure she was with me on Saturday almost two hours." They said it was impossible, for they must have seen her if she had. In comes Captain Watson, while they were in dispute, and said that Mrs. Veal was certainly dead, and the escutcheons were making. This strangely surprised Mrs. Bargrave, when she sent to the person immediately who had the care of them, and found it true. Then she related the whole story to Captain Watson's family; and what gown she had on, and how striped; and that Mrs. Veal told her that it was scoured. Then Mrs. Watson cried out, "You have seen her indeed, for none knew but Mrs. Veal and myself that the gown was scoured." And Mrs. Watson owned that she described the gown exactly; "for," said she, "I helped her to make it up." This Mrs. Watson blazed all about the town, and avouched the demonstration of truth of Mrs. Bargrave's seeing Mrs. Veal's apparition. And Captain Watson carried two gentlemen immediately to Mrs. Bargrave's house to hear the relation from her own mouth. And when it spread so fast that gentlemen and persons of quality, the judicious and sceptical part of the world, flocked in upon her, it at last became such a task that she was forced to go out of the way; for they were in general extremely satisfied of the truth of the thing, and plainly saw that Mrs. Bargrave was no hypochondriac, for she always appears with such a cheerful air and pleasing mien that she has gained the favor and esteem of all the gentry, and it is thought a great favor if they can but get the relation from her own mouth. I should have told you before that Mrs. Veal told Mrs. Bargrave that her sister and brother-in-law were just come down from London to see her. Says Mrs. Bargrave, "How came you to order matters so strangely?" "It could not be helped," said Mrs. Veal. And her brother and sister did come to see her, and entered the town of Dover just as Mrs. Veal was expiring. Mrs. Bargrave asked her whether she would drink some tea. Says Mrs. Veal, "I do not care if I do; but I'll warrant you this mad fellow"—meaning Mrs. Bargrave's husband—"has broke all your trinkets." "But," says Mrs. Bargrave, "I'll get something to drink in for all that"; but Mrs. Veal waived it, and said, "It is no matter; let it alone"; and so it passed.

All the time I sat with Mrs. Bargrave, which was some hours, she recollected fresh sayings of Mrs. Veal. And one material thing more she told Mrs. Bargrave, that old Mr. Bretton allowed Mrs. Veal ten pounds a year, which was a secret, and unknown to Mrs. Bargrave till Mrs. Veal told her.

Mrs. Bargrave never varies in her story, which puzzles those who doubt of the truth, or are unwilling to believe it. A servant in the neighbor's yard adjoining to Mrs. Bargrave's house heard her talking to somebody an hour of the time Mrs. Veal was with her. Mrs. Bargrave went out to her next neighbor's the very moment she parted with Mrs. Veal, and told her what ravishing conversation she had had with an old friend, and told the whole of it. Drelincourt's Book of Death is, since this happened, bought up strangely. And it is to be observed that, notwithstanding all the trouble and fatigue Mrs. Bargrave has undergone upon this account, she never took the value of a farthing, nor suffered her daughter to take anything of anybody, and therefore can have no interest in telling the story.

But Mr. Veal does what he can to stifle the matter, and said he would see Mrs. Bargrave; but yet it is certain matter of fact that he has been at Captain Watson's since the death of his sister, and yet never went near Mrs. Bargrave; and some of his friends report her to be a liar, and that she knew of Mr. Bretton's ten pounds a year. But the person who pretends to say so has the reputation to be a notorious liar among persons whom I know to be of undoubted credit. Now, Mr. Veal is more of a gentleman than to say she lies, but says a bad husband has crazed her; but she needs only present herself, and it will effectually confute that pretence. Mr. Veal says he asked his sister on her death-bed whether she had a mind to dispose of anything. And she said no. Now the things which Mrs. Veal's apparition would have disposed of were so trifling, and nothing of justice aimed at in the disposal, that the design of it appears to me to be only in order to make Mrs. Bargrave satisfy the world of the reality thereof as to what she had seen and heard, and to secure her reputation among the reasonable and understanding part of mankind. And then, again, Mr. Veal owns that there was a purse of gold; but it was not found in her cabinet, but in a comb-box. This looks improbable; for that Mrs. Watson owned that Mrs. Veal was so very careful of the key of her cabinet that she would trust nobody with it; and if so, no doubt she would not trust her gold out of it.

And Mrs. Veal's often drawing her hands over her eyes, and asking Mrs. Bargrave whether her fits had not impaired her, looks to me as if she did it on purpose to remind Mrs. Bargrave of her fits, to prepare her not to think it strange that she should put her upon writing to her brother, to dispose of rings and gold, which look so much like a dying person's request; and it took accordingly with Mrs. Bargrave as the effect of her fits coming upon her, and was one of the many instances of her wonderful love to her and care of her, that she should not be affrighted, which, indeed, appears in her whole management, particularly in her coming to her in the daytime, waiving the salutation, and when she was alone; and then the manner of her parting, to prevent a second attempt to salute her.

Now, why Mr. Veal should think this relation a reflection—as it is plain he does, by his endeavoring to stifle it—I cannot imagine; because the generality believe her to be a good spirit, her discourse was so heavenly. Her two great errands were, to comfort Mrs. Bargrave in her affliction, and to ask her forgiveness for her breach of friendship, and with a pious discourse to encourage her. So that, after all, to suppose that Mrs. Bargrave could hatch such an invention as this, from Friday noon to Saturday noon—supposing that she knew of Mrs. Veal's death the very first moment—without jumbling circumstances, and without any interest, too, she must be more witty, fortunate, and wicked, too, than any indifferent person, I dare say, will allow. I asked Mrs. Bargrave several times if she was sure she felt the gown. She answered, modestly, "If my senses be to be relied on, I am sure of it." I asked her if she heard a sound when she clapped her hand upon her knee. She said she did not remember she did, but said she appeared to be as much a substance as I did who talked with her. "And I may," said she, "be as soon persuaded that your apparition is talking to me now as that I did not really see her; for I was under no manner of fear, and received her as a friend, and parted with her as such. I would not," says she, "give one farthing to make any one believe it; I have no interest in it; nothing but trouble is entailed upon me for a long time, for aught I know; and, had it not come to light by accident, it would never have been made public." But now she says she will make her own private use of it, and keep herself out of the way as much as she can; and so she has done since. She says she had a gentleman who came thirty miles to her to hear the relation; and that she had told it to a roomful of people at the time. Several particular gentlemen have had the story from Mrs. Bargrave's own mouth.

This thing has very much affected me, and I am as well satisfied as I am of the best-grounded matter of fact. And why we should dispute matter of fact, because we cannot solve things of which we can have no certain or demonstrative notions, seems strange to me; Mrs. Bargrave's authority and sincerity alone would have been undoubted in any other case.

THE MYSTERIOUS BRIDE[17]

James Hogg (1770-1835)

A great number of people nowadays are beginning broadly to insinuate that there are no such things as ghosts, or spiritual beings visible to mortal sight. Even Sir Walter Scott is turned renegade, and, with his stories made up of half-and-half, like Nathaniel Gow's toddy, is trying to throw cold water on the most certain, though most impalpable, phenomena of human nature. The bodies are daft. Heaven mend their wits! Before they had ventured to assert such things, I wish they had been where I have often been; or, in particular, where the Laird of Birkendelly was on St. Lawrence's Eve, in the year 1777, and sundry times subsequent to that.

Be it known, then, to every reader of this relation of facts that happened in my own remembrance that the road from Birkendelly to the great muckle village of Balmawhapple (commonly called the muckle town, in opposition to the little town that stood on the other side of the burn)—that road, I say, lay between two thorn-hedges, so well kept by the Laird's hedger, so close, and so high, that a rabbit could not have escaped from the highway into any of the adjoining fields. Along this road was the Laird riding on the Eve of St. Lawrence, in a careless, indifferent manner, with his hat to one side, and his cane dancing a hornpipe before him. He was, moreover, chanting a song to himself, and I have heard people tell what song it was too. There was once a certain, or rather uncertain, bard, ycleped Robert Burns, who made a number of good songs; but this that the Laird sang was an amorous song of great antiquity, which, like all the said bard's best songs, was sung one hundred and fifty years before he was born. It began thus:

> "I am the Laird of Windy-wa's,
> I cam nae here without a cause,
> An' I hae gotten forty fa's
> In coming o'er the knowe, joe.
> The night it is baith wind and weet;
> The morn it will be snaw and sleet;
> My shoon are frozen to my feet;
> O, rise an' let me in, joe!
> Let me in this ae night," etc.

---

[17] From Tales and Sketches, by the Ettrick Shepherd.

This song was the Laird singing, while, at the same time, he was smudging and laughing at the catastrophe, when, ere ever aware, he beheld, a short way before him, an uncommonly elegant and beautiful girl walking in the same direction with him. "Aye," said the Laird to himself, "here is something very attractive indeed! Where the deuce can she have sprung from? She must have risen out of the earth, for I never saw her till this breath. Well, I declare I have not seen such a female figure—I wish I had such an assignation with her as the Laird of Windy-wa's had with his sweetheart."

As the Laird was half-thinking, half-speaking this to himself, the enchanting creature looked back at him with a motion of intelligence that she knew what he was half-saying, half-thinking, and then vanished over the summit of the rising ground before him, called the Birky Brow. "Aye, go your ways!" said the Laird; "I see by you, you'll not be very hard to overtake. You cannot get off the road, and I'll have a chat with you before you make the Deer's Den."

The Laird jogged on. He did not sing the Laird of Windy-wa's any more, for he felt a stifling about his heart; but he often repeated to himself, "She's a very fine woman!—a very fine woman indeed!— and to be walking here by herself! I cannot comprehend it."

When he reached the summit of the Birky Brow he did not see her, although he had a longer view of the road than before. He thought this very singular, and began to suspect that she wanted to escape him, although apparently rather lingering on him before. "I shall have another look at her, however," thought the Laird, and off he set at a flying trot. No. He came first to one turn, then another. There was nothing of the young lady to be seen. "Unless she take wings and fly away, I shall be up with her," quoth the Laird, and off he set at the full gallop.

In the middle of his career he met with Mr. McMurdie, of Aulton, who hailed him with, "Hilloa, Birkendelly! Where the deuce are you flying at that rate?"

"I was riding after a woman," said the Laird, with great simplicity, reining in his steed.

"Then I am sure no woman on earth can long escape you, unless she be in an air balloon."

"I don't know that. Is she far gone?"

"In which way do you mean?"

"In this."

"Aha-ha-ha! Hee-hee-hee!" nichered McMurdie, misconstruing the Laird's meaning.

"What do you laugh at, my dear sir? Do you know her, then?"

"Ho-ho-ho! Hee-hee-hee! How should I, or how can I, know her, Birkendelly, unless you inform me who she is?"

"Why, that is the very thing I want to know of you. I mean the young lady whom you met just now."

"You are raving, Birkendelly. I met no young lady, nor is there a single person on the road I have come by, while you know that for a mile and a half forward your way she could not get out of it."

"I know that," said the Laird, biting his lip and looking greatly puzzled; "but confound me if I understand this; for I was within speech of her just now on the top of the Birky Brow there, and, when I think of it, she could not have been even thus far as yet. She had on a pure white gauze frock, a small green bonnet and feathers, and a green veil, which, flung back over her left shoulder, hung below her waist, and was altogether such an engaging figure that no man could have passed her on the road without taking some note of her. Are you not making game of me? Did you not really meet with her?"

"On my word of truth and honor, I did not. Come, ride back with me, and we shall meet her still, depend on it. She has given you the go-by on the road. Let us go; I am only to call at the mill about some barley for the distillery, and will return with you to the big town."

Birkendelly returned with his friend. The sun was not yet set, yet M'Murdie could not help observing that the Laird looked thoughtful and confused, and not a word could he speak about anything save this lovely apparition with the white frock and the green veil; and lo! when they reached the top of Birky Brow there was the maiden again before them, and exactly at the same spot where the Laird first saw her before, only walking in the contrary direction.

"Well, this is the most extraordinary thing that I ever knew!" exclaimed the Laird.

"What is it, sir?" said M'Murdie.

"How that young lady could have eluded me," returned the Laird. "See, here she is still!"

"I beg your pardon, sir, I don't see her. Where is she?"

"There, on the other side of the angle; but you are shortsighted. See, there she is ascending the other eminence in her white frock and green veil, as I told you. What a lovely creature!"

"Well, well, we have her fairly before us now, and shall see what she is like at all events," said McMurdie.

Between the Birky Brow and this other slight eminence there is an obtuse angle of the road at the part where it is lowest, and, in passing this, the two friends necessarily lost sight of the object of their curiosity. They pushed on at a quick pace, cleared the low angle—the maiden was not there! They rode full speed to the top of

the eminence from whence a long extent of road was visible before
them—there was no human creature in view. McMurdie laughed
aloud, but the Laird turned pale as death and bit his lip. His friend
asked him good-humoredly why he was so much affected. He said,
because he could not comprehend the meaning of this singular
apparition or illusion, and it troubled him the more as he now
remembered a dream of the same nature which he had, and which
terminated in a dreadful manner.

"Why, man, you are dreaming still," said McMurdie. "But never
mind; it is quite common for men of your complexion to dream of
beautiful maidens with white frocks, and green veils, bonnets,
feathers, and slender waists. It is a lovely image, the creation of your
own sanguine imagination, and you may worship it without any
blame. Were her shoes black or green? And her stockings—did you
note them? The symmetry of the limbs, I am sure you did! Good-
bye; I see you are not disposed to leave the spot. Perhaps she will
appear to you again."

So saying, McMurdie rode on toward the mill, and Birkendelly,
after musing for some time, turned his beast's head slowly round,
and began to move toward the great muckle village.

The Laird's feelings were now in terrible commotion. He was
taken beyond measure with the beauty and elegance of the figure he
had seen, but he remembered, with a mixture of admiration and
horror, that a dream of the same enchanting object had haunted his
slumbers all the days of his life; yet, how singular that he should
never have recollected the circumstance till now! But farther, with
the dream there were connected some painful circumstances which,
though terrible in their issue, he could not recollect so as to form
them into any degree of arrangement.

As he was considering deeply of these things and riding slowly
down the declivity, neither dancing his cane nor singing the Laird of
Windy-wa's, he lifted up his eyes, and there was the girl on the same
spot where he saw her first, walking deliberately up the Birky Brow.
The sun was down, but it was the month of August and a fine
evening, and the Laird, seized with an unconquerable desire to see
and speak with that incomparable creature, could restrain himself
no longer, but shouted out to her to stop till he came up. She
beckoned acquiescence, and slackened her pace into a slow
movement. The Laird turned the corner quickly, but when he had
rounded it the maiden was still there, though on the summit of the
brow. She turned round, and, with an ineffable smile and curtsy,
saluted him, and again moved slowly on. She vanished gradually
beyond the summit, and while the green feathers were still nodding
in view, and so nigh that the Laird could have touched them with a

fishing-rod, he reached the top of the brow himself. There was no living soul there, nor onward, as far as his view reached. He now trembled in every limb, and, without knowing what he did, rode straight on to the big town, not daring well to return and see what he had seen for three several times; and certain he would see it again when the shades of evening were deepening, he deemed it proper and prudent to decline the pursuit of such a phantom any farther.

He alighted at the Queen's Head, called for some brandy and water, quite forgot what was his errand to the great muckle town that afternoon, there being nothing visible to his mental sight but lovely images, with white gauze frocks and green veils. His friend M'Murdie joined him; they drank deep, bantered, reasoned, got angry, reasoned themselves calm again, and still all would not do. The Laird was conscious that he had seen the beautiful apparition, and, moreover, that she was the very maiden, or the resemblance of her, who, in the irrevocable decrees of Providence, was destined to be his. It was in vain that M'Murdie reasoned of impressions on the imagination, and

> "Of fancy moulding in the mind,
> Light visions on the passing wind."

Vain also was a story that he told him of a relation of his own, who was greatly harassed by the apparition of an officer in a red uniform that haunted him day and night, and had very nigh put him quite distracted several times, till at length his physician found out the nature of this illusion so well that he knew, from the state of his pulse, to an hour when the ghost of the officer would appear, and by bleeding, low diet, and emollients contrived to keep the apparition away altogether.

The Laird admitted the singularity of this incident, but not that it was one in point; for the one, he said, was imaginary, the other real, and that no conclusions could convince him in opposition to the authority of his own senses. He accepted of an invitation to spend a few days with M'Murdie and his family, but they all acknowledged afterward that the Laird was very much like one bewitched.

As soon as he reached home he went straight to the Birky Brow, certain of seeing once more the angelic phantom, but she was not there. He took each of his former positions again and again, but the desired vision would in no wise make its appearance. He tried every day and every hour of the day, all with the same effect, till he grew absolutely desperate, and had the audacity to kneel on the spot and entreat of Heaven to see her. Yes, he called on Heaven to see her once more, whatever she was, whether a being of earth, heaven, or hell.

He was now in such a state of excitement that he could not exist; he grew listless, impatient, and sickly, took to his bed, and sent for M'Murdie and the doctor; and the issue of the consultation was that Birkendelly consented to leave the country for a season, on a visit to his only sister in Ireland, whither we must accompany him for a short space.

His sister was married to Captain Bryan, younger, of Scoresby, and they two lived in a cottage on the estate, and the Captain's parents and sisters at Scoresby Hall. Great was the stir and preparation when the gallant young Laird of Birkendelly arrived at the cottage, it never being doubted that he came to forward a second bond of connection with the family, which still contained seven dashing sisters, all unmarried, and all alike willing to change that solitary and helpless state for the envied one of matrimony—a state highly popular among the young women of Ireland. Some of the Misses Bryan had now reached the years of womanhood, several of them scarcely, but these small disqualifications made no difference in the estimation of the young ladies themselves; each and all of them brushed up for the competition with high hopes and unflinching resolutions. True, the elder ones tried to check the younger in their good-natured, forthright Irish way; but they retorted, and persisted in their superior pretensions. Then there was such shopping in the county town! It was so boundless that the credit of the Hall was finally exhausted, and the old Squire was driven to remark that "Och, and to be sure it was a dreadful and tirrabell concussion, to be put upon the equipment of seven daughters all at the same moment, as if the young gentleman could marry them all! Och, then, poor dear shoul, he would be after finding that one was sufficient, if not one too many. And therefore there was no occasion, none at all, at all, and that there was not, for any of them to rig out more than one."

It was hinted that the Laird had some reason for complaint at this time, but as the lady sided with her daughters, he had no chance. One of the items of his account was thirty-seven buckling-combs, then greatly in vogue. There were black combs, pale combs, yellow combs, and gilt ones, all to suit or set off various complexions; and if other articles bore any proportion at all to these, it had been better for the Laird and all his family that Birkendelly had never set foot in Ireland.

The plan was all concocted. There was to be a grand dinner at the Hall, at which the damsels were to appear in all their finery. A ball to follow, and note be taken which of the young ladies was their guest's choice, and measures taken accordingly. The dinner and the ball took place; and what a pity I may not describe that entertainment, the dresses, and the dancers, for they were all exquisite in their way, and outré beyond measure. But such details only serve to derange a winter evening's tale such as this.

Birkendelly having at this time but one model for his choice among womankind, all that ever he did while in the presence of ladies was to look out for some resemblance to her, the angel of his fancy; and it so happened that in one of old Bryan's daughters named Luna, or, more familiarly, Loony, he perceived, or thought he perceived, some imaginary similarity in form and air to the lovely apparition. This was the sole reason why he was incapable of taking his eyes off from her the whole of that night; and this incident settled the point, not only with the old people, but even the young ladies were forced, after every exertion on their own parts, to "yild the p'int to their sister Loony, who certainly was not the mist genteelest nor mist handsomest of that guid-lucking fimily."

The next day Lady Luna was dispatched off to the cottage in grand style, there to live hand in glove with her supposed lover. There was no standing all this. There were the two parrocked together, like a ewe and a lamb, early and late; and though the Laird really appeared to have, and probably had, some delight in her company, it was only in contemplating that certain indefinable air of resemblance which she bore to the sole image impressed on his heart. He bought her a white gauze frock, a green bonnet and feather, with a veil, which she was obliged to wear thrown over her left shoulder, and every day after, six times a day, was she obliged to walk over a certain eminence at a certain distance before her lover. She was delighted to oblige him; but still, when he came up, he looked disappointed, and never said, "Luna, I love you; when are we to be married?" No, he never said any such thing, for all her looks and expressions of fondest love; for, alas! in all this dalliance he was only feeding a mysterious flame that preyed upon his vitals, and proved too severe for the powers either of reason or religion to extinguish. Still, time flew lighter and lighter by, his health was restored, the bloom of his cheek returned, and the frank and simple confidence of Luna had a certain charm with it that reconciled him to his sister's Irish economy. But a strange incident now happened to him which deranged all his immediate plans.

He was returning from angling one evening, a little before sunset, when he saw Lady Luna awaiting him on his way home. But instead of brushing up to meet him as usual, she turned, and walked up the rising ground before him. "Poor sweet girl! how condescending she is," said he to himself, "and how like she is in reality to the angelic being whose form and features are so deeply impressed on my heart! I now see it is no fond or fancied resemblance. It is real! real! real! How I long to clasp her in my arms, and tell her how I love her; for, after all, that is the girl that is to be mine, and the former a vision to impress this the more on my heart."

He posted up the ascent to overtake her. When at the top she turned, smiled, and curtsied. Good heavens! it was the identical lady of his fondest adoration herself, but lovelier, far lovelier, than ever. He expected every moment that she would vanish, as was her wont; but she did not—she awaited him, and received his embraces with open arms. She was a being of real flesh and blood, courteous, elegant, and affectionate. He kissed her hand, he kissed her glowing cheek, and blessed all the powers of love who had thus restored her to him again, after undergoing pangs of love such as man never suffered.

"But, dearest heart, here we are standing in the middle of the highway," said he; "suffer me to conduct you to my sister's house, where you shall have an apartment with a child of nature having some slight resemblance to yourself." She smiled, and said, "No, I will not sleep with Lady Luna to-night. Will you please to look round you, and see where you are." He did so, and behold they were standing on the Birky Brow, on the only spot where he had ever seen her. She smiled at his embarrassed look, and asked if he did not remember aught of his coming over from Ireland. He said he thought he did remember something of it, but love with him had long absorbed every other sense. He then asked her to his own house, which she declined, saying she could only meet him on that spot till after their marriage, which could not be before St. Lawrence's Eve come three years. "And now," said she, "we must part. My name is Jane Ogilvie, and you were betrothed to me before you were born. But I am come to release you this evening, if you have the slightest objection."

He declared he had none; and kneeling, swore the most solemn oath to be hers forever, and to meet her there on St. Lawrence's Eve next, and every St. Lawrence's Eve until that blessed day on which she had consented to make him happy by becoming his own forever. She then asked him affectionately to change rings with her, in pledge of their faith and troth, in which he joyfully acquiesced; for she could not have then asked any conditions which, in the fulness of his heart's love, he would not have granted; and after one fond and affectionate kiss, and repeating all their engagements over again, they parted.

Birkendelly's heart was now melted within him, and all his senses overpowered by one overwhelming passion. On leaving his fair and kind one, he got bewildered, and could not find the road to his own house, believing sometimes that he was going there, and sometimes to his sister's, till at length he came, as he thought, upon the Liffey, at its junction with Loch Allan; and there, in attempting to call for a boat, he awoke from a profound sleep, and found himself lying in his bed within his sister's house, and the day sky just breaking.

If he was puzzled to account for some things in the course of his dream, he was much more puzzled to account for them now that he was wide awake. He was sensible that he had met his love, had embraced, kissed, and exchanged vows and rings with her, and, in token of the truth and reality of all these, her emerald ring was on his finger, and his own away; so there was no doubt that they had met—by what means it was beyond the power of man to calculate.

There was then living with Mrs. Bryan an old Scotswoman, commonly styled Lucky Black. She had nursed Birkendelly's mother, and been dry-nurse to himself and sister; and having more than a mother's attachment for the latter, when she was married, old Lucky left her country to spend the last of her days in the house of her beloved young lady. When the Laird entered the breakfast-parlor that morning she was sitting in her black velvet hood, as usual, reading The Fourfold State of Man, and, being paralytic and somewhat deaf, she seldom regarded those who went or came. But chancing to hear him say something about the 9th of August, she quitted reading, turned round her head to listen, and then asked, in a hoarse, tremulous voice: "What's that he's saying? What's the unlucky callant saying about the 9th of August? Aih? To be sure it is St. Lawrence's Eve, although the 10th be his day. It's ower true, ower true, ower true for him an' a' his kin, poor man! Aih? What was he saying then?"

The men smiled at her incoherent earnestness, but the lady, with true feminine condescension, informed her, in a loud voice, that Allan had an engagement in Scotland on St. Lawrence's Eve. She then started up, extended her shrivelled hands, that shook like the aspen, and panted out: "Aih, aih? Lord preserve us! Whaten an engagement has he on St. Lawrence's Eve? Bind him! bind him! Shackle him wi' bands of steel, and of brass, and of iron! O may He whose blessed will was pleased to leave him an orphan sae soon, preserve him from the fate which I tremble to think on!"

She then tottered round the table, as with supernatural energy, and seizing the Laird's right hand, she drew it close to her unstable eyes, and then perceiving the emerald ring chased in blood, she threw up her arms with a jerk, opened her skinny jaws with a fearful gape, and uttering a shriek that made all the house yell, and every one within it to tremble, she fell back lifeless and rigid on the floor. The gentlemen both fled, out of sheer terror; but a woman never deserts her friends in extremity. The lady called her maids about her, had her old nurse conveyed to bed, where every means were used to restore animation. But, alas, life was extinct! The vital spark had fled forever, which filled all their hearts with grief, disappointment, and horror, as some dreadful tale of mystery was now sealed up from their knowledge which, in all likelihood, no other could reveal. But to say the truth, the Laird did not seem greatly disposed to probe it to the bottom.

Not all the arguments of Captain Bryan and his lady, nor the simple entreaties of Lady Luna, could induce Birkendelly to put off his engagement to meet his love on the Birky Brow on the evening of the 9th of August; but he promised soon to return, pretending that some business of the utmost importance called him away. Before he went, however, he asked his sister if ever she had heard of such a lady in Scotland as Jane Ogilvie. Mrs. Bryan repeated the name many times to herself, and said that name undoubtedly was once familiar to her, although she thought not for good, but at that moment she did not recollect one single individual of the name. He then showed her the emerald ring that had been the death of Lucky Black; but the moment the lady looked at it, she made a grasp at it to take it off by force, which she had very nearly effected. "Oh, burn it! burn it!" cried she; "it is not a right ring! Burn it!"

"My dear sister, what fault is in the ring?" said he. "It is a very pretty ring, and one that I set great value by."

"Oh, for Heaven's sake, burn it, and renounce the giver!" cried she. "If you have any regard for your peace here or your soul's welfare hereafter, burn that ring! If you saw with your own eyes, you would easily perceive that that is not a ring befitting a Christian to wear."

This speech confounded Birkendelly a good deal. He retired by himself and examined the ring, and could see nothing in it unbecoming a Christian to wear. It was a chased gold ring, with a bright emerald, which last had a red foil, in some lights giving it a purple gleam, and inside was engraven "Elegit," much defaced, but that his sister could not see; therefore he could not comprehend her vehement injunctions concerning it. But that it might no more give her offence, or any other, he sewed it within his vest, opposite his heart, judging that there was something in it which his eyes were withholden from discerning.

Thus he left Ireland with his mind in great confusion, groping his way, as it were, in a hole of mystery, yet with the passion that preyed on his heart and vitals more intense than ever. He seems to have had an impression all his life that some mysterious fate awaited him, which the correspondence of his dreams and day visions tended to confirm. And though he gave himself wholly up to the sway of one overpowering passion, it was not without some yearnings of soul, manifestations of terror, and so much earthly shame, that he never more mentioned his love, or his engagements, to any human being, not even to his friend M'Murdie, whose company he forthwith shunned.

It is on this account that I am unable to relate what passed between the lovers thenceforward. It is certain they met at the Birky Brow that St. Lawrence's Eve, for they were seen in company together; but of the engagements, vows, or dalliance that passed between them I can say nothing; nor of all their future meetings, until the beginning of August, 1781, when the Laird began decidedly to make preparations for his approaching marriage; yet not as if he and his betrothed had been to reside at Birkendelly, all his provisions rather bespeaking a meditated journey.

On the morning of the 9th he wrote to his sister, and then arraying himself in his new wedding suit, and putting the emerald ring on his finger, he appeared all impatience, until toward evening, when he sallied out on horseback to his appointment. It seems that his mysterious inamorata had met him, for he was seen riding through the big town before sunset, with a young lady behind him, dressed in white and green, and the villagers affirmed that they were riding at the rate of fifty miles an hour! They were seen to pass a cottage called Mosskilt, ten miles farther on, where there was no highway, at the same tremendous speed; and I could never hear that they were any more seen, until the following morning, when Birkendelly's fine bay horse was found lying dead at his own stable door; and shortly after his master was likewise discovered lying, a blackened corpse, on the Birky Brow at the very spot where the mysterious but lovely dame had always appeared to him. There was neither wound, bruise, nor dislocation in his whole frame; but his skin was of a livid color, and his features terribly distorted.

This woful catastrophe struck the neighborhood with great consternation, so that nothing else was talked of. Every ancient tradition and modern incident were raked together, compared, and combined; and certainly a most rare concatenation of misfortunes was elicited. It was authenticated that his father had died on the same spot that day twenty years, and his grandfather that day forty years, the former, as was supposed, by a fall from his horse when in liquor, and the latter, nobody knew how; and now this Allan was the last of his race, for Mrs. Bryan had no children.

It was, moreover, now remembered by many, and among the rest by the Rev. Joseph Taylor, that he had frequently observed a young lady, in white and green, sauntering about the spot on a St. Lawrence's Eve.

When Captain Bryan and his lady arrived to take possession of the premises, they instituted a strict inquiry into every circumstance; but nothing further than what was related to them by Mr. M'Murdie could be learned of this Mysterious Bride, besides what the Laird's own letter bore. It ran thus:

"DEAREST SISTER,—I shall before this time to-morrow be the most happy, or most miserable, of mankind, having solemnly engaged myself this night to wed a young and beautiful lady, named Jane Ogilvie, to whom it seems I was betrothed before I was born. Our correspondence has been of a most private and mysterious nature; but my troth is pledged, and my resolution fixed. We set out on a far journey to the place of her abode on the nuptial eve, so that it will be long before I see you again. Yours till death,

"ALLAN GEORGE SANDISON.
"BIRKENDELLY, August 8, 1781."

That very same year, an old woman, named Marion Haw, was returned upon that, her native parish, from Glasgow. She had led a migratory life with her son—who was what he called a bell-hanger, but in fact a tinker of the worst grade—for many years, and was at last returned to the muckle town in a state of great destitution. She gave the parishioners a history of the Mysterious Bride, so plausibly correct, but withal so romantic, that everybody said of it (as is often said of my narratives, with the same narrow-minded prejudice and injustice) that it was a made story. There were, however, some strong testimonies of its veracity.

She said the first Allan Sandison, who married the great heiress of Birkendelly, was previously engaged to a beautiful young lady named Jane Ogilvie, to whom he gave anything but fair play; and, as she believed, either murdered her, or caused her to be murdered, in the midst of a thicket of birch and broom, at a spot which she mentioned; and she had good reason for believing so, as she had seen the red blood and the new grave, when she was a little girl, and ran home and mentioned it to her grandfather, who charged her as she valued her life never to mention that again, as it was only the nombles and hide of a deer which he himself had buried there. But when, twenty years subsequent to that, the wicked and unhappy

41

Allan Sandison was found dead on that very spot, and lying across the green mound, then nearly level with the surface, which she had once seen a new grave, she then for the first time ever thought of a Divine Providence; and she added, "For my grandfather, Neddy Haw, he dee'd too; there's naebody kens how, nor ever shall."

As they were quite incapable of conceiving from Marion's description anything of the spot, Mr. M'Murdie caused her to be taken out to the Birky Brow in a cart, accompanied by Mr. Taylor and some hundreds of the town's folks; but whenever she saw it, she said, "Aha, birkies! the haill kintra's altered now. There was nae road here then; it gaed straight ower the tap o' the hill. An' let me see—there's the thorn where the cushats biggit; an' there's the auld birk that I ance fell aff an' left my shoe sticking i' the cleft. I can tell ye, birkies, either the deer's grave or bonny Jane Ogilvie's is no twa yards aff the place where that horse's hind-feet are standin'; sae ye may howk, an' see if there be ony remains."

The minister and M'Murdie and all the people stared at one another, for they had purposely caused the horse to stand still on the very spot where both the father and son had been found dead. They digged, and deep, deep below the road they found part of the slender bones and skull of a young female, which they deposited decently in the church-yard. The family of the Sandisons is extinct, the Mysterious Bride appears no more on the Eve of St. Lawrence, and the wicked people of the great muckle village have got a lesson on divine justice written to them in lines of blood.

THE DEVIL AND TOM WALKER[18]

Washington Irving (1783-1859)

A few miles from Boston, in Massachusetts, there is a deep inlet winding several miles into the interior of the country from Charles Bay, and terminating in a thickly wooded swamp or morass. On one side of this inlet is a beautiful dark grove; on the opposite side the land rises abruptly from the water's edge into a high ridge, on which grow a few scattered oaks of great age and immense size. Under one of these gigantic trees, according to old stories, there was a great amount of treasure buried by Kidd the pirate. The inlet allowed a facility to bring the money in a boat secretly, and at night, to the very foot of the hill; the elevation of the place permitted a good lookout to be kept that no one was at hand; while the remarkable trees formed good landmarks by which the place might easily be found again. The old stories add, moreover, that the devil presided at the hiding of the money, and took it under his guardianship; but this, it is well known, he always does with buried treasure, particularly when it has been ill-gotten. Be that as it may, Kidd never returned to recover his wealth; being shortly after seized at Boston, sent out to England, and there hanged for a pirate.

About the year 1727, just at the time that earthquakes were prevalent in New England, and shook many tall sinners down upon their knees, there lived near this place a meagre, miserly fellow, of the name of Tom Walker. He had a wife as miserly as himself; they were so miserly that they even conspired to cheat each other. Whatever the woman could lay hands on she hid away; a hen could not cackle but she was on the alert to secure the new-laid egg. Her husband was continually prying about to detect her secret hoards, and many and fierce were the conflicts that took place about what ought to have been common property. They lived in a forlorn-looking house that stood alone and had an air of starvation. A few straggling savin-trees, emblems of sterility, grew near it; no smoke ever curled from its chimney; no traveller stopped at its door. A miserable horse, whose ribs were as articulate as the bars of a gridiron, stalked about a field, where a thin carpet of moss, scarcely covering the ragged beds of pudding-stone, tantalized and balked his hunger; and sometimes he would lean his head over the fence,

---

[18] From The Money-diggers.

look piteously at the passer-by, and seem to petition deliverance from this land of famine.

The house and its inmates had altogether a bad name. Tom's wife was a tall termagant, fierce of temper, loud of tongue, and strong of arm. Her voice was often heard in wordy warfare with her husband; and his face sometimes showed signs that their conflicts were not confined to words. No one ventured, however, to interfere between them. The lonely wayfarer shrank within himself at the horrid clamor and clapper-clawing; eyed the den of discord askance; and hurried on his way, rejoicing, if a bachelor, in his celibacy.

One day that Tom Walker had been to a distant part of the neighborhood, he took what he considered a short-cut homeward, through the swamp. Like most short-cuts, it was an ill-chosen route. The swamp was thickly grown with great, gloomy pines and hemlocks, some of them ninety feet high, which made it dark at noonday and a retreat for all the owls of the neighborhood. It was full of pits and quagmires, partly covered with weeds and mosses, where the green surface often betrayed the traveller into a gulf of black, smothering mud; there were also dark and stagnant pools, the abodes of the tadpole, the bull-frog, and the water-snake, where the trunks of pines and hemlocks lay half-drowned, half-rotting, looking like alligators sleeping in the mire.

Tom had long been picking his way cautiously through this treacherous forest, stepping from tuft to tuft of rushes and roots, which afforded precarious footholds among deep sloughs, or pacing carefully, like a cat, along the prostrate trunks of trees, startled now and then by the sudden screaming of the bittern, or the quacking of a wild duck, rising on the wing from some solitary pool. At length he arrived at a firm piece of ground, which ran like a peninsula into the deep bosom of the swamp. It had been one of the strongholds of the Indians during their wars with the first colonists. Here they had thrown up a kind of fort, which they had looked upon as almost impregnable, and had used as a place of refuge for their squaws and children. Nothing remained of the old Indian fort but a few embankments, gradually sinking to the level of the surrounding earth, and already overgrown in part by oaks and other forest trees, the foliage of which formed a contrast to the dark pines and hemlocks of the swamps.

It was late in the dusk of evening when Tom Walker reached the old fort, and he paused there awhile to rest himself. Any one but he would have felt unwilling to linger in this lonely, melancholy place, for the common people had a bad opinion of it, from the stories handed down from the times of the Indian wars, when it was asserted that the savages held incantations here and made sacrifices to the Evil Spirit.

Tom Walker, however, was not a man to be troubled with any fears of the kind. He reposed himself for some time on the trunk of a fallen hemlock, listening to the boding cry of the tree-toad, and delving with his walking-staff into a mound of black mould at his feet. As he turned up the soil unconsciously, his staff struck against something hard. He raked it out of the vegetable mould, and lo! a cloven skull, with an Indian tomahawk buried deep in it, lay before him. The rust on the weapon showed the time that had elapsed since this death-blow had been given. It was a dreary memento of the fierce struggle that had taken place in this last foothold of the Indian warriors.

"Humph!" said Tom Walker, as he gave it a kick to shake the dirt from it.

"Let that skull alone!" said a gruff voice. Tom lifted up his eyes and beheld a great black man seated directly opposite him, on the stump of a tree. He was exceedingly surprised, having neither heard nor seen any one approach; and he was still more perplexed on observing, as well as the gathering gloom would permit, that the stranger was neither negro nor Indian. It is true he was dressed in a rude Indian garb, and had a red belt or sash swathed round his body; but his face was neither black nor copper-color, but swarthy and dingy, and begrimed with soot, as if he had been accustomed to toil among fires and forges. He had a shock of coarse black hair, that stood out from his head in all directions, and bore an axe on his shoulder.

He scowled for a moment at Tom with a pair of great red eyes.

"What are you doing on my grounds?" said the black man, with a hoarse, growling voice.

"Your grounds!" said Tom, with a sneer; "no more your grounds than mine; they belong to Deacon Peabody."

"Deacon Peabody be damned," said the stranger, "as I flatter myself he will be, if he does not look more to his own sins and less to those of his neighbors. Look yonder, and see how Deacon Peabody is faring."

Tom looked in the direction that the stranger pointed, and beheld one of the great trees, fair and flourishing without, but rotten at the core, and saw that it had been nearly hewn through, so that the first high wind was likely to blow it down. On the bark of the tree was scored the name of Deacon Peabody, an eminent man who had waxed wealthy by driving shrewd bargains with the Indians. He now looked around, and found most of the tall trees marked with the name of some great man of the colony, and all more or less scored by the axe. The one on which he had been seated, and which had evidently just been hewn down, bore the name of Crowninshield; and he recollected a mighty rich man of that name, who made a vulgar display of wealth, which it was whispered he had acquired by buccaneering.

"He's just ready for burning!" said the black man, with a growl of triumph. "You see I am likely to have a good stock of firewood for winter."

"But what right have you," said Tom, "to cut down Deacon Peabody's timber?"

"The right of a prior claim," said the other. "This woodland belonged to me long before one of your white-faced race put foot upon the soil."

"And, pray, who are you, if I may be so bold?" said Tom.

"Oh, I go by various names. I am the wild huntsman in some countries; the black miner in others. In this neighborhood I am known by the name of the black woodsman. I am he to whom the red men consecrated this spot, and in honor of whom they now and then roasted a white man, by way of sweet-smelling sacrifice. Since the red men have been exterminated by you white savages, I amuse myself by presiding at the persecutions of Quakers and Anabaptists; I am the great patron and prompter of slave-dealers and the grand-master of the Salem witches."

"The upshot of all which is, that, if I mistake not," said Tom, sturdily, "you are he commonly called Old Scratch."

"The same, at your service!" replied the black man, with a half-civil nod.

Such was the opening of this interview, according to the old story; though it has almost too familiar an air to be credited. One would think that to meet with such a singular personage in this wild, lonely place would have shaken any man's nerves; but Tom was a hard-minded fellow, not easily daunted, and he had lived so long with a termagant wife that he did not even fear the devil.

It is said that after this commencement they had a long and earnest conversation together, as Tom returned homeward. The black man told him of great sums of money buried by Kidd the pirate under the oak-trees on the high ridge, not far from the morass. All these were under his command, and protected by his power, so that none could find them but such as propitiated his favor. These he offered to place within Tom Walker's reach, having conceived an especial kindness for him; but they were to be had only on certain conditions. What these conditions were may be easily surmised, though Tom never disclosed them publicly. They must have been very hard, for he required time to think of them, and he was not a man to stick at trifles when money was in view. When they had reached the edge of the swamp, the stranger paused. "What proof have I that all you have been telling me is true?" said Tom. "There's my signature," said the black man, pressing his finger on Tom's forehead. So saying, he turned off among the thickets of the swamp, and seemed, as Tom said, to go down, down, down, into the earth, until nothing but his head and shoulders could be seen, and so on, until he totally disappeared.

When Tom reached home he found the black print of a finger burned, as it were, into his forehead, which nothing could obliterate.

The first news his wife had to tell him was the sudden death of Absalom Crowninshield, the rich buccaneer. It was announced in the papers, with the usual flourish, that "A great man had fallen in Israel."

Tom recollected the tree which his black friend had just hewn down, and which was ready for burning. "Let the freebooter roast," said Tom; "who cares!" He now felt convinced that all he had heard and seen was no illusion.

He was not prone to let his wife into his confidence; but as this was an uneasy secret, he willingly shared it with her. All her avarice was awakened at the mention of hidden gold, and she urged her husband to comply with the black man's terms, and secure what would make them wealthy for life. However Tom might have felt disposed to sell himself to the devil, he was determined not to do so to oblige his wife; so he flatly refused, out of the mere spirit of contradiction. Many and bitter were the quarrels they had on the subject; but the more she talked, the more resolute was Tom not to be damned to please her.

At length she determined to drive the bargain on her own account, and, if she succeeded, to keep all the gain to herself. Being of the same fearless temper as her husband, she set off for the old Indian fort toward the close of a summer's day. She was many hours absent. When she came back, she was reserved and sullen in her replies. She spoke something of a black man, whom she had met about twilight hewing at the root of a tall tree. He was sulky, however, and would not come to terms; she was to go again with a propitiatory offering, but what it was she forbore to say.

The next evening she set off again for the swamp, with her apron heavily laden. Tom waited and waited for her, but in vain; midnight came, but she did not make her appearance; morning, noon, night returned, but still she did not come. Tom now grew uneasy for her safety, especially as he found she had carried off in her apron the silver tea-pot and spoons, and every portable article of value. Another night elapsed, another morning came; but no wife. In a word, she was never heard of more.

What was her real fate nobody knows, in consequence of so many pretending to know. It is one of those facts which have become confounded by a variety of historians. Some asserted that she lost her way among the tangled mazes of the swamp, and sank into some pit or slough; others, more uncharitable, hinted that she had eloped with the household booty, and made off to some other province; while others surmised that the tempter had decoyed her into a dismal quagmire, on the top of which her hat was found lying. In confirmation of this, it was said a great black man, with an axe on his shoulder, was seen late that very evening coming out of the swamp, carrying a bundle tied in a check apron, with an air of surly triumph.

The most current and probable story, however, observes that Tom Walker grew so anxious about the fate of his wife and his property that he set out at length to seek them both at the Indian fort. During a long summer's afternoon he searched about the gloomy place, but no wife was to be seen. He called her name repeatedly, but she was nowhere to be heard. The bittern alone responded to his voice, as he flew screaming by; or the bull-frog croaked dolefully from a neighboring pool. At length, it is said, just in the brown hour of twilight, when the owls began to hoot and the bats to flit about, his attention was attracted by the clamor of carrion crows hovering about a cypress-tree. He looked up and beheld a bundle tied in a check apron and hanging in the branches of the tree, with a great vulture perched hard by, as if keeping watch upon it. He leaped with joy, for he recognized his wife's apron, and supposed it to contain the household valuables.

"Let us get hold of the property," said he, consolingly, to himself, "and we will endeavor to do without the woman."

As he scrambled up the tree, the vulture spread its wide wings and sailed off, screaming, into the deep shadows of the forest. Tom seized the checked apron, but, woful sight! found nothing but a heart and liver tied up in it!

Such, according to this most authentic old story, was all that was to be found of Tom's wife. She had probably attempted to deal with the black man as she had been accustomed to deal with her husband; but though a female scold is generally considered a match for the devil, yet in this instance she appears to have had the worst of it. She must have died game, however; for it is said Tom noticed many prints of cloven feet deeply stamped about the tree, and found handfuls of hair, that looked as if they had been plucked from the coarse black shock of the woodsman. Tom knew his wife's prowess by experience. He shrugged his shoulders as he looked at the signs of fierce clapper-clawing. "Egad," said he to himself, "Old Scratch must have had a tough time of it!"

Tom consoled himself for the loss of his property, with the loss of his wife, for he was a man of fortitude. He even felt something like gratitude toward the black woodsman, who, he considered, had done him a kindness. He sought, therefore, to cultivate a further acquaintance with him, but for some time without success; the old black-legs played shy, for, whatever people may think, he is not always to be had for the calling; he knows how to play his cards when pretty sure of his game.

At length, it is said, when delay had whetted Tom's eagerness to the quick and prepared him to agree to anything rather than not gain the promised treasure, he met the black man one evening in his usual woodsman's dress, with his axe on his shoulder, sauntering along the swamp and humming a tune. He affected to receive Tom's advances with great indifference, made brief replies, and went on humming his tune.

By degrees, however, Tom brought him to business, and they began to haggle about the terms on which the former was to have the pirate's treasure. There was one condition which need not be mentioned, being generally understood in all cases where the devil grants favors; but there were others about which, though of less importance, he was inflexibly obstinate. He insisted that the money found through his means should be employed in his service. He proposed, therefore, that Tom should employ it in the black traffic; that is to say, that he should fit out a slave-ship. This, however, Tom resolutely refused; he was bad enough in all conscience, but the devil himself could not tempt him to turn slave-trader.

Finding Tom so squeamish on this point, he did not insist upon it, but proposed, instead, that he should turn usurer; the devil being extremely anxious for the increase of usurers, looking upon them as his peculiar people.

To this no objections were made, for it was just to Tom's taste.

"You shall open a broker's shop in Boston next month," said the black man.

"I'll do it to-morrow, if you wish," said Tom Walker.

"You shall lend money at two per cent. a month."

"Egad, I'll charge four!" replied Tom Walker.

"You shall extort bonds, foreclose mortgages, drive the merchants to bankruptcy—"

"I'll drive them to the devil," cried Tom Walker.

"You are the usurer for my money!" said black-legs with delight. "When will you want the rhino?"

"This very night."

"Done!" said the devil.

"Done!" said Tom Walker. So they shook hands and struck a bargain.

A few days' time saw Tom Walker seated behind his desk in a counting-house in Boston.

His reputation for a ready-moneyed man, who would lend money out for a good consideration, soon spread abroad. Everybody remembers the time of Governor Belcher, when money was particularly scarce. It was a time of paper credit. The country had been deluged with government bills; the famous Land Bank had been established; there had been a rage for speculating; the people had run mad with schemes for new settlements, for building cities in the wilderness; land-jobbers went about with maps of grants and townships and Eldorados, lying nobody knew where, but which everybody was ready to purchase. In a word, the great speculating fever which breaks out every now and then in the country had raged to an alarming degree, and everybody was dreaming of making sudden fortunes from nothing. As usual, the fever had subsided, the dream had gone off, and the imaginary fortunes with it; the patients were left in doleful plight, and the whole country resounded with the consequent cry of "hard times."

At this propitious time of public distress did Tom Walker set up as usurer in Boston. His door was soon thronged by customers. The needy and adventurous, the gambling speculator, the dreaming land-jobber, the thriftless tradesman, the merchant with cracked credit—in short, everyone driven to raise money by desperate means and desperate sacrifices hurried to Tom Walker.

Thus Tom was the universal friend to the needy, and acted like "a friend in need"; that is to say, he always exacted good pay and security. In proportion to the distress of the applicant was the hardness of his terms. He accumulated bonds and mortgages, gradually squeezed his customers closer and closer, and sent them at length, dry as a sponge, from his door.

In this way he made money hand over hand, became a rich and mighty man, and exalted his cocked hat upon "Change." He built himself, as usual, a vast house, out of ostentation, but left the greater part of it unfinished and unfurnished, out of parsimony. He even set up a carriage in the fulness of his vain-glory, though he nearly starved the horses which drew it; and, as the ungreased wheels groaned and screeched on the axle-trees, you would have thought you heard the souls of the poor debtors he was squeezing.

As Tom waxed old, however, he grew thoughtful. Having secured the good things of this world, he began to feel anxious about those of the next. He thought with regret of the bargain he had made with his black friend, and set his wits to work to cheat him out of the conditions. He became, therefore, all of a sudden, a violent church-goer. He prayed loudly and strenuously, as if heaven were to be taken by force of lungs. Indeed, one might always tell when he had sinned most during the week by the clamor of his Sunday devotion. The quiet Christians who had been modestly and steadfastly travelling Zionward were struck with self-reproach at seeing themselves so suddenly outstripped in their career by this new-made convert. Tom was as rigid in religious as in money matters; he was a stern supervisor and censurer of his neighbors, and seemed to think every sin entered up to their account became a credit on his own side of the page. He even talked of the expediency of reviving the persecution of Quakers and Anabaptists. In a word, Tom's zeal became as notorious as his riches.

Still, in spite of all this strenuous attention to forms, Tom had a lurking dread that the devil, after all, would have his due. That he might not be taken unawares, therefore, it is said he always carried a small Bible in his coat-pocket. He had also a great folio Bible on his counting-house desk, and would frequently be found reading it when people called on business; on such occasions he would lay his green spectacles in the book, to mark the place, while he turned round to drive some usurious bargain.

Some say that Tom grew a little crack-brained in his old days, and that, fancying his end approaching, he had his horse new shod, saddled, and bridled, and buried with his feet uppermost; because he supposed that at the last day the world would be turned upside-down; in which case he should find his horse standing ready for mounting, and he was determined at the worst to give his old friend a run for it. This, however, is probably a mere old wives' fable. If he really did take such a precaution, it was totally superfluous; at least so says the authentic old legend, which closes his story in the following manner:

One hot summer afternoon in the dog-days, just as a terrible black thunder-gust was coming up, Tom sat in his counting-house, in his white linen cap and India silk morning-gown. He was on the point of foreclosing a mortgage, by which he would complete the ruin of an unlucky land-speculator for whom he had professed the greatest friendship. The poor land-jobber begged him to grant a few months' indulgence. Tom had grown testy and irritated, and refused another delay.

"My family will be ruined, and brought upon the parish," said the land-jobber.

"Charity begins at home," replied Tom; "I must take care of myself in these hard times."

"You have made so much money out of me," said the speculator.

Tom lost his patience and his piety. "The devil take me," said he, "if I have made a farthing!"

Just then there were three loud knocks at the street door. He stepped out to see who was there. A black man was holding a black horse, which neighed and stamped with impatience.

"Tom, you're come for," said the black fellow, gruffly. Tom shrank back, but too late. He had left his little Bible at the bottom of his coat-pocket and his big Bible on the desk buried under the mortgage he was about to foreclose: never was sinner taken more unawares. The black man whisked him like a child into the saddle, gave the horse the lash, and away he galloped, with Tom on his back, in the midst of the thunder-storm. The clerks stuck their pens behind their ears, and stared after him from the windows. Away went Tom Walker, dashing down the streets, his white cap bobbing up and down, his morning-gown fluttering in the wind, and his steed striking fire out of the pavement at every bound. When the clerks turned to look for the black man, he had disappeared.

Tom Walker never returned to foreclose the mortgage. A countryman, who lived on the border of the swamp, reported that in the height of the thunder-gust he had heard a great clattering of hoofs and a howling along the road, and running to the window caught sight of a figure, such as I have described, on a horse that galloped like mad across the fields, over the hills, and down into the black hemlock swamp toward the old Indian fort, and that shortly after a thunder-bolt falling in that direction seemed to set the whole forest in a blaze.

The good people of Boston shook their heads and shrugged their shoulders, but had been so much accustomed to witches and goblins, and tricks of the devil, in all kinds of shapes, from the first settlement of the colony, that they were not so much horror-struck as might have been expected. Trustees were appointed to take charge of Tom's effects. There was nothing, however, to administer upon. On searching his coffers, all his bonds and mortgages were reduced to cinders. In place of gold and silver, his iron chest was filled with chips and shavings; two skeletons lay in his stable instead of his half-starved horses, and the very next day his great house took fire and was burned to the ground.

Such was the end of Tom Walker and his ill-gotten wealth. Let all gripping money-brokers lay this story to heart. The truth of it is not to be doubted. The very hole under the oak-trees, whence he dug Kidd's money, is to be seen to this day; and the neighboring swamp and old Indian fort are often haunted in stormy nights by a figure on horseback, in morning-gown and white cap, which is doubtless the troubled spirit of the usurer. In fact, the story has resolved itself into a proverb, and is the origin of that popular saying, so prevalent throughout New England, of "The devil and Tom Walker."

DR. HEIDEGGER'S EXPERIMENT

Nathaniel Hawthorne (1807-1864)

That very singular man, old Doctor Heidegger, once invited four venerable friends to meet him in his study. There were three white-bearded gentlemen, Mr. Medbourne, Colonel Killigrew, and Mr. Gascoigne, and a withered gentlewoman whose name was the Widow Wycherley. They were all melancholy old creatures, who had been unfortunate in life, and whose greatest misfortune it was that they were not long ago in their graves. Mr. Medbourne, in the vigor of his age, had been a prosperous merchant, but had lost his all by a frantic speculation, and was no little better than a mendicant. Colonel Killigrew had wasted his best years, and his health and substance, in the pursuit of sinful pleasures, which had given birth to a brood of pains, such as the gout and divers other torments of soul and body. Mr. Gascoigne was a ruined politician, a man of evil fame, or at least had been so, till time had buried him from the knowledge of the present generation, and made him obscure instead of infamous. As for the Widow Wycherley, tradition tells us that she was a great beauty in her day; but, for a long while past, she had lived in deep seclusion, on account of certain scandalous stories which had prejudiced the gentry of the town against her. It is a circumstance worth mentioning that each of these three old gentlemen, Mr. Medbourne, Colonel Killigrew, and Mr. Gascoigne, were early lovers of the Widow Wycherley, and had once been on the point of cutting each other's throats for her sake. And, before proceeding further, I will merely hint that Doctor Heidegger and all his four guests were sometimes thought to be a little beside themselves; as is not unfrequently the case with old people, when worried either by present troubles or woful recollections.

"My dear friends," said Doctor Heidegger, motioning them to be seated, "I am desirous of your assistance in one of those little experiments with which I amuse myself here in my study."

If all stories were true, Doctor Heidegger's study must have been a very curious place. It was a dim, old-fashioned chamber, festooned with cobwebs and besprinkled with antique dust. Around the walls stood several oaken bookcases, the lower shelves of which were filled with rows of gigantic folios and black-letter quartos, and the upper with little parchment-covered duodecimos. Over the central bookcase was a bronze bust of Hippocrates, with which, according to some authorities, Doctor Heidegger was accustomed to hold consultations in all difficult cases of his practice. In the obscurest corner of the room stood a tall and narrow oaken closet, with its door ajar, within which doubtfully appeared a skeleton. Between two of the bookcases hung a looking-glass, presenting its high and dusty plate within a tarnished gilt frame. Among many wonderful stories related of this mirror, it was fabled that the spirits of all the doctor's deceased patients dwelt within its verge, and would stare him in the face whenever he looked thitherward. The opposite side of the chamber was ornamented with the full-length portrait of a young lady, arrayed in the faded magnificence of silk, satin, and brocade, and with a visage as faded as her dress. Above half a century ago Doctor Heidegger had been on the point of marriage with this young lady; but, being affected with some slight disorder, she had swallowed one of her lover's prescriptions, and died on the bridal evening. The greatest curiosity of the study remains to be mentioned; it was a ponderous folio volume, bound in black leather, with massive silver clasps. There were no letters on the back, and nobody could tell the title of the book. But it was well known to be a book of magic; and once, when a chambermaid had lifted it, merely to brush away the dust, the skeleton had rattled in its closet, the picture of the young lady had stepped one foot upon the floor, and several ghastly faces had peeped forth from the mirror; while the brazen head of Hippocrates frowned, and said: "Forbear!"

Such was Doctor Heidegger's study. On the summer afternoon of our tale a small round table, as black as ebony, stood in the centre of the room, sustaining a cut-glass vase of beautiful form and workmanship. The sunshine came through the window, between the heavy festoons of two faded damask curtains, and fell directly across this vase; so that a mild splendor was reflected from it on the ashen visages of the five old people who sat around. Four champagne glasses were also on the table.

"My dear old friends," repeated Doctor Heidegger, "may I reckon on your aid in performing an exceedingly curious experiment?"

Now Doctor Heidegger was a very strange old gentleman, whose eccentricity had become the nucleus for a thousand fantastic stories. Some of these fables, to my shame be it spoken, might possibly be traced back to mine own veracious self; and if any passages of the present tale should startle the reader's faith, I must be content to bear the stigma of a fiction-monger.

When the doctor's four guests heard him talk of his proposed experiment, they anticipated nothing more wonderful than the murder of a mouse in an air-pump or the examination of a cobweb by the microscope, or some similar nonsense, with which he was constantly in the habit of pestering his intimates. But without waiting for a reply, Doctor Heidegger hobbled across the chamber, and returned with the same ponderous folio, bound in black leather, which common report affirmed to be a book of magic. Undoing the silver clasps, he opened the volume, and took from among its black-letter pages a rose, or what was once a rose, though now the green leaves and crimson petals had assumed one brownish hue, and the ancient flower seemed ready to crumble to dust in the doctor's hands.

"This rose," said Doctor Heidegger, with a sigh, "this same withered and crumbling flower, blossomed five and fifty years ago. It was given me by Sylvia Ward, whose portrait hangs yonder, and I meant to wear it in my bosom at our wedding. Five and fifty years it has been treasured between the leaves of this old volume. Now, would you deem it possible that this rose of half a century could ever bloom again?"

"Nonsense!" said the Widow Wycherley, with a peevish toss of her head. "You might as well ask whether an old woman's wrinkled face could ever bloom again."

"See!" answered Doctor Heidegger.

He uncovered the vase, and threw the faded rose into the water which it contained. At first, it lay lightly on the surface of the fluid, appearing to imbibe none of its moisture. Soon, however, a singular change began to be visible. The crushed and dried petals stirred, and assumed a deepening tinge of crimson, as if the flower were reviving from a death-like slumber; the slender stalk and twigs of foliage became green; and there was the rose of half a century, looking as fresh as when Sylvia Ward had first given it to her lover. It was scarcely full blown; for some of its delicate red leaves curled modestly around its moist bosom, within which two or three dewdrops were sparkling.

"That is certainly a very pretty deception," said the doctor's friends; careless, however, for they had witnessed greater miracles at a conjurer's show; "pray how was it effected?"

"Did you ever hear of the 'Fountain of Youth,'" asked Doctor Heidegger, "which Ponce de Leon, the Spanish adventurer, went in search of, two or three centuries ago?"

"But did Ponce de Leon ever find it?" said the Widow Wycherley.

"No," answered Doctor Heidegger, "for he never sought it in the right place. The famous Fountain of Youth, if I am rightly informed, is situated in the southern part of the Floridian peninsula, not far from Lake Macaco. Its source is overshadowed by several magnolias, which, though numberless centuries old, have been kept as fresh as violets, by the virtues of this wonderful water. An acquaintance of mine, knowing my curiosity in such matters, has sent me what you see in the vase."

"Ahem!" said Colonel Killigrew, who believed not a word of the doctor's story; "and what may be the effect of this fluid on the human frame?"

"You shall judge for yourself, my dear Colonel," replied Doctor Heidegger; "and all of you, my respected friends, are welcome to so much of this admirable fluid as may restore to you the bloom of youth. For my own part, having had much trouble in growing old, I am in no hurry to grow young again. With your permission, therefore, I will merely watch the progress of the experiment."

While he spoke, Doctor Heidegger had been filling the four champagne glasses with the water of the Fountain of Youth. It was apparently impregnated with an effervescent gas; for little bubbles were continually ascending from the depths of the glasses, and bursting in silvery spray at the surface. As the liquor diffused a pleasant perfume, the old people doubted now that it possessed cordial and comfortable properties; and though utter sceptics as to its rejuvenescent power, they were inclined to swallow it at once. But Doctor Heidegger besought them to stay a moment.

"Before you drink, my respectable old friends," said he, "it would be well that, with the experience of a lifetime to direct you, you should draw up a few general rules for your guidance, in passing a second time through the perils of youth. Think what a sin and shame it would be if, with your peculiar advantages, you should not become patterns of virtue and wisdom to all the young people of the age!"

The doctor's four venerable friends made him no answer, except by a feeble and tremulous laugh; so very ridiculous was the idea that, knowing how closely repentance treads behind the steps of error, they should ever go astray again.

"Drink, then," said the doctor, bowing: "I rejoice that I have so well selected the subjects of my experiment."

With palsied hands they raised the glasses to their lips. The liquor, if it really possessed such virtues as Doctor Heidegger imputed to it, could not have been bestowed on four human beings who needed it more wofully. They looked as if they had never known what youth or pleasure was, but had been the offspring of nature's dotage, and always the gray, decrepit, sapless, miserable creatures, who now sat stooping round the doctor's table, without life enough in their souls or bodies to be animated even by the prospect of growing young again. They drank off the water, and replaced their glasses on the table.

Assuredly there was an almost immediate improvement in the aspect of the party, not unlike what might have been produced by a glass of generous wine, together with a sudden glow of cheerful sunshine, brightening over all their visages at once. There was a healthful suffusion on their cheeks, instead of the ashen hue that had made them look so corpselike. They gazed at one another, and fancied that some magic power had really begun to smooth away the deep and sad inscriptions which Father Time had been so long engraving on their brows. The Widow Wycherley adjusted her cap, for she felt almost like a woman again.

"Give us more of this wondrous water!" cried they, eagerly. "We are younger—but we are still too old! Quick—give us more!"

"Patience! patience!" quoth Doctor Heidegger, who sat watching the experiment with philosophic coolness. "You have been a long time growing old. Surely you might be content to grow young in half an hour! But the water is at your service."

Again he filled their glasses with the liquor of youth, enough of which still remained in the vase to turn half the old people in the city to the age of their own grandchildren. While the bubbles were yet sparkling on the brim, the doctor's four guests snatched their glasses from the table, and swallowed the contents at a single gulp. Was it delusion? Even while the draught was passing down their throats it seemed to have wrought a change on their whole systems. Their eyes grew clear and bright; a dark shade deepened among their silvery locks; they sat round the table, three gentlemen of middle age, and a woman hardly beyond her buxom prime.

"My dear widow, you are charming!" cried Colonel Killigrew, whose eyes had been fixed upon her face, while the shadows of age were flitting from it like darkness from the crimson daybreak.

The fair widow knew of old that Colonel Killigrew's compliments were not always measured by sober truth; so she started up and ran to the mirror, still dreading that the ugly visage of an old woman would meet her gaze. Meanwhile the three gentlemen behaved in such a manner as proved that the water of the Fountain of Youth possessed some intoxicating qualities, unless, indeed, their exhilaration of spirits were merely a lightsome dizziness, caused by the sudden removal of the weight of years. Mr. Gascoigne's mind seemed to run on political topics, but whether relating to the past, present, or future could not easily be determined, since the same ideas and phrases have been in vogue these fifty years. Now he rattled forth full-throated sentences about patriotism, national glory, and the people's rights; now he muttered some perilous stuff or other, in a sly and doubtful whisper, so cautiously that even his own conscience could scarcely catch the secret; and now, again, he spoke in measured accents and a deeply deferential tone, as if a royal ear were listening to his well-turned periods. Colonel Killigrew all this time had been trolling forth a jolly battle-song, and ringing his glass toward the buxom figure of the Widow Wycherley. On the other side of the table Mr. Medbourne was involved in a calculation of dollars and cents, with which was strangely intermingled a project for supplying the East Indies with ice, by harnessing a team of whales to the polar icebergs.

As for the Widow Wycherley, she stood before the mirror, courtesying and simpering to her own image, and greeting it as the friend whom she loved better than all the world beside. She thrust her face close to the glass to see whether some long-remembered wrinkle or crow's-foot had indeed vanished. She examined whether the snow had so entirely melted from her hair that the venerable cap could be safely thrown aside. At last, turning briskly away, she came with a sort of dancing step to the table.

"My dear old doctor," cried she, "pray favor me with another glass!"

"Certainly, my dear madam, certainly!" replied the complaisant doctor. "See! I have already filled the glasses."

There, in fact, stood the four glasses, brimful of this wonderful water, the delicate spray of which, as it effervesced from the surface, resembled the tremulous glitter of diamonds. It was now so nearly sunset that the chamber had grown duskier than ever; but a mild and moon-like splendor gleamed from within the vase, and rested alike on the four guests, and on the doctor's venerable figure. He sat in a high-backed, elaborately carved oaken chair, with a gray dignity of aspect that might have well befitted that very Father Time, whose power had never been disputed, save by this fortunate company. Even while quaffing the third draught of the Fountain of Youth, they were almost awed by the expression of his mysterious visage.

But the next moment the exhilarating gush of young life shot through their veins. They were now in the happy prime of youth. Age, with its miserable train of cares, and sorrows, and diseases, was remembered only as the trouble of a dream, from which they had joyously awoke. The fresh gloss of the soul, so early lost, and without which the world's successive scenes had been but a gallery of faded pictures, again threw its enchantment over all their prospects. They felt like new-created beings in a new-created universe.

"We are young! We are young!" they cried, exultingly.

Youth, like the extremity of age, had effaced the strongly marked characteristics of middle life, and mutually assimilated them all. They were a group of merry youngsters, almost maddened with the exuberant frolicsomeness of their years. The most singular effect of their gayety was an impulse to mock the infirmity and decrepitude of which they had so lately been the victims. They laughed loudly at their old-fashioned attire—the wide-skirted coats and flapped waistcoats of the young men, and the ancient cap and gown of the blooming girl. One limped across the floor like a gouty grandfather; one set a pair of spectacles astride of his nose, and pretended to pore over the black-letter pages of the book of magic; a third seated himself in an arm-chair, and strove to imitate the venerable dignity of Doctor Heidegger. Then all shouted mirthfully, and leaped about the room. The Widow Wycherley—if so fresh a damsel could be called a widow—tripped up to the doctor's chair with a mischievous merriment in her rosy face.

"Doctor, you dear old soul," cried she, "get up and dance with me!" And then the four young people laughed louder than ever, to think what a queer figure the poor old doctor would cut.

"Pray excuse me," answered the doctor, quietly. "I am old and rheumatic, and my dancing days were over long ago. But either of these gay young gentlemen will be glad of so pretty a partner."

"Dance with me, Clara!" cried Colonel Killigrew.

"She promised me her hand fifty years ago!" exclaimed Mr. Medbourne.

They all gathered round her. One caught both her hands in his passionate grasp—another threw his arm about her waist—the third buried his hand among the curls that clustered beneath the widow's cap. Blushing, panting, struggling, chiding, laughing, her warm breath fanning each of their faces by turns, she strove to disengage herself, yet still remained in their triple embrace. Never was there a livelier picture of youthful rivalship, with bewitching beauty for the prize. Yet, by a strange deception, owing to the duskiness of the chamber and the antique dresses which they still wore, the tall mirror is said to have reflected the figures of the three old, gray, withered grand-sires, ridiculously contending for the skinny ugliness of a shrivelled grandam.

But they were young: their burning passions proved them so. Inflamed to madness by the coquetry of the girl-widow, who neither granted nor quite withheld her favors, the three rivals began to interchange threatening glances. Still keeping hold of the fair prize, they grappled fiercely at one another's throats. As they struggled to and fro, the table was overturned, and the vase dashed into a thousand fragments. The precious Water of Youth flowed in a bright stream across the floor, moistening the wings of a butterfly, which, grown old in the decline of summer, had alighted there to die. The insect fluttered lightly through the chamber, and settled on the snowy head of Doctor Heidegger.

"Come, come, gentlemen!—come, Madame Wycherley!" exclaimed the doctor, "I really must protest against this riot."

They stood still and shivered; for it seemed as if gray Time were calling them back from their sunny youth, far down into the chill and darksome vale of years. They looked at old Doctor Heidegger, who sat in his carved arm-chair, holding the rose of half a century which he had rescued from among the fragments of the shattered vase. At the motion of his hand the rioters resumed their seats, the more readily because their violent exertions had wearied them, youthful though they were.

"My poor Sylvia's rose!" ejaculated Doctor Heidegger, holding it in the light of the sunset clouds; "it appears to be fading again."

And so it was. Even while the party were looking at it the flower continued to shrivel up, till it became as dry and fragile as when the doctor had first thrown it into the vase. He shook off the few drops of moisture which clung to its petals.

"I love it as well thus as in its dewy freshness," observed he, pressing the withered rose to his withered lips. While he spoke, the butterfly fluttered down from the doctor's snowy head, and fell upon the floor.

His guests shivered again. A strange dullness, whether of the body or spirit they could not tell, was creeping gradually over them all. They gazed at one another, and fancied that each fleeting moment snatched away a charm, and left a deepening furrow where none had been before. Was it an illusion? Had the changes of a lifetime been crowded into so brief a space, and were they now four aged people, sitting with their old friend, Doctor Heidegger?

"Are we grown old again so soon?" cried they, dolefully.

In truth, they had. The Water of Youth possessed merely a virtue more transient than that of wine. The delirium which it created had effervesced away. Yes, they were old again! With a shuddering impulse, that showed her a woman still, the widow clasped her skinny hands over her face, and wished that the coffin lid were over it, since it could be no longer beautiful.

"Yes, friends, ye are old again," said Doctor Heidegger; "and lo! the Water of Youth is all lavished on the ground. Well, I bemoan it not; for if the fountain gushed at my doorstep, I would not stoop to bathe my lips in it—no, though its delirium were for years instead of moments. Such is the lesson ye have taught me!"

But the doctor's four friends had taught no such lesson to themselves. They resolved forthwith to make a pilgrimage to Florida, and quaff at morning, noon, and night from the Fountain of Youth.

THE PURLOINED LETTER[19]

Edgar Allan Poe (1809-1849)

At Paris, just after dark one gusty evening in the autumn of 18—, I was enjoying the twofold luxury of meditation and a meerschaum, in company with my friend, C. Auguste Dupin, in his little back library, or book-closet, au troisième, No. 33 Rue Dunôt, Faubourg St. Germain. For one hour at least we had maintained a profound silence, while each, to any casual observer, might have seemed intently and exclusively occupied with the curling eddies of smoke that oppressed the atmosphere of the chamber. For myself, however, I was mentally discussing certain topics which had formed matter for conversation between us at an earlier period of the evening; I mean the affair of the Rue Morgue, and the mystery attending the murder of Marie Rogêt. I looked upon it, therefore, as something of a coincidence, when the door of our apartment was thrown open and admitted our old acquaintance, Monsieur G——, the Prefect of the Parisian police.

We gave him a hearty welcome; for there was nearly half as much of the entertaining as of the contemptible about the man, and we had not seen him for several years. We had been sitting in the dark, and Dupin now arose for the purpose of lighting a lamp, but sat down again, without doing so, upon G——'s saying that he had called to consult us, or rather to ask the opinion of my friend, about some official business which had occasioned a great deal of trouble.

"If it is any point requiring reflection," observed Dupin, as he forebore to enkindle the wick, "we shall examine it to better purpose in the dark."

"That is another of your odd notions," said the Prefect, who had the fashion of calling everything "odd" that was beyond his comprehension, and thus lived amid an absolute legion of "oddities."

"Very true," said Dupin, as he supplied his visitor with a pipe, and rolled toward him a comfortable chair.

"And what is the difficulty now?" I asked. "Nothing more in the assassination way, I hope?"

"Oh no, nothing of that nature. The fact is, the business is very simple indeed, and I make no doubt that we can manage it sufficiently well ourselves; but then I thought Dupin would like to hear the details of it, because it is so excessively odd."

---

[19] The pattern in method for all detective stories.

"Simple and odd," said Dupin.

"Why, yes; and not exactly that, either. The fact is, we have all been a good deal puzzled because the affair is so simple, and yet baffles us altogether."

"Perhaps it is the very simplicity of the thing which puts you at fault," said my friend.

"What nonsense you do talk!" replied the Prefect, laughing heartily.

"Perhaps the mystery is a little too plain," said Dupin.

"Oh, good heavens! who ever heard of such an idea?"

"A little too self-evident."

"Ha! ha! ha!—ha! ha! ha!—ho! ho! ho!" roared our visitor, profoundly amused, "Oh, Dupin, you will be the death of me yet!"

"And what, after all, is the matter on hand?" I asked.

"Why, I will tell you," replied the Prefect, as he gave a long, steady, and contemplative puff, and settled himself in his chair. "I will tell you in a few words; but, before I begin, let me caution you that this is an affair demanding the greatest secrecy, and that I should most probably lose the position I now hold were it known that I confided it to any one."

"Proceed," said I.

"Or not," said Dupin.

"Well, then; I have received personal information, from a very high quarter, that a certain document of the last importance has been purloined from the royal apartments. The individual who purloined it is known; this beyond a doubt; he was seen to take it. It is known, also, that it still remains in his possession."

"How is this known?" asked Dupin.

"It is clearly inferred," replied the Prefect, "from the nature of the document, and from the non-appearance of certain results which would at once arise from its passing out of the robber's possession—that is to say, from his employing it as he must design in the end to employ it."

"Be a little more explicit," I said.

"Well, I may venture so far as to say that the paper gives its holder a certain power in a certain quarter where such power is immensely valuable." The Prefect was fond of the cant of diplomacy.

"Still I do not quite understand," said Dupin.

"No? Well, the disclosure of the document to a third person, who shall be nameless, would bring in question the honor of a personage of the most exalted station, and this fact gives the holder of the document an ascendancy over the illustrious personage whose honor and peace are so jeopardized."

"But this ascendancy," I interposed, "would depend upon the

robber's knowledge of the loser's knowledge of the robber. Who would dare—"

"The thief," said G——, "is the Minister D——, who dares all things, those unbecoming as well as those becoming a man. The method of the theft was not less ingenious than bold. The document in question—a letter, to be frank—had been received by the personage robbed while alone in the royal boudoir. During its perusal she was suddenly interrupted by the entrance of the other exalted personage from whom especially it was her wish to conceal it. After a hurried and vain endeavor to thrust it in a drawer, she was forced to place it, open as it was, upon a table. The address, however, was uppermost, and, the contents thus unexposed, the letter escaped notice. At this juncture enters the Minister D——. His lynx eye immediately perceives the paper, recognizes the handwriting of the address, observes the confusion of the personage addressed, and fathoms her secret. After some business transactions, hurried through in his ordinary manner, he produces a letter somewhat similar to the one in question, opens it, pretends to read it, and then places it in close juxtaposition to the other. Again he converses, for some fifteen minutes, upon the public affairs. At length, in taking leave, he takes also from the table the letter to which he had no claim. Its rightful owner saw, but of course, dared not call attention to the act, in the presence of the third personage who stood at her elbow. The Minister decamped, leaving his own letter—one of no importance—upon the table."

"Here, then," said Dupin to me, "you have precisely what you demand to make the ascendancy complete—the robber's knowledge of the loser's knowledge of the robber."

"Yes," replied the Prefect, "and the power thus attained has, for some months past, been wielded, for political purposes, to a very dangerous extent. The personage robbed is more thoroughly convinced, every day, of the necessity of reclaiming her letter. But this, of course, cannot be done openly. In fine, driven to despair, she has committed the matter to me."

"Than whom," said Dupin, amid a perfect whirlwind of smoke, "no more sagacious agent could, I suppose, be desired, or even imagined."

"You flatter me," replied the Prefect; "but it is possible that some such opinion may have been entertained."

"It is clear," said I, "as you observe, that the letter is still in the possession of the Minister; since it is this possession, and not any employment of the letter, which bestows the power. With the employment the power departs."

"True," said G——; "and upon this conviction I proceeded. My

first care was to make thorough search of the Minister's hotel; and here my chief embarrassment lay in the necessity of searching without his knowledge. Beyond all things, I have been warned of the danger which would result from giving him reason to suspect our design."

"But," said I, "you are quite au fait in these investigations. The Parisian police have done this thing often before."

"Oh yes, and for this reason I did not despair. The habits of the Minister gave me, too, a great advantage. He is frequently absent from home all night. His servants are by no means numerous. They sleep at a distance from their master's apartment, and, being chiefly Neapolitans, are readily made drunk. I have keys, as you know, with which I can open any chamber or cabinet in Paris. For three months a night has not passed during the greater part of which I have not been engaged, personally, in ransacking the D—— Hotel. My honor is interested, and, to mention a great secret, the reward is enormous. So I did not abandon the search until I had become fully satisfied that the thief is a more astute man than myself. I fancy that I have investigated every nook and corner of the premises in which it is possible that the paper can be concealed."

"But is it not possible," I suggested, "that although the letter may be in the possession of the Minister, as it unquestionably is, he may have concealed it elsewhere than upon his own premises?"

"This is barely possible," said Dupin. "The present peculiar condition of affairs at court, and especially of those intrigues in which D—— is known to be involved, would render the instant availability of the document—its susceptibility of being produced at a moment's notice—a point of nearly equal importance with its possession."

"Its susceptibility of being produced?" said I.

"That is to say, of being destroyed," said Dupin.

"True," I observed; "the paper is clearly, then, upon the premises. As for its being upon the person of the Minister, we may consider that as out of the question."

"Entirely," said the Prefect. "He has been twice waylaid, as if by footpads, and his person rigidly searched under my own inspection."

"You might have spared yourself this trouble," said Dupin. "D——, I presume, is not altogether a fool; and, if not, must have anticipated these waylayings, as a matter of course."

"Not altogether a fool," said G——; "but, then, he is a poet, which I take to be only one remove from a fool."

"True," said Dupin, after a long and thoughtful whiff from his meerschaum, "although I have been guilty of certain doggrel myself."

"Suppose you detail," said I, "the particulars of your search."

"Why, the fact is, we took our time, and we searched everywhere. I have had long experience in these affairs. I took the entire building, room by room, devoting the nights of a whole week to each. We examined, first, the furniture of each apartment. We opened every possible drawer; and I presume you know that, to a properly trained police-agent, such a thing as a 'secret' drawer is impossible. Any man is a dolt who permits a 'secret' drawer to escape him in a search of this kind. The thing is so plain. There is a certain amount of bulk—of space—to be accounted for in every cabinet. Then we have accurate rules. The fiftieth part of a line could not escape us. After the cabinets we took the chairs. The cushions we probed with the fine long needles you have seen me employ. From the tables we removed the tops."

"Why so?"

"Sometimes the top of a table, or other similarly arranged piece of furniture, is removed by the person wishing to conceal an article; then the leg is excavated, the article deposited within the cavity, and the top replaced. The bottoms and tops of bedposts are employed in the same way."

"But could not the cavity be detected by sounding?" I asked.

"By no means, if, when the article is deposited, a sufficient wadding of cotton be placed around it. Besides, in our case, we were obliged to proceed without noise."

"But you could not have removed—you could not have taken to pieces all articles of furniture in which it would have been possible to make a deposit in the manner you mention. A letter may be compressed into a thin spiral roll, not differing much in shape or bulk from a large knitting-needle, and in this form it might be inserted into the rung of a chair, for example. You did not take to pieces all the chairs?"

"Certainly not; but we did better—we examined the rungs of every chair in the hotel, and, indeed, the jointings of every description of furniture, by the aid of a most powerful microscope. Had there been any traces of recent disturbance we should not have failed to detect it instantly. A single grain of gimlet-dust, for example, would have been as obvious as an apple. Any disorder in the gluing—any unusual gaping in the joints—would have sufficed to insure detection."

"I presume you looked to the mirrors, between the boards and the plates, and you probed the beds and the bedclothes, as well as the curtains and carpets."

"That, of course; and when we had absolutely completed every particle of the furniture in this way, then we examined the house itself. We divided its entire surface into compartments, which we numbered, so that none might be missed; then we scrutinized each individual square inch throughout the premises, including the two houses immediately adjoining, with the microscope, as before."

"The two houses adjoining!" I exclaimed. "You must have had a great deal of trouble."

"We had; but the reward offered is prodigious."

"You include the grounds about the houses?"

"All the grounds are paved with brick. They gave us comparatively little trouble. We examined the moss between the bricks, and found it undisturbed."

"You looked among D——'s papers, of course, and into the books of the library?"

"Certainly; we opened every package and parcel; we not only opened every book, but we turned over every leaf in each volume, not contenting ourselves with a mere shake, according to the fashion of some of our police officers. We also measured the thickness of every book-cover, with the most accurate admeasurement, and applied to each the most jealous scrutiny of the microscope. Had any of the bindings been recently meddled with, it would have been utterly impossible that the fact should have escaped observation. Some five or six volumes, just from the hands of the binder, we carefully probed, longitudinally, with the needles."

"You explored the floors beneath the carpets?"

"Beyond doubt. We removed every carpet, and examined the boards with the microscope."

"And the paper on the walls?"

"Yes."

"You looked into the cellars?"

"We did."

"Then," I said, "you have been making a miscalculation, and the letter is not upon the premises, as you suppose."

"I fear you are right there," said the Prefect. "And now, Dupin, what would you advise me to do?"

"To make a thorough research of the premises."

"That is absolutely needless," replied G——. "I am not more sure that I breathe than I am that the letter is not at the hotel."

"I have no better advice to give you," said Dupin. "You have, of course, an accurate description of the letter?"

"Oh yes!" And here the Prefect, producing a memorandum book, proceeded to read aloud a minute account of the internal, and especially of the external, appearance of the missing document.

Soon after finishing the perusal of this description, he took his departure, more entirely depressed in spirits than I had ever known the good gentleman before.

In about a month afterward he paid us another visit, and found us occupied very nearly as before. He took a pipe and a chair, and entered into some ordinary conversation. At length I said:

"Well, but, G——, what of the purloined letter? I presume you have at last made up your mind that there is no such thing as overreaching the Minister?"

"Confound him, say I—yes; I made the re-examination, however, as Dupin suggested—but it was all labor lost, as I knew it would be."

"How much was the reward offered, did you say?" asked Dupin.

"Why, a very great deal—a very liberal reward—I don't like to say how much, precisely; but one thing I will say, that I wouldn't mind giving my individual check for fifty thousand francs to any one who could obtain me that letter. The fact is, it is becoming of more and more importance every day; and the reward has been lately doubled. If it were trebled, however, I could do no more than I have done."

"Why, yes," said Dupin, drawling, between the whiffs of his meerschaum, "I really—think, G——, you have not exerted yourself—to the utmost in this matter. You might—do a little more, I think; eh?"

"How?—in what way?"

"Why"—puff, puff—"you might"—puff, puff—"employ counsel in the matter, eh"—puff, puff, puff. "Do you remember the story they tell of Abernethy?"

"No; hang Abernethy!"

"To be sure! Hang him and welcome. But, once upon a time, a certain miser conceived the design of spunging upon this Abernethy for a medical opinion. Getting up, for this purpose, an ordinary conversation in a private company, he insinuated his case to the physician as that of an imaginary individual."

"'We will suppose,' said the miser, 'that his symptoms are such and such; now, doctor, what would you have directed him to take?'

"'Take!' said Abernethy. 'Why, take advice, to be sure.'"

"But," said the Prefect, a little discomposed, "I am perfectly willing to take advice, and to pay for it. I would really give fifty thousand francs to any one who would aid me in the matter."

"In that case," replied Dupin, opening a drawer, and producing a check-book, "you may as well fill me up a check for the amount mentioned. When you have signed it, I will hand you the letter."

I was astounded. The Prefect appeared absolutely thunder-stricken. For some minutes he remained speechless and motionless, looking incredulously at my friend with open mouth, and eyes that seemed starting from their sockets; then apparently recovering himself in some measure, he seized a pen, and after several pauses and vacant stares, finally filled up and signed a check for fifty thousand francs, and handed it across the table to Dupin. The latter examined it carefully and deposited it in his pocket-book; then, unlocking an escritoire, took thence a letter and gave it to the Prefect. This functionary grasped it in a perfect agony of joy, opened it with a trembling hand, cast a rapid glance at its contents, and then, scrambling and struggling to the door, rushed at length unceremoniously from the room and from the house, without having uttered a syllable since Dupin had requested him to fill up the check.

When he had gone, my friend entered into some explanation.

"The Parisian police," he said, "are exceedingly able in their way. They are persevering, ingenious, cunning, and thoroughly versed in the knowledge which their duties seem chiefly to demand. Thus, when G—— detailed to us his mode of searching the premises at the Hotel D——, I felt entire confidence in his having made a satisfactory investigation—so far as his labors extended."

"So far as his labors extended?" said I.

"Yes," said Dupin. "The measures adopted were not only the best of their kind, but carried out to absolute perfection. Had the letter been deposited within the range of their search, these fellows would, beyond a question, have found it."

I merely laughed—but he seemed quite serious in all that he said.

"The measures, then," he continued, "were good in their kind, and well executed; their defect lay in their being inapplicable to the case and to the man. A certain set of highly ingenious resources are, with the Prefect, a sort of Procrustean bed, to which he forcibly adapts his designs. But he perpetually errs by being too deep or too shallow for the matter in hand, and many a school-boy is a better reasoner than he. I knew one about eight years of age, whose success at guessing in the game of 'even and odd' attracted universal admiration. This game is simple, and is played with marbles. One player holds in his hand a number of these toys, and demands of another whether that number is even or odd. If the guess is right, the guesser wins one; if wrong, he loses one. The boy to whom I allude won all the marbles of the school. Of course, he had some principle of guessing; and this lay in mere observation and admeasurement of the astuteness of his opponents. For example, an arrant simpleton is his opponent, and, holding up his closed hand, asks, 'Are they even or odd?' Our school-boy replies, 'Odd,' and loses; but upon the second trial he wins, for he then says to himself: 'The simpleton had them even upon the first trial, and his amount of cunning is just sufficient to make him have them odd upon the second; I will therefore guess odd'; he guesses odd, and wins. Now, with a simpleton a degree above the first, he would have reasoned thus;

'This fellow finds that in the first instance I guessed odd, and, in the second, he will propose to himself, upon the first impulse, a simple variation from even to odd, as did the first simpleton; but then a second thought will suggest that this is too simple a variation, and finally he will decide upon putting it even as before. I will therefore guess even'; he guesses even, and wins. Now this mode of reasoning in the school-boy, whom his fellows termed 'Lucky,' what, in its last analysis, is it?"

"It is merely," I said, "an identification of the reasoner's intellect with that of his opponent."

"It is," said Dupin; "and, upon inquiring of the boy by what means he effected the thorough identification in which his success consisted, I received answer as follows: 'When I wish to find out how wise, or how stupid, or how good, or how wicked, is any one, or what are his thoughts at the moment, I fashion the expression of my face, as accurately as possible, in accordance with the expression of his, and then wait to see what thoughts or sentiments arise in my mind or heart, as if to match or correspond with the expression.' This response of the school-boy lies at the bottom of all the spurious profundity which has been attributed to Rochefoucault, to La Bougive, to Machiavelli, and to Campanella."

"And the identification," I said, "of the reasoner's intellect with that of his opponent, depends, if I understand you aright, upon the accuracy with which the opponent's intellect is admeasured."

"For its practical value it depends upon this," replied Dupin; "and the Prefect and his cohort fail so frequently, first, by default of this identification, and, secondly, by ill-admeasurement, or rather through non-admeasurement, of the intellect with which they are engaged. They consider only their own ideas of ingenuity; and, in searching for anything hidden, advert only to the modes in which they would have hidden it. They are right in this much—that their own ingenuity is a faithful representative of that of the mass; but when the cunning of the individual felon is diverse in character from their own, the felon foils them of course. This always happens when it is above their own, and very usually when it is below. They have no variation of principle in their investigations; at best, when urged by some unusual emergency—by some extraordinary reward—they extend or exaggerate their old modes of practice, without touching their principles. What, for example, in this case of D——, has been done to vary the principle of action? What is all this boring, and probing, and sounding, and scrutinizing with the microscope, and dividing the surface of the building into registered square inches—what is it all but an exaggeration of the application of the one principle or set of principles of search, which are based upon the one set of notions retarding human ingenuity, to which the Prefect, in the long routine of his duty, has been accustomed? Do you not see he had taken it for granted that all men proceed to conceal a letter, not exactly in a gimlet-hole bored in a chair-leg, but, at least, in some out-of-the-way hole or corner suggested by the same tenor of thought which would urge a man to secrete a letter in a gimlet-hole bored in a chair-leg? And do you not see, also, that such recherché nooks for concealment are adapted only for ordinary occasions, and would be adopted only by ordinary intellects; for, in all cases of concealment, a disposal of the article concealed—a disposal of it in this recherché manner—is, in the very first instance, presumable and presumed; and thus its discovery depends, not at all upon the acumen, but altogether upon the mere care, patience, and determination of the seekers; and where the case is of importance—or, when the reward is of magnitude—the qualities in question have never been known to fail. You will now understand what I meant in suggesting that, had the purloined letter been hidden anywhere within the limits of the Prefect's examination—in other words, had the principle of its concealment been comprehended within the principles of the Prefect—its discovery would have been a matter altogether beyond question. This functionary, however, has been thoroughly mystified; and the remote source of his defeat lies in the supposition that the Minister is a fool, because he has acquired renown as a poet. All fools are poets; this the Prefect feels; and he is merely guilty of a non distributio medii in thence inferring that all poets are fools. I mean to say, that if the Minister had been no more than a mathematician, the Prefect would have been under no necessity of giving me this check. I knew him, however, as both mathematician and poet, and my measures were adapted to his capacity, with reference to the circumstances by which he was surrounded. I knew him as a courtier, too, and as a bold intriguant. Such a man, I considered, could not fail to be aware of the ordinary political modes of action. He could not have failed to anticipate—and events have proved that he did not fail to anticipate—the waylayings to which he was subjected. He must have foreseen, I reflected, the secret investigations of his premises. His frequent absences from home at night, which were hailed by the Prefect as certain aids to his success, I regarded only as ruses, to afford opportunity for thorough search to the police, and thus the sooner to impress them with the conviction to which G——, in fact, did finally arrive—the conviction that the letter was not upon the premises. I felt, also, that the whole train of thought, which I was at some pains in detailing to you just now, concerning the invariable principle of political action in searches for articles concealed—I felt that this whole train of thought would necessarily pass through the mind of the Minister. It would imperatively lead him to despise all the ordinary nooks of concealment. He could not, I reflected, be so weak as not to see that the most intricate and remote recess of his hotel would be as open as his commonest closets to the eyes, to the probes, to the gimlets, and to the microscopes of the Prefect. I saw, in fine, that he would be driven, as a matter of course, to simplicity, if not deliberately induced to it as a matter of choice. You will remember, perhaps, how desperately the Prefect laughed when I suggested, upon our first interview, that it was just possible this mystery troubled him so much on account of its being so very self-evident."

"Yes," said I, "I remember his merriment well. I really thought he would have fallen into convulsions."

"The material world," continued Dupin, "abounds with very strict analogies to the immaterial; and thus some color of truth has been given to the rhetorical dogma that metaphor, or simile, may be made to strengthen an argument as well as to embellish a description. The principle of the vis inertiae, for example, seems to be identical in physics and metaphysics. It is not more true, in the former, that a large body is with more difficulty set in motion than a smaller one, and that its subsequent momentum is commensurate with this difficulty, than it is, in the latter, that intellects of the vaster capacity, while more forcible, more constant, and more eventful in their movements than those of inferior grade, are yet the less readily moved, and more embarrassed, and full of hesitation in the first few steps of their progress. Again: have you ever noticed which of the street signs, over the shop doors, are the most attractive of attention?"

"I have never given the matter a thought," I said.

"There is a game of puzzles," he resumed, "which is played upon a map. One party playing requires another to find a given word—the name of town, river, state, or empire—any word, in short, upon the motley and perplexed surface of the chart. A novice in the game generally seeks to embarrass his opponents by giving them the most minutely lettered names; but the adept selects such words as stretch, in large characters, from one end of the chart to the other. These, like the over-largely lettered signs and placards of the street, escape observation by dint of being excessively obvious; and here the physical oversight is precisely analogous with the moral inapprehension by which the intellect suffers to pass unnoticed those considerations which are too obtrusively and too palpably self-evident. But this is a point, it appears, somewhat above or beneath the understanding of the Prefect. He never once thought it probable, or possible, that the Minister had deposited the letter immediately beneath the nose of the whole world, by way of best preventing any portion of that world from perceiving it.

"But the more I reflected upon the daring, dashing, and discriminating ingenuity of D——; upon the fact that the document must always have been at hand, if he intended to use it to good purpose; and upon the decisive evidence, obtained by the Prefect, that it was not hidden within the limits of that dignitary's ordinary search, the more satisfied I became that, to conceal this letter, the Minister had resorted to the comprehensive and sagacious expedient of not attempting to conceal it.

"Full of these ideas, I prepared myself with a pair of green spectacles, and called one fine morning, quite by accident, at the Ministerial hotel. I found D—— at home, yawning, lounging, and dawdling, as usual, and pretending to be in the last extremity of ennui. He is, perhaps, the most really energetic human being now alive—but that is only when nobody sees him.

"To be even with him, I complained of my weak eyes, and lamented the necessity of the spectacles, under cover of which I cautiously and thoroughly surveyed the whole apartment, while seemingly intent only upon the conversation of my host.

"I paid especial attention to a large writing-table near which he sat, and upon which lay confusedly some miscellaneous letters and other papers, with one or two musical instruments and a few books. Here, however, after a long and very deliberate scrutiny, I saw nothing to excite particular suspicion.

"At length my eyes, in going the circuit of the room, fell upon a trumpery filigree card-rack of pasteboard that hung dangling by a dirty blue ribbon from a little brass knob just beneath the middle of the mantelpiece. In this rack, which had three or four compartments, were five or six soiled cards and a solitary letter. This last was much soiled and crumpled. It was torn nearly in two, across the middle—as if a design, in the first instance, to tear it entirely up as worthless had been altered or stayed in the second. It had a large black seal, bearing the D—— cipher very conspicuously, and was addressed, in a diminutive female hand, to D——, the

Minister, himself. It was thrust carelessly, and even, as it seemed, contemptuously, into one of the uppermost divisions of the rack.

"No sooner had I glanced at this letter than I concluded it to be that of which I was in search. To be sure, it was, to all appearance, radically different from the one of which the Prefect had read us so minute a description. Here the seal was large and black, with the D—— cipher; there it was small and red, with the ducal arms of the S—— family. Here the address, to the Minister, was diminutive and feminine; there the superscription, to a certain royal personage, was markedly bold and decided; the size alone formed a point of correspondence. But, then, the radicalness of these differences, which was excessive; the dirt; the soiled and torn condition of the paper, so inconsistent with the true methodical habits of D——, and so consistent of a design to delude the beholder into an idea of the worthlessness of the document—these things, together with the hyperobtrusive situation of this document, full in the view of every visitor, and thus exactly in accordance with the conclusions to which I had previously arrived—these things, I say, were strongly corroborative of suspicion in one who came with the intention to suspect.

"I protracted my visit as long as possible, and, while I maintained a most animated discussion with the Minister upon a topic which I knew well had never failed to interest and excite him, I kept my attention riveted upon the letter. In this examination I committed to memory its external appearance and arrangement in the rack, and also fell, at length, upon a discovery which set at rest whatever trivial doubt I might have entertained. In scrutinizing the edges of the paper, I observed them to be more chafed than seemed necessary. They presented the broken appearance which is manifested when a stiff paper, having been once folded and pressed with a folder, is refolded in a reversed direction, in the same creases or edges which formed the original fold. This discovery was sufficient. It was clear to me that the letter had been turned, as a glove, inside out, re-directed and re-sealed. I bade the Minister good-morning, and took my departure at once, leaving a gold snuff-box upon the table.

"The next morning I called for the snuff-box, when we resumed, quite eagerly, the conversation of the preceding day. While thus engaged, however, a loud report, as if of a pistol, was heard immediately beneath the windows of the hotel, and was succeeded by a series of fearful screams and the shoutings of a terrified mob. D—— rushed to a casement, threw it open, and looked out. In the mean time I stepped to the card-rack, took the letter, put it in my pocket, and replaced it by a facsimile (so far as regards externals), which I had carefully prepared at my lodgings—imitating the D——cipher, very readily, by means of a seal formed of bread.

"The disturbance in the street had been occasioned by the frantic behavior of a man with a musket. He had fired it among a crowd of women and children. It proved, however, to have been without ball, and the fellow was suffered to go his way as a lunatic or a drunkard. When he had gone, D—— came from the window, whither I had followed him immediately upon securing the object in view. Soon afterward I bade him farewell. The pretended lunatic was a man in my own pay."

"But what purpose had you," I asked, "in replacing the letter by a facsimile? Would it not have been better, at the first visit, to have seized it openly and departed?"

"D——," replied Dupin, "is a desperate man and a man of nerve. His hotel, too, is not without attendants devoted to his interests. Had I made the wild attempt you suggest, I might never have left the Ministerial presence alive. The good people of Paris might have heard of me no more. But I had an object apart from these considerations. You know my political prepossessions. In this matter I act as a partisan of the lady concerned. For eighteen months the Minister has had her in his power. She has now him in hers—since, being unaware that the letter is not in his possession, he will proceed with his exactions as if it was. Thus will he inevitably commit himself, at once, to his political destruction. His downfall, too, will not be more precipitate than awkward. It is all very well to talk about the facilis descensus Averni; but in all kinds of climbing, as Catalani said of singing, it is far more easy to get up than to come down. In the present instance I have no sympathy—at least no pity—for him who descends. He is that monstrum horrendum, an unprincipled man of genius. I confess, however, that I should like very well to know the precise character of his thoughts, when, being defied by her whom the Prefect terms 'a certain personage,' he is reduced to opening the letter I left for him in the card-rack."

"How? Did you put anything particular in it?"

"Why—it did not seem altogether right to leave the interior blank—that would have been insulting. D——, at Vienna once, did me an evil turn, which I told him, quite good-humoredly, that I should remember. So, as I knew he would feel some curiosity in regard to the identity of the person who had outwitted him, I thought it a pity not to give him a clew. He is well acquainted with my MS., and I just copied into the middle of the blank sheet the words:

"'——

... Un dessein si funeste,

S'il n'est digne d'Atrée, este digne de Thyeste.'

They are to be found in Crébillon's Atrée."

RAB AND HIS FRIENDS

Dr. John Brown (1810-1882)

Four-and-thirty years ago, Bob Ainslie and I were coming up Infirmary Street from the High School, our heads together, and our arms intertwisted as only lovers and boys know how or why.

When we got to the top of the street and turned north we espied a crowd at the Tron Church. "A dog-fight!" shouted Bob, and was off; and so was I, both of us all but praying that it might not be over before we got up! And is not this boy-nature, and human nature, too? And don't we all wish a house on fire not to be out before we see it? Dogs like fighting; old Isaac says they "delight" in it, and for the best of all reasons; and boys are not cruel because they like to see the fight. They see three of the great cardinal virtues of dog or man—courage, endurance, and skill—in intense action. This is very different from a love of making dogs fight, and aggravating and making gain by their pluck. A boy—be he ever so fond himself of fighting, if he be a good boy, hates and despises all this, but he would have run off with Bob and me fast enough; it is a natural, and a not wicked, interest that all boys and men have in witnessing intense energy in action.

Does any curious and finely ignorant woman wish to know how Bob's eye at a glance announced a dog-fight to his brain? He did not—he could not—see the dogs fighting; it was a flash of an inference, a rapid induction. The crowd round a couple of dogs fighting is a crowd masculine mainly, with an occasional active, compassionate woman fluttering wildly round the outside and using her tongue and her hands freely upon the men, as so many "brutes"; it is a crowd annular, compact, and mobile; a crowd centripetal, having its eyes and its heads all bent downward and inward to one common focus.

Well, Bob and I are up, and find it is not over; a small thoroughbred, white bull-terrier is busy throttling a large shepherd's dog, unaccustomed to war but not to be trifled with. They are hard at it; the scientific little fellow doing his work in great style, his pastoral enemy fighting wildly, but with the sharpest of teeth and a great courage. Science and breeding, however, soon had their own; the Game Chicken, as the premature Bob called him, working his way up, took his final grip of poor Yarrow's throat—and he lay gasping and done for. His master, a brown, handsome, big, young shepherd from Tweedsmuir, would have liked to have knocked down any man, would "drink up Esil, or eat a crocodile,"

for that part, if he had a chance; it was no use kicking the little dog;
that would only make him hold the closer. Many were the means
shouted out in mouthfuls of the best possible ways of ending it.
"Water!" but there was none near, and many cried for it who might
have got it from the well at Blackfriar's Wynd. "Bite the tail!" and a
large, vague, benevolent, middle-aged man, more desirous than
wise, with some struggle got the bushy end of Yarrow's tail into his
ample mouth and bit it with all his might. This was more than
enough for the much-enduring, much-perspiring shepherd, who,
with a gleam of joy over his broad visage, delivered a terrific facer
upon our large, vague, benevolent, middle-aged friend, who went
down like a shot.

Still the Chicken holds; death not far off. "Snuff! a pinch of
snuff!" observed a calm, highly dressed young buck with an eye-
glass in his eye. "Snuff, indeed!" growled the angry crowd, affronted
and glaring. "Snuff! a pinch of snuff!" again observes the buck, but
with more urgency; whereon were produced several open boxes,
and from a mull which may have been at Culloden he took a pinch,
knelt down, and presented it to the nose of the Chicken, The laws of
physiology and of snuff take their course; the Chicken sneezes, and
Yarrow is free!

The young pastoral giant stalks off with Yarrow in his arms—
comforting him.

But the bull-terrier's blood is up, and his soul unsatisfied; he
grips the first dog he meets, and, discovering she is not a dog, in
Homeric phrase, he makes a brief sort of amende and is off. The
boys, with Bob and me at their head, are after him: down Niddry
Street he goes, bent on mischief; up the Cowgate like an arrow—Bob
and I, and our small men; panting behind.

There, under the single arch of the South Bridge, is a huge
mastiff, sauntering down the middle of the causeway, as if with his
hands in his pockets; he is old, brindled, as big as a little Highland
bull, and has the Shakespearean dewlaps shaking as he goes.

The Chicken makes straight at him, and fastens on his throat.
To our astonishment, the great creature does nothing but stand still,
hold himself up, and roar—yes, roar, a long, serious, remonstrative
roar. How is this? Bob and I are up to them. He is muzzled! The
bailies had proclaimed a general muzzling, and his master, studying
strength and economy mainly, had encompassed his huge jaws in a
home-made apparatus constructed out of the leather of some
ancient breechin. His mouth was open as far as it could; his lips
curled up in rage—a sort of terrible grin; his teeth gleaming, ready,
from out the darkness; the strap across his mouth tense as a
bowstring; his whole frame stiff with indignation and surprise; his

roar asking us all round, "Did you ever see the like of this?" He looked a statue of anger and astonishment done in Aberdeen granite.

We soon had a crowd; the Chicken held on. "A knife!" cried Bob; and a cobbler gave him his knife; you know the kind of knife, worn obliquely to a point and always keen. I put its edge to the tense leather; it ran before it; and then!—one sudden jerk of that enormous head, a sort of dirty mist about his mouth, no noise, and the bright and fierce little fellow is dropped, limp and dead. A solemn pause; this was more than any of us had bargained for. I turned the little fellow over, and saw he was quite dead: the mastiff had taken him by the small of the back like a rat and broken it.

He looked down at his victim appeased, ashamed, and amazed; sniffed him all over, stared at him, and, taking a sudden thought, turned round and trotted off. Bob took the dead dog up, and said, "John, we'll bury him after tea." "Yes," said I, and was off after the mastiff. He made up the Cowgate at a rapid swing; he had forgotten some engagement. He turned up the Candlemaker Row, and stopped at the Harrow Inn.

There was a carrier's cart ready to start, and a keen, thin, impatient, black-a-vised little man, his hand at his gray horse's head, looking about angrily for something. "Rab, ye thief!" said he, aiming a kick at my great friend, who drew cringing up, and, avoiding the heavy shoe with more agility than dignity and watching his master's eye? slunk dismayed under the cart—his ears down, and as much as he had of tail down, too.

What a man this must be—thought I—to whom my tremendous hero turns tail! The carrier saw the muzzle hanging, cut and useless, from his neck, and I eagerly told him the story, which Bob and I always thought, and still think, Homer, or King David, or Sir Walter alone were worthy to rehearse. The severe little man was mitigated, and condescended to say, "Rab, ma man—puir Rabbie," whereupon the stump of a tail rose up, the ears were cocked, the eyes filled and were comforted; the two friends were reconciled. "Hupp!" and a stroke of the whip were given to Jess, and off went the three.

Bob and I buried the Game Chicken that night (we had not much of a tea) in the back-green of his house, in Melville Street, No. 17, with considerable gravity and silence; and being at the time in the Iliad, and, like all boys, Trojans, we of course called him Hector.

Six years have passed—a long time for a boy and a dog; Bob Ainslie is off to the wars; I am a medical student, and clerk at Minto House Hospital.

Rab I saw almost every week, on the Wednesday, and we had much pleasant intimacy. I found the way to his heart by frequent scratching of his huge head and an occasional bone. When I did not notice him he would plant himself straight before me and stand wagging that bud of a tail, and looking up, with his head a little to the one side. His master I occasionally saw; he used to call me "Maister John," but was laconic as any Spartan.

One fine October afternoon I was leaving the hospital, when I saw the large gate open, and in walked Rab, with that great and easy saunter of his. He looked as if taking possession of the place, like the Duke of Wellington entering a subdued city, satiated with victory and peace. After him came Jess, now white from age, with her cart; and in it a woman carefully wrapped up—the carrier leading the horse anxiously and looking back. When he saw me, James (for his name was James Noble) made a curt and grotesque "boo," and said, "Maister John, this is the mistress; she's got a trouble in her breest—some kind o' an income, we're thinkin'."

By this time I saw the woman's face; she was sitting on a sack filled with straw, with her husband's plaid round her, and his big-coat, with its large, white metal buttons, over her feet.

I never saw a more unforgettable face—pale, serious, lonely, delicate, sweet, without being at all what we call fine. She looked sixty, and had on a mutch, white as snow, with its black ribbon; her silvery, smooth hair setting off her dark-gray eyes—eyes such as one sees only twice or thrice in a lifetime, full of suffering, full also of the overcoming of it; her eyebrows black and delicate, and her mouth firm, patient, and contented, which few mouths ever are.

As I have said, I never saw a more beautiful countenance, or one more subdued to settled quiet. "Ailie," said James, "this is Maister John, the young doctor; Rab's friend, ye ken. We often speak aboot you, doctor." She smiled and made a movement, but said nothing, and prepared to come down, putting her plaid aside and rising. Had Solomon, in all his glory, been handing down the Queen of Sheba at his palace gate, he could not have done it more daintily, more tenderly, more like a gentleman than James, the Howland carrier, when he lifted down Ailie, his wife. The contrast of his small, swarthy, weather-beaten, keen, worldly face to hers—pale, subdued, and beautiful—was something wonderful. Rab looked on concerned and puzzled, but ready for anything that might turn up, were it to strangle the nurse, the porter, or even me. Ailie and he seemed great friends.

"As I was sayin', she's got a kind o' trouble in her breest, doctor; wull ye tak' a look at it?" We walked into the consulting-room, all four; Rab, grim and comic, willing to be happy and confidential if cause should be shown, willing also to be the reverse on the same terms. Ailie sat down, undid her open gown and her lawn handkerchief round her neck, and, without a word, showed me her right breast. I looked at it and examined it carefully, she and James watching me, and Rab eying all three. What could I say? There it was, that had once been so soft, so shapely, so white, so gracious and bountiful, so "full of all blessed condition," hard as a stone, a centre of horrid pain, making that pale face, with its gray, lucid, reasonable eyes, and its sweet, resolved mouth, express the full measure of suffering overcome. Why was that gentle, modest, sweet woman, clean and lovable, condemned by God to bear such a burden?

I got her away to bed. "May Rab and me bide?" said James. "You may; and Rab, if he will behave himself." "I'se warrant he's do that, doctor." And in slunk the faithful beast. There are no such dogs now. He belonged to a lost tribe. As I have said, he was brindled, and gray like Rubislaw granite; his hair short, hard, and close, like a lion's; his body thick-set, like a little bull—a sort of compressed Hercules of a dog. He must have been ninety pounds' weight, at the least; he had a large, blunt head; his muzzle black as night; his mouth blacker than any night; a tooth or two—being all he had— gleaming out of his jaws of darkness. His head was scarred with the records of old wounds, a sort of series of fields of battles all over it; one eye out, one ear cropped as close as was Archbishop Leighton's father's; the remaining eye had the power of two; and above it, and in constant communication with it, was a tattered rag of an ear, which was forever unfurling itself, like an old flag; and then that bud of a tail, about one inch long, if it could in any sense be said to be long, being as broad as long—the mobility, the instantaneousness of that bud were very funny and surprising, and its expressive twinklings and winkings, the intercommunications between the eye, the ear, and it, were of the oddest and swiftest.

Rab had the dignity and simplicity of great size; and, having fought his way all along the road to absolute supremacy, he was as mighty in his own line as Julius Caesar or the Duke of Wellington, and had the gravity of all great fighters.

You must have often observed the likeness of certain men to certain animals, and of certain dogs to men. Now, I never looked at Rab without thinking of the great Baptist preacher, Andrew Fuller. The same large, heavy, menacing, combative, sombre, honest countenance, the same deep, inevitable eye; the same look, as of thunder asleep, but ready—neither a dog nor a man to be trifled with.

Next day my master, the surgeon, examined Ailie. There could be no doubt it must kill her, and soon. If it could be removed—it might never return—it would give her speedy relief—she should have it done. She curtsied, looked at James, and said, "When?" "To-morrow," said the kind surgeon—a man of few words. She and James and Rab and I retired. I noticed that he and she spoke little, but seemed to anticipate everything in each other. The following day, at noon, the students came in, hurrying up the great stair. At the first landing-place, on a small, well-known blackboard, was a bit of paper fastened by wafers, and many remains of old wafers beside it. On the paper were the words:

"An operation to-day.—J.B., Clerk."

Up ran the youths, eager to secure good places; in they crowded, full of interest and talk. "What's the case?" "Which side is it?"

Don't think them heartless; they are neither better nor worse than you or I; they get over their professional horrors, and into their proper work; and in them pity, as an emotion, ending in itself or at best in tears and a long-drawn breath, lessens, while pity, as a motive, is quickened, and gains power and purpose. It is well for poor human nature that it is so.

The operating-theatre is crowded; much talk and fun, and all the cordiality and stir of youth. The surgeon with his staff of assistants is there. In comes Ailie; one look at her quiets and abates the eager students. That beautiful old woman is too much for them; they sit down, and are dumb, and gaze at her. These rough boys feel the power of her presence. She walks in quietly, but without haste; dressed in her mutch, her neckerchief, her white dimity short-gown, her black bombazeen petticoat, showing her white worsted stockings and her carpet shoes. Behind her was James with Rab. James sat down in the distance, and took that huge and noble head between his knees. Rab looked perplexed and dangerous—forever cocking his ear and dropping it as fast.

Ailie stepped up on a seat, and laid herself on the table, as her friend the surgeon told her; arranged herself, gave a rapid look at James, shut her eyes, rested herself on me, and took my hand. The operation was at once begun; it was necessarily slow; and chloroform—one of God's best gifts to his suffering children—was then unknown. The surgeon did his work. The pale face showed its pain, but was still and silent. Rab's soul was working within him; he saw something strange was going on, blood flowing from his mistress, and she suffering; his ragged ear was up and importunate; he growled and gave now and then a sharp, impatient yelp; he would have liked to have done something to that man. But James had him firm, and gave him a glower from time to time, and an intimation of a possible kick; all the better for James—it kept his eye and his mind off Ailie.

It is over; she is dressed, steps gently and decently down from the table, looks for James; then turning to the surgeon and the students, she curtsies, and in a low, clear voice, begs their pardon if she has behaved ill. The students—all of us—wept like children; the surgeon wrapped her up carefully, and, resting on James and me, Ailie went to her room, and Rab followed. We put her to bed. James took off his heavy shoes, crammed with tackets, heel-capped and toe-capped, and put them carefully under the table, saying: "Maister John, I'm for nane o' yer strynge nurse bodies for Ailie. I'll be her nurse, and I'll gang aboot on my stockin' soles as canny as pussy." And so he did; and handy and clever, and swift and tender as any woman was that horny-handed, snell, peremptory little man. Everything she got he gave her; he seldom slept; and often I saw his small, shrewd eyes out of the darkness, fixed on her. As before, they spoke little.

Rab behaved well, never moving, showing us how meek and gentle he could be, and occasionally, in his sleep, letting us know that he was demolishing some adversary. He took a walk with me every day, generally to the Candlemaker Row; but he was sombre and mild; declined doing battle, though some fit cases offered, and indeed submitted to sundry indignities; and was always very ready to turn, and came faster back, and trotted up the stair with much lightness, and went straight to that door.

Jess, the mare, had been sent, with her weather-beaten cart, to Howgate, and had doubtless her own dim and placid meditations and confusions on the absence of her master and Rab and her unnatural freedom from the road and her cart.

For some days Ailie did well. The wound healed "by the first intention"; for as James said, "Oor Ailie's skin's ower clean to beil." The students came in quiet and anxious, and surrounded her bed. She said she liked to see their young, honest faces. The surgeon dressed her, and spoke to her in his own short, kind way, pitying her through his eyes, Rab and James outside the circle—Rab being now reconciled, and even cordial, and having made up his mind that as yet nobody required worrying, but, as you may suppose, semper paratus.

So far well; but, four days after the operation, my patient had a sudden and long shivering, a "groosin," as she called it. I saw her soon after; her eyes were too bright, her cheek colored; she was restless, and ashamed of being so; the balance was lost; mischief had begun. On looking at the wound, a blush of red told the secret; her pulse was rapid, her breathing anxious and quick; she wasn't herself, as she said, and was vexed at her restlessness. We tried what we could. James did everything, was everywhere, never in the way, never out of it; Rab subsided under the table into a dark place, and was motionless, all but his eye, which followed every one. Ailie got worse; began to wander in her mind, gently; was more demonstrative in her ways to James, rapid in her questions, and sharp at times. He was vexed, and said, "She was never that way afore, no, never." For a time she knew her head was wrong, and was always asking our pardon—the dear, gentle old woman; then delirium set in strong, without pause. Her brain gave way, and then came that terrible spectacle,

"The intellectual power, through words and things,
Went sounding on, a dim and perilous way";

she sang bits of old songs and Psalms, stopping suddenly, mingling the Psalms of David and the diviner words of his Son and Lord with homely odds and ends of ballads.

Nothing more touching, or in a sense more strangely beautiful, did I ever witness. Her tremulous, rapid, affectionate, eager, Scotch voice—the swift, aimless, bewildered mind, the baffled utterance, the bright and perilous eye; some wild words, some household cares, something for James, the names of the dead, Rab called rapidly and in a "fremyt" voice, and he starting up, surprised, and slinking off as if he were to blame somehow, or had been dreaming he heard. Many eager questions and beseechings which James and I could make nothing of, and on which she seemed to set her all, and then sink back ununderstood. It was very sad, but better than many things that are not called sad. James hovered about, put out and miserable, but active and exact as ever; read to her, when there was a lull, short bits from the Psalms, prose and metre, chanting the latter in his own rude and serious way, showing great knowledge of the fit words, bearing up like a man, and doating over her as his "ain Ailie." "Ailie, ma woman!" "Ma ain bonnie wee dawtie!"

The end was drawing on; the golden bowl was breaking; the silver cord was fast being loosed—that animula, blandula, vagula, hospes, comesque, was about to flee. The body and the soul—companions for sixty years—were being sundered and taking leave. She was walking, alone, through the valley of that shadow into which one day we must all enter—and yet she was not alone, for we know whose rod and staff were comforting her.

One night she had fallen quiet, and, as we hoped, asleep; her eyes were shut. We put down the gas, and sat watching her. Suddenly she sat up in bed, and, taking a bedgown which was lying on it rolled up, she held it eagerly to her breast—to the right side. We could see her eyes bright with a surprising tenderness and joy, bending over this bundle of clothes. She held it as a woman holds her sucking child; opening out her night-gown impatiently, and holding it close and brooding over it and murmuring foolish little words, as over one whom his mother comforteth, and who sucks and is satisfied. It was pitiful and strange to see her wasted, dying look, keen and yet vague—her immense love.

"Preserve me!" groaned James, giving way. And then she rocked back and forward, as if to make it sleep, hushing it, and wasting on it her infinite fondness. "Wae's me, doctor; I declare she's thinkin' it's that bairn." "What bairn?" "The only bairn we ever had; our wee Mysie, and she's in the Kingdom forty years and mair." It was plainly true; the pain in the breast, telling its urgent story to a bewildered, ruined brain, was misread and mistaken; it suggested to her the uneasiness of a breast full of milk, and then the child; and so again once more they were together, and she had her ain wee Mysie on her bosom.

This was the close. She sank rapidly; the delirium left her; but, as she whispered, she was "clean silly"; it was the lightening before the final darkness. After having for some time lain still, her eyes shut, she said, "James!" He came close to her, and, lifting up her calm, clear, beautiful eyes, she gave him a long look, turned to me kindly but shortly, looked for Rab but could not see him, then turned to her husband again, as if she would never leave off looking, shut her eyes, and composed herself. She lay for some time breathing quick, and passed away so gently that, when we thought she was gone, James, in his old-fashioned way, held the mirror to her face. After a long pause, one small spot of dimness was breathed out; it vanished away, and never returned, leaving the blank, clear darkness without a stain. "What is our life? It is even as a vapor, which appeareth for a little time, and then vanisheth away."

Rab all this time had been full awake and motionless; he came forward beside us; Ailie's hand, which James had held, was hanging down; it was soaked with his tears; Rab licked it all over carefully, looked at her, and returned to his place under the table.

James and I sat, I don't know how long, but for some time. Saying nothing, he started up abruptly, and with some noise went to the table, and, putting his right fore and middle fingers each into a shoe, pulled them out and put them on, breaking one of the leather latchets, and muttering in anger, "I never did the like o' that afore!"

I believe he never did; nor after either. "Rab!" he said, roughly, and, pointing with his thumb to the bottom of the bed. Rab leaped up and settled himself, his head and eye to the dead face. "Maister John, ye'll wait for me," said the carrier; and disappeared in the darkness, thundering down-stairs in his heavy shoes. I ran to a front window; there he was, already round the house and out at the gate, fleeing like a shadow.

I was afraid about him, and yet not afraid; so I sat down beside Rab, and, being wearied, fell asleep. I awoke from a sudden noise outside. It was November, and there had been a heavy fall of snow. Rab was in statu quo; he heard the noise, too, and plainly knew it, but never moved. I looked out; and there, at the gate, in the dim morning—for the sun was not up—was Jess and the cart, a cloud of steam rising from the old mare. I did not see James; he was already at the door, and came up the stairs and met me. It was less than three hours since he left, and he must have posted out—who knows how?—to Howgate, full nine miles off, yoked Jess, and driven her astonished into town. He had an armful of blankets, and was streaming with perspiration. He nodded to me, and spread out on the floor two pairs of clean old blankets having at their corners, "A.G., 1794," in large letters in red worsted. These were the initials of Alison Graeme, and James may have looked in at her from without—himself unseen but not unthought of—when he was "wat, wat, and weary," and, after having walked many a mile over the hills, may have seen her sitting, while "a' the lave were sleeping," and by the firelight working her name on the blankets for her ain James's bed.

He motioned Rab down, and, taking his wife in his arms, laid her in the blankets, and happed her carefully and firmly up, leaving the face uncovered; and then, lifting her, he nodded again sharply to me, and with a resolved but utterly miserable face strode along the passage and down-stairs, followed by Rab. I followed with a light; but he didn't need it. I went out, holding stupidly the candle in my hand in the calm, frosty air; we were soon at the gate. I could have helped him, but I saw he was not to be meddled with, and he was strong, and did not need it. He laid her down as tenderly, as safely, as he had lifted her out ten days before—as tenderly as when he had her first in his arms when she was only "A.G."—sorted her, leaving that beautiful sealed face open to the heavens; and then, taking Jess by the head, he moved away. He did not notice me, neither did Rab, who presided behind the cart.

I stood till they passed through the long shadow of the College and turned up Nicolson Street. I heard the solitary cart sound through the streets, and die away and come again; and I returned, thinking of that company going up Libberton Brae, then along Roslin Muir, the morning light touching the Pentlands, and making them like onlooking ghosts; then down the hill through Auchindinny woods, past "haunted Woodhouselee"; and as daybreak came sweeping up the bleak Lammermuirs, and fell on his own door, the company would stop, and James would take the key, and lift Ailie up again, laying her on her own bed, and, having put Jess up, would return with Rab and shut the door.

James buried his wife, with his neighbors mourning, Rab watching the proceedings from a distance. It was snow, and that black, ragged hole would look strange in the midst of the swelling, spotless cushion of white. James looked after everything; then rather suddenly fell ill, and took to bed; was insensible when the doctor came, and soon died. A sort of low fever was prevailing in the village, and his want of sleep, his exhaustion, and his misery made him apt to take it. The grave was not difficult to reopen. A fresh fall of snow had again made all things white and smooth; Rab once more looked on, and slunk home to the stable.

And what of Rab? I asked for him next week at the new carrier who got the good-will of James's business and was now master of Jess and her cart. "How's Rab?" He put me off, and said, rather rudely, "What's your business wi' the dowg?" I was not to be so put off. "Where's Rab?" He, getting confused and red, and intermeddling with his hair, said, "'Deed, sir, Rab's deid." "Dead! What did he die of?" "Weel, sir," said he, getting redder, "he didna' exactly dee; he was killed. I had to brain him wi' a rack-pin; there was nae doin' wi' him. He lay in the treviss wi' the mear, and wadna come oot. I tempit him wi' kail and meat, but he wad tak naething, and keepit me frae feeding the beast, and he was aye gurrin', and grup, gruppin' me by the legs. I was laith to mak' awa' wi' the auld dowg, his like wasna atween this and Thornhill—but, 'deed, sir, I could do naething else." I believed him. Fit end for Rab, quick and complete. His teeth and his friends gone, why should he keep the peace and be civil?

He was buried in the braeface, near the burn, the children of the village, his companions, who used to make very free with him and sit on his ample stomach as he lay half asleep at the door in the sun, watching the solemnity.

THE BOOTS AT THE HOLLY-TREE INN

Charles Dickens (1812-1870)

Where had he been in his time? he repeated, when I asked him the question, Lord, he had been everywhere! And what had he been? Bless you, he had been everything you could mention, a'most!

Seen a good deal? Why, of course he had. I should say so, he could assure me, if I only knew about a twentieth part of what had come in his way. Why, it would be easier for him, he expected, to tell what he hadn't seen than what he had. Ah! a deal, it would.

What was the curiousest thing he had seen? Well! He didn't know. He couldn't momently name what was the curiousest thing he had seen—unless it was a Unicorn—and he see him once at a fair. But supposing a young gentleman not eight year old was to run away with a fine young woman of seven, might I think that a queer start? Certainly. Then that was a start as he himself had had his blessed eyes on, and he had cleaned the shoes they run away in— and they was so little he couldn't get his hand into 'em.

Master Harry Walmers' father, you see, he lived at the Elmses, down away by Shooter's Hill there, six or seven miles from Lunnon. He was a gentleman of spirit, and good-looking, and held his head up when he walked, and had what you call Fire about him. He wrote poetry, and he rode, and he ran, and he cricketed, and he danced, and he acted, and he done it all equally beautiful. He was uncommon proud of Master Harry as was his only child; but he didn't spoil him neither. He was a gentleman that had a will of his own and a eye of his own, and that would be minded. Consequently, though he made quite a companion of the fine bright boy, and was delighted to see him so fond of reading his fairy-books, and was never tired of hearing him say my name is Norval, or hearing him sing his songs about Young May Moons is beaming love, and When he as adores thee has left but the name, and that; still he kept the command over the child, and the child was a child, and it's to be wished more of 'em was.

How did Boots happen to know all this? Why, through being under-gardener. Of course he couldn't be under-gardener, and he always about, in the summer-time, near the windows on the lawn, a-mowing, and sweeping, and weeding, and pruning, and this and that, without getting acquainted with the ways of the family. Even supposing Master Harry hadn't come to him one morning early, and said, "Cobbs, how should you spell Norah, if you was asked?" and then began cutting it in print all over the fence.

He couldn't say that he had taken particular notice of children before that; but really it was pretty to see them two mites a-going about the place together, deep in love. And the courage of the boy! Bless your soul, he'd have throwed off his little hat, and tucked up his little sleeves, and gone in at a lion, he would, if they had happened to meet one, and she had been frightened of him. One day he stops, along with her, where Boots was hoeing weeds in the gravel, and says, speaking up, "Cobbs," he says, "I like you." "Do you, sir? I'm proud to hear it." "Yes, I do, Cobbs. Why do I like you, do you think, Cobbs?" "Don't know, Master Harry, I am sure." "Because Norah likes you, Cobbs." "Indeed, sir? That's very gratifying." "Gratifying, Cobbs? It's better than millions of the brightest diamonds to be liked by Norah." "Certainly, sir." "Would you like another situation, Cobbs?" "Well, sir, I shouldn't object if it was a good 'un." "Then, Cobbs," says he, "you shall be our Head Gardener when we are married." And he tucks her, in her little sky-blue mantle, under his arm, and walks away.

Boots could assure me that it was better than a picter, and equal to a play, to see them babies, with their long, bright, curling hair, their sparkling eyes, and their beautiful light tread, a-rambling about the garden, deep in love. Boots was of opinion that the birds believed they was birds, and kept up with 'em, singing to please 'em. Sometimes they would creep under the tulip-tree, and would sit there with their arms round one another's necks, and their soft cheeks touching, a-reading about the Prince and the Dragon, and the good and bad enchanters, and the king's fair daughter. Sometimes he would hear them planning about a house in a forest, keeping bees and a cow, and living entirely on milk and honey. Once he came upon them by the pond, and heard Master Harry say, "Adorable Norah, kiss me, and say you love me to distraction, or I'll jump in head foremost." And Boots made no question he would have done it if she hadn't complied. On the whole, Boots said it had a tendency to make him feel he was in love himself—only he didn't exactly know who with.

"Cobbs," said Master Harry, one evening, when Cobbs was watering the flowers, "I am going on a visit, this present midsummer, to my grandmamma's at York."

"Are you, indeed, sir? I hope you'll have a pleasant time. I am going into Yorkshire, myself, when I leave here."

"Are you going to your grandmamma's, Cobbs?"

"No, sir. I haven't got such a thing."

"Not as a grandmamma, Cobbs?"

"No, sir."

The boy looked on at the watering of the flowers for a little while, and then said, "I shall be very glad indeed to go, Cobbs—Norah's going."

"You'll be all right, then, sir," says Cobbs, "with your beautiful sweetheart by your side."

"Cobbs," returned the boy, flushing, "I never let anybody joke about it when I can prevent them."

"It wasn't a joke, sir," says Cobbs, with humility—"wasn't so meant."

"I am glad of that, Cobbs, because I like you, you know, and you're going to live with us. Cobbs!"

"Sir."

"What do you think my grandmamma gives me when I go down there?"

"I couldn't so much as make a guess, sir."

"A Bank-of-England five-pound note, Cobbs."

"Whew!" says Cobbs, "that's a spanking sum of money, Master Harry."

"A person could do a great deal with such a sum of money as that—couldn't a person, Cobbs?"

"I believe you, sir!"

"Cobbs," said the boy, "I'll tell you a secret. At Norah's house they have been joking her about me, and pretending to laugh at our being engaged—pretending to make game of it, Cobbs!"

"Such, sir," says Cobbs, "is the depravity of human natur'."

The boy, looking exactly like his father, stood for a few minutes with his glowing face toward the sunset, and then departed with, "Good-night, Cobbs. I'm going in."

If I was to ask Boots how it happened that he was a-going to leave that place just at that present time, well, he couldn't rightly answer me. He did suppose he might have stayed there till now if he had been anyways inclined. But you see, he was younger then, and he wanted change. That's what he wanted—change. Mr. Walmers, he said to him when he gave him notice of his intentions to leave, "Cobbs," he says, "have you anythink to complain of? I make the inquiry, because if I find that any of my people really has anythink to complain of, I wish to make it right if I can." "No, sir," says Cobbs; "thanking you, sir, I find myself as well sitiwated here as I could hope to be anywheres. The truth is, sir, that I'm a-going to seek my fortun'." "Oh, indeed, Cobbs!" he says; "I hope you may find it." And Boots could assure me—which he did, touching his hair with his bootjack, as a salute in the way of his present calling—that he hadn't found it yet.

Well, sir! Boots left the Elmses when his time was up, and Master Harry, he went down to the old lady's at York, which old lady would have given that child the teeth out of her head (if she had had any), she was so wrapped up in him. What does that Infant do— for Infant you may call him, and be within the mark—but cut away from that old lady's with his Norah, on a expedition to go to Gretna Green and be married!

Sir, Boots was at this identical Holly-Tree Inn (having left it several times to better himself, but always come back through one thing or another), when, one summer afternoon, the coach drives up, and out of the coach gets them two children. The Guard says to our Governor, "I don't quite make out these little passengers, but the young gentleman's words was, that they was to be brought here." The young gentleman gets out; hands his lady out; gives the Guard something for himself; says to our Governor, "We're to stop here to-night, please. Sitting-room and two bedrooms will be required. Chops and cherry-pudding for two!" and tucks her in her little sky-blue mantle, under his arm, and walks into the house much bolder than Brass.

Boots leaves me to judge what the amazement of that establishment was, when these two tiny creatures all alone by themselves was marched into the Angel—much more so when he, who had seen them without their seeing him, give the Governor his views upon the expedition they was upon. "Cobbs," says the Governor, "if this is so, I must set off myself to York, and quiet their friends' minds. In which case you must keep your eye upon 'em, and humor 'em till I come back. But before I take these measures, Cobbs, I should wish you to find from themselves whether your opinions is correct." "Sir, to you," says Cobbs, "that shall be done directly."

So Boots goes up-stairs to the Angel, and there he finds Master Harry, on a e'normous sofa—immense at any time, but looking like the Great Bed of Ware, compared with him—a-drying the eyes of Miss Norah with his pocket-hankecher. Their little legs was entirely off the ground, of course, and it really is not possible for Boots to express to me how small them children looked.

"It's Cobbs! It's Cobbs!" cries Master Harry, and comes running to him on t'other side, and catching hold of his t'other hand, and they both jump for joy.

"I see you a-getting out, sir," says Cobbs. "I thought it was you. I thought I couldn't be mistaken in your height and figure. What's the object of your journey, sir? Matrimonial?"

"We're going to be married, Cobbs, at Gretna Green," returned the boy. "We have run away on purpose. Norah has been in rather low spirits, Cobbs; but she'll be happy, now we have found you to be our friend."

"Thank you, sir, and thank you, miss," says Cobbs, "for your good opinion. Did you bring any luggage with you, sir?"

If I will believe Boots when he gives me his word and honor upon it, the lady had got a parasol, a smelling-bottle, a round and a half of cold buttered toast, eight peppermint drops, and a hair-brush—seemingly a doll's. The gentleman had got about half a dozen yards of string, a knife, three or four sheets of writing-paper, folded up surprising small, a orange, and a Chaney mug with his name upon it.

"What may be the exact nature of your plans, sir?" says Cobbs.

"To go on," replied the boy—which the courage of that boy was something wonderful!—"in the morning, and be married to-morrow."

"Just so, sir," says Cobbs. "Would it meet your views, sir, if I was to accompany you?"

When Cobbs said this, they both jumped for joy again, and cried out, "Oh yes, yes, Cobbs! Yes!"

"Well, sir!" says Cobbs. "If you will excuse me having the freedom to give an opinion, what I should recommend would be this. I am acquainted with a pony, sir, which, put in a pheayton that I could borrow, would take you and Mrs. Harry Walmers, Junior (myself driving, if you approved), to the end of your journey in a very short space of time. I am not altogether sure, sir, that this pony will be at liberty to-morrow, but even if you had to wait over to-morrow for him, it might be worth your while. As to the small account here, sir, in case you was to find yourself running at all short, that don't signify; because I am a part proprietor of this inn, and it could stand over."

Boots assures me that when they clapped their hands, and jumped for joy again, and called him "Good Cobbs!" and "Dear Cobbs!" and bent across him to kiss one another in the delight of their confiding hearts, he felt himself the meanest rascal for deceiving 'em that ever was born.

"Is there anything you want just at present, sir?" says Cobbs, mortally ashamed of himself.

"We should like some cakes after dinner," answered Master Harry, folding his arms, putting out one leg, and looking straight at him, "and two apples and jam. With dinner we should like to have toast and water. But Norah has always been accustomed to half a glass of currant wine at dessert. And so have I."

"It shall be ordered at the bar, sir," says Cobbs; and away he went.

Boots has the feeling as fresh upon him this moment of speaking as he had then, that he would far rather have had it out in half a dozen rounds with the Governor than have combined with him; and that he wished with all his heart there was any impossible place where two babies could make an impossible marriage, and live impossibly happy ever afterward. However, as it couldn't be, he went into the Governor's plans, and the Governor set off for York in half an hour.

The way in which the women of that house—without exception—every one of 'em—married and single—took to that boy when they heard the story, Boots considers surprising. It was as much as he could do to keep 'em from dashing into the room and kissing him. They climbed up all sorts of places, at the risk of their lives, to look at him through a pane of glass. They was seven deep at the keyhole. They was out of their minds about him and his bold spirit.

In the evening, Boots went into the room to see how the runaway couple was getting on. The gentleman was on the window-seat, supporting the lady in his arms. She had tears upon her face, and was lying, very tired and half asleep, with her head upon his shoulder.

"Mrs. Harry Walmers, Junior, fatigued, sir?" says Cobbs.

"Yes, she is tired, Cobbs; but she is not used to be away from home, and she has been in low spirits again. Cobbs, do you think you could bring a biffin, please?"

"I ask your pardon, sir," says Cobbs. "What was it you—"

"I think a Norfolk biffin would rouse her, Cobbs. She is very fond of them."

Boots withdrew in search of the required restorative, and, when he brought it in, the gentleman handed it to the lady, and fed her with a spoon, and took a little himself; the lady being heavy with sleep, and rather cross. "What should you think, sir," says Cobbs, "of a chamber candlestick?" The gentleman approved; the chambermaid went first, up the great staircase; the lady, in her sky-blue mantle, followed, gallantly escorted by the gentleman; the gentleman embraced her at her door, and retired to his own apartment, where Boots softly locked him in.

Boots couldn't but feel with increased acuteness what a base deceiver he was, when they consulted him at breakfast (they had ordered sweet milk-and-water, and toast and currant jelly, over-night) about the pony. It really was as much as he could do, he don't mind confessing to me, to look them two young things in the face, and think what a wicked old father of lies he had grown up to be. Howsomever, he went on a-lying like a Trojan about the pony. He told 'em that it did so unfortunately happen that the pony was half clipped, you see, and that he couldn't be taken out in that state, for fear it should strike to his inside. But that he'd be finished clipping in the course of the day, and that to-morrow morning at eight o'clock the pheayton would be ready. Boots' view of the whole case, looking back on it in my room, is, that Mrs. Harry Walmers, Junior, was beginning to give in. She hadn't had her hair curled when she went to bed, and she didn't seem quite up to brushing it herself, and its getting in her eyes put her out. But nothing put out Master Harry. He sat behind his breakfast-cup, a-tearing away at the jelly, as if he had been his own father.

After breakfast Boots is inclined to consider they drawed soldiers—at least he knows that many such was found in the fireplace, all on horseback. In the course of the morning Master Harry rang the bell—it was surprising how that there boy did carry on—and said, in a sprightly way, "Cobbs, is there any good walks in this neighborhood?"

"Yes, sir," says Cobbs. "There's Love Lane."

"Get out with you, Cobbs!"—that was that there boy's expression—"you're joking."

"Begging your pardon, sir," says Cobbs, "there really is Love Lane. And a pleasant walk it is, and proud shall I be to show it to yourself and Mrs. Harry Walmers, Junior."

"Norah, dear," says Master Harry, "this is curious. We really ought to see Love Lane. Put on your bonnet, my sweetest darling, and we will go there with Cobbs."

Boots leaves me to judge what a Beast he felt himself to be, when that young pair told him, as they all three jogged along together, that they had made up their minds to give him two thousand guineas a year as Head Gardener, on account of his being so true a friend to 'em. Boots could have wished at the moment that the earth would have opened and swallowed him up, he felt so mean, with their beaming eyes a-looking at him, and believing him. Well, sir, he turned the conversation as well as he could, and he took 'em down Love Lane to the water-meadows, and there Master Harry would have drowned himself in half a moment more, a-getting out a water-lily for her—but nothing daunted that boy. Well, sir, they was tired out. All being so new and strange to 'em, they was tired as tired could be. And they laid down on a bank of daisies, like the children in the wood, leastways meadows, and fell asleep.

Boots don't know—perhaps I do—but never mind, it don't signify either way—why it made a man fit to make a fool of himself to see them two pretty babies a-lying there in the clear, still day, not dreaming half so hard when they was asleep as they done when they was awake. But, Lord! when you come to think of yourself, you know, and what a game you have been up to ever since you was in your own cradle, and what a poor sort of chap you are, and how it's always either Yesterday with you, or To-morrow, and never To-day, that's where it is!

Well, sir, they woke up at last, and then one thing was getting pretty clear to Boots—namely, that Mrs. Harry Walmerses, Junior's, temper was on the move. When Master Harry took her round the waist, she said he "teased her so"; and when he says, "Norah, my young May Moon, your Harry tease you?" she tells him, "Yes; and I want to go home."

A biled fowl and baked bread-and-butter pudding brought Mrs. Walmers up a little; but Boots could have wished, he must privately own to me, to have seen her more sensible of the woice of love, and less abandoning of herself to currants. However, Master Harry, he kept up, and his noble heart was as fond as ever. Mrs. Walmers turned very sleepy about dusk, and began to cry. Therefore, Mrs. Walmers went off to bed as per yesterday; and Master Harry ditto repeated.

About eleven or twelve at night comes back the Governor in a chaise, along with Mr. Walmers and a elderly lady. Mr. Walmers looks amused and very serious, both at once, and says to our Missis: "We are much indebted to you, ma'am; for your kind care of our little children, which we can never sufficiently acknowledge. Pray, ma'am, where is my boy?" Our Missis says: "Cobbs has the dear child in charge, sir. Cobbs, show Forty!" Then he says to Cobbs: "Ah, Cobbs, I am glad to see you! I understood you was here!" And Cobbs says: "Yes, sir. Your most obedient, sir."

I may be surprised to hear Boots say it, perhaps; but Boots assures me that his heart beat like a hammer, going up-stairs. "I beg your pardon, sir," says he, while unlocking the door; "I do hope you are not angry with Master Harry. For Master Harry is a fine boy, sir, and will do you credit and honor." And Boots signifies to me that, if the fine boy's father had contradicted him in the daring state of mind in which he then was, he thinks he should have "fetched him a crack," and taken the consequences.

But Mr. Walmers only says: "No, Cobbs. No, my good fellow. Thank you!" And, the door being opened, goes in.

Boots goes in, too, holding the light, and he sees Mr. Walmers go up to the bedside, bend gently down, and kiss the little sleeping face. Then he stands looking at it for a minute, looking wonderfully like it (they do say he ran away with Mrs. Walmers); and then he gently shakes the little shoulder.

"Harry, my dear boy! Harry!"

Master Harry starts up and looks at him. Looks at Cobbs, too.

Such is the honor of that mite, that he looks at Cobbs, to see whether he has brought him into trouble.

"I'm not angry, my child. I only want you to dress yourself and come home."

"Yes, pa."

Master Harry dresses himself quickly. His breast begins to swell when he has nearly finished, and it swells more and more as he stands, at last, a-looking at his father; his father standing a-looking at him, the quiet image of him.

"Please may I"—the spirit of that little creatur', and the way he kept his rising tears down!—"please, dear pa—may I—kiss Norah before I go?"

"You may, my child."

So he takes Master Harry in his hand, and Boots leads the way with the candle, and they come to that other bedroom, where the elderly lady is seated by the bed, and poor little Mrs. Harry Walmers, Junior, is fast asleep. There the father lifts the child up to the pillow, and he lays his little face down for an instant by the little warm face of poor unconscious little Mrs. Harry Walmers, Junior, and gently draws it to him—a sight so touching to the chambermaids, who are peeping through the door, that one of them called out, "It's a shame to part 'em!" But this chambermaid was always, as Boots informs us, a softhearted one. Not that there was any harm in that girl. Far from it.

Finally, Boots says, that's all about it. Mr. Walmers drove away in the chaise, having hold of Master Harry's hand. The elderly lady and Mrs. Walmers, Junior, that was never to be (she married a Captain long afterward, and died in India), went off next day. In conclusion, Boots puts it to me whether I hold with him in two opinions: firstly, that there are not many couples on their way to be married who are half as innocent of guile as those two children; secondly, that it would be a jolly good thing for a great many couples on their way to be married, if they could only be stopped in time, and brought back separately.

A STORY OF SEVEN DEVILS[20]

Frank R. Stockton (1834-1902)

The negro church which stood in the pine woods near the little village of Oxford Cross Roads, in one of the lower counties of Virginia, was presided over by an elderly individual, known to the community in general as Uncle Pete; but on Sundays the members of his congregation addressed him as Brudder Pete. He was an earnest and energetic man, and, although he could neither read nor write, he had for many years expounded the Scriptures to the satisfaction of his hearers. His memory was good, and those portions of the Bible, which from time to time he had heard read, were used by him, and frequently with powerful effect, in his sermons. His interpretations of the Scriptures were generally entirely original, and were made to suit the needs, or what he supposed to be the needs, of his congregation.

Whether as "Uncle Pete" in the garden and corn-field, or "Brudder Pete" in the church, he enjoyed the good opinion of everybody excepting one person, and that was his wife. She was a high-tempered and somewhat dissatisfied person, who had conceived the idea that her husband was in the habit of giving too much time to the church, and too little to the acquisition of corn-bread and pork. On a certain Saturday she gave him a most tremendous scolding, which so affected the spirits of the good man that it influenced his decision in regard to the selection of the subject for his sermon the next day.

His congregation was accustomed to being astonished, and rather liked it, but never before had their minds received such a shock as when the preacher announced the subject of his discourse. He did not take any particular text, for this was not his custom, but he boldly stated that the Bible declared that every woman in this world was possessed by seven devils; and the evils which this state of things had brought upon the world, he showed forth with much warmth and feeling. Subject-matter, principally from his own experience, crowded in upon his mind, and he served it out to his audience hot and strong. If his deductions could have been proved to be correct, all women were creatures who, by reason of their sevenfold diabolic possession, were not capable of independent thought or action, and who should in tears and humility place

---

20 From Amos Kilbright and Other Stories. 1888.

themselves absolutely under the direction and authority of the other sex.

When he approached the conclusion of his sermon, Brother Peter closed with a bang the Bible, which, although he could not read a word of it, always lay open before him while he preached, and delivered the concluding exhortation of his sermon.

"Now, my dear brev'ren ob dis congregation," he said, "I want you to understan' dat dar's nuffin in dis yer sarmon wot you've jus' heerd ter make you think yousefs angels. By no means, brev'ren; you was all brung up by women, an' you've got ter lib wid' em, an ef anythin' in dis yer worl' is ketchin', my dear brev'ren, it's habin debbils, an' from wot I've seen ob some ob de men ob dis worl' I 'spect dey is persest ob 'bout all de debbils dey got room fur. But de Bible don' say nuffin p'intedly on de subjec' ob de number ob debbils in man, an' I 'spec' dose dat's got 'em—an' we ought ter feel pow'ful thankful, my dear brev'ren, dat de Bible don' say we all's got 'em—has 'em 'cordin to sarcumstances. But wid de women it's dif'rent; dey's got jus' sebin, an' bless my soul, brev'ren, I think dat's 'nuff.

"While I was a-turnin' ober in my min' de subjec' ob dis sarmon, dere come ter me a bit ob Scripter wot I heerd at a big preachin' an' baptizin' at Kyarter's Mills, 'bout ten year' ago. One ob de preachers was a-tellin' about ole mudder Ebe a-eatin' de apple, and says he: De sarpint fus' come along wid a red apple, an' says he: 'You gib dis yer to your husban', an' he think it so mighty good dat when he done eat it he gib you anything you ax him fur, ef you tell him whar de tree is.' Ebe, she took one bite, an' den she frew dat apple away. 'Wot you mean, you triflin' sarpint,' says she, 'a fotchin' me dat apple wot ain't good fur nuffin but ter make cider wid?' Den de sarpint he go fotch her a yaller apple, an' she took one bite, an' den says she: 'Go 'long wid ye, you fool sarpint, wot you fotch me dat June apple wot ain't got no taste to it?' Den de sarpint he think she like sumpin' sharp, an' he fotch her a green apple. She takes one bite ob it, an' den she frows it at his head, an' sings out: 'Is you 'spectin' me to gib dat apple to yer Uncle Adam an' gib him de colic?' Den de debbil he fotch her a lady-apple, but she say she won't take no sich triflin' nubbins as dat to her husban', an' she took one bite ob it, an' frew it away. Den he go fotch her two udder kin' ob apples, one yaller wid red stripes, an' de udder one red on one side an' green on de udder—mighty good-lookin' apples, too—de kin' you git two dollars a bar'l fur at the store. But Ebe, she wouldn't hab neider ob 'em, an' when she done took one bite out ob each one, she frew it away. Den de ole debbil-sarpint, he scratch he head, an' he say to hese'f: 'Dis yer Ebe, she pow'ful 'ticklar 'bout her apples. Reckin I'll have ter wait till after fros', an' fotch her a real good one,' An' he done wait till after fros', and then he fotch her a' Albemarle pippin, an' when she took one bite ob dat, she jus' go 'long an' eat it all up, core, seeds, an' all. 'Look h'yar, sarpint,' says she, 'hab you got anudder ob dem apples in your pocket?' An' den he tuk one out, an' gib it to her. ''Cuse me,' says she, 'I's gwine ter look up Adam, an' ef he don' want ter know war de tree is wot dese apples grow on, you can hab him fur a corn-field han'.'

"An' now, my dear brev'ren," said Brother Peter, "while I was a-turnin' dis subjec' ober in my min', an' wonderin' how de women come ter hab jus' seben debbils apiece, I done reckerleck dat bit ob Scripter wot I heerd at Kyarter's Mills, an' I reckon dat 'splains how de debbils got inter woman. De sarpint he done fotch mudder Ebe seben apples, an' ebery one she take a bite out of gib her a debbil."

As might have been expected, this sermon produced a great sensation, and made a deep impression on the congregation. As a rule, the men were tolerably well satisfied with it; and when the services were over many of them made it the occasion of shy but very plainly pointed remarks to their female friends and relatives.

But the women did not like it at all. Some of them became angry, and talked very forcibly, and feelings of indignation soon spread among all the sisters of the church. If their minister had seen fit to stay at home and preach a sermon like this to his own wife (who, it may be remarked, was not present on this occasion), it would have been well enough, provided he had made no allusions to outsiders; but to come there and preach such things to them was entirely too much for their endurance. Each one of the women knew she had not seven devils, and only a few of them would admit of the possibility of any of the others being possessed by quite so many.

Their preacher's explanation of the manner in which every woman came to be possessed of just so many devils appeared to them of little importance. What they objected to was the fundamental doctrine of his sermon, which was based on his assertion that the Bible declared every woman had seven devils. They were not willing to believe that the Bible said any such thing. Some of them went so far as to state it was their opinion that Uncle Pete had got this fool notion from some of the lawyers at the court-house when he was on a jury a month or so before. It was quite noticeable that, although Sunday afternoon had scarcely begun, the majority of the women of the congregation called their minister Uncle Pete. This was very strong evidence of a sudden decline in his popularity.

Some of the more vigorous-minded women, not seeing their minister among the other people in the clearing in front of the log church, went to look for him, but he was not to be found. His wife had ordered him to be home early, and soon after the congregation had been dismissed he departed by a short cut through the woods. That afternoon an irate committee, composed principally of women, but including also a few men who had expressed disbelief in the new doctrine, arrived at the cabin of their preacher, but found there only his wife, cross-grained old Aunt Rebecca. She informed them that her husband was not at home.

"He's done 'gaged hisse'f," she said, "ter cut an' haul wood fur Kunnel Martin ober on Little Mount'n fur de whole ob nex' week. It's fourteen or thirteen mile' from h'yar, an' ef he'd started ter-morrer mawnm', he'd los' a'mos' a whole day. 'Sides dat, I done tole him dat ef he git dar ter-night he'd have his supper frowed in. Wot you all want wid him? Gwine to pay him fur preachin'?"

Any such intention as this was instantaneously denied, and Aunt Rebecca was informed of the subject upon which her visitors had come to have a very plain talk with her husband.

Strange to say, the announcement of the new and startling dogma had apparently no disturbing effect upon Aunt Rebecca. On the contrary, the old woman seemed rather to enjoy the news.

"Reckin he oughter know all 'bout dat," she said. "He's done had three wives, an' he ain't got rid o' dis one yit."

Judging from her chuckles and waggings of the head when she made this remark, it might be imagined that Aunt Rebecca was rather proud of the fact that her husband thought her capable of exhibiting a different kind of diabolism every day in the week.

The leader of the indignant church-members was Susan Henry; a mulatto woman of a very independent turn of mind. She prided herself that she never worked in anybody's house but her own, and this immunity from outside service gave her a certain pre-eminence among her sisters. Not only did Susan share the general resentment with which the startling statement of old Peter had been received, but she felt that its promulgation had affected her position in the community. If every woman was possessed by seven devils, then, in this respect, she was no better nor worse than any of the others; and at this her proud heart rebelled. If the preacher had said some women had eight devils and others six, it would have been better. She might then have made a mental arrangement in regard to her relative position which would have somewhat consoled her. But now there was no chance for that. The words of the preacher had equally debased all women.

A meeting of the disaffected church-members was held the next night at Susan Henry's cabin, or rather in the little yard about it, for the house was not large enough to hold the people who attended it.

The meeting was not regularly organized, but everybody said what he or she had to say, and the result was a great deal of clamor, and a general increase of indignation against Uncle Pete.

"Look h'yar!" cried Susan, at the end of some energetic remarks, "is dar enny pusson h'yar who kin count up figgers?"

Inquiries on the subject ran through the crowd, and in a few moments a black boy, about fourteen, was pushed forward as an expert in arithmetic.

"Now, you Jim," said Susan, "you's been, to school, an' you kin count up figgers. 'Cordin' ter de chu'ch books dar's forty-seben women b'longin' to our meetin', an' ef each one ob dem dar has got seben debbils in her, I jus' wants you ter tell me how many debbils come to chu'ch ebery clear Sunday ter hear dat ole Uncle Pete preach."

This view of the case created a sensation, and much interest was shown in the result of Jim's calculations, which were made by the aid of a back of an old letter and a piece of pencil furnished by Susan. The result was at last announced as three hundred and nineteen, which, although not precisely correct, was near enough to satisfy the company.

"Now, you jus' turn dat ober in you all's minds," said Susan. "More'n free hundred debbils in chu'ch ebery Sunday, an' we women fotchin 'em. Does anybody s'pose I's gwine ter b'lieve dat fool talk?"

A middle-aged man now lifted up his voice and said: "I's been thinkin' ober dis h'yar matter and I's 'cluded dat p'r'aps de words ob de preacher was used in a figgeratous form o' sense. P'r'aps de seben debbils meant chillun."

These remarks were received with no favor by the assemblage.

"Oh, you git out!" cried Susan. "Your ole woman's got seben chillun, shore 'nuf, an' I s'pec' dey's all debbils. But dem sent'ments don't apply ter all de udder women h'yar, 'tic'larly ter dem dar young uns wot ain't married yit."

This was good logic, but the feeling on the subject proved to be even stronger, for the mothers in the company became so angry at their children being considered devils that for a time there seemed to be danger of an Amazonian attack on the unfortunate speaker. This was averted, but a great deal of uproar now ensued, and it was the general feeling that something ought to be done to show the deep-seated resentment with which the horrible charge against the mothers and sisters of the congregation had been met. Many violent propositions were made, some of the younger men going so far as to offer to burn down the church. It was finally agreed, quite unanimously, that old Peter should be unceremoniously ousted from his place in the pulpit which he had filled so many years.

As the week passed on, some of the older men of the congregation who had friendly feelings toward their old companion and preacher talked the matter over among themselves, and afterward, with many of their fellow-members, succeeded at last in gaining the general consent that Uncle Pete should be allowed a chance to explain himself, and give his grounds and reasons for his astounding statement in regard to womankind. If he could show biblical authority for this, of course nothing more could be said. But if he could not, then he must get down from the pulpit, and sit for the rest of his life on a back seat of the church. This proposition met with the more favor, because even those who were most indignant had an earnest curiosity to know what the old man would say for himself.

During all this time of angry discussion, good old Peter was quietly and calmly cutting and hauling wood on the Little Mountain. His mind was in a condition of great comfort and peace, for not only had he been able to rid himself, in his last sermon, of many of the hard thoughts concerning women that had been gathering themselves together for years, but his absence from home had given him a holiday from the harassments of Aunt Rebecca's tongue, so that no new notions of woman's culpability had risen within him. He had dismissed the subject altogether, and had been thinking over a sermon regarding baptism, which he thought he could make convincing to certain of the younger members of his congregation.

He arrived at home very late on Saturday night, and retired to his simple couch without knowing anything of the terrible storm which had been gathering through the week, and which was to burst upon him on the morrow. But the next morning, long before church time, he received warning enough of what was going to happen. Individuals and deputations gathered in and about his cabin—some to tell him all that had been said and done; some to inform him what was expected of him; some to stand about and look at him; some to scold; some to denounce; but, alas! not one to encourage; nor one to call him "Brudder Pete," that Sunday appellation dear to his ears. But the old man possessed a stubborn soul, not easily to be frightened.

"Wot I says in de pulpit," he remarked, "I'll 'splain in de pulpit, an' you all ud better git 'long to de chu'ch, an' when de time fur de sarvice come, I'll be dar."

This advice was not promptly acted upon, but in the course of half an hour nearly all the villagers and loungers had gone off to the church in the woods; and when Uncle Peter had put on his high black hat, somewhat battered, but still sufficiently clerical looking for that congregation, and had given something of a polish to his cowhide shoes, he betook himself by the accustomed path to the log building where he had so often held forth to his people. As soon as he entered the church he was formally instructed by a committee of the leading members that before he began to open the services, he must make it plain to the congregation that what he had said on the preceding Sunday about every woman being possessed by seven devils was Scripture truth, and not mere wicked nonsense out of his own brain. If he could not do that, they wanted no more praying or preaching from him.

Uncle Peter made no answer, but, ascending the little pulpit, he put his hat on the bench behind him where it was used to repose, took out his red cotton handkerchief and blew his nose in his accustomed way, and looked about him. The house was crowded. Even Aunt Rebecca was there.

After a deliberate survey of his audience, the preacher spoke: "Brev'eren an' sisters, I see afore me Brudder Bill Hines, who kin read de Bible, an' has got one. Ain't dat so, Brudder?"

Bill Hines having nodded and modestly grunted assent, the preacher continued. "An' dars' Ann' Priscilla's boy, Jake, who ain't a brudder yit, though he's plenty old 'nuf, min', I tell ye; an' he kin read de Bible, fus' rate, an' has read it ter me ober an' ober ag'in. Ain't dat so, Jake?"

Jake grinned, nodded, and hung his head, very uncomfortable at being thus publicly pointed out.

"An' dar's good ole Aun' Patty, who knows more Scripter dan ennybuddy h'yar, havin' been teached by de little gals from Kunnel Jasper's an' by dere mudders afore 'em. I reckin she know' de hull Bible straight froo, from de Garden of Eden to de New Jerus'lum. An' dar are udders h'yar who knows de Scripters, some one part an' some anudder. Now I axes ebery one ob you all wot know de Scripters ef he don' 'member how de Bible tells how our Lor' when he was on dis yearth cas' seben debbils out o' Mary Magdalum?"

A murmur of assent came from the congregation, Most of them remembered that.

"But did enny ob you ebber read, or hab read to you, dat he ebber cas' 'em out o' enny udder woman?"

Negative grunts and shakes of the head signified that nobody had ever heard of this.

"Well, den," said the preacher, gazing blandly around, "all de udder women got 'em yit."

A deep silence fell upon the assembly, and in a few moments an elderly member arose. "Brudder Pete," he said, "I reckin you mought as well gib out de hyme."

A DOG'S TALE[21]

Mark Twain (1835)

I

My father was a St. Bernard, my mother was a collie, but I am a Presbyterian. This is what my mother told me; I do not know these nice distinctions myself. To me they are only fine large words meaning nothing. My mother had a fondness for such; she liked to say them, and see other dogs look surprised and envious, as wondering how she got so much education. But, indeed, it was not real education; it was only show: she got the words by listening in the dining-room and drawing-room when there was company, and by going with the children to Sunday-school and listening there; and whenever she heard a large word she said it over to herself many times, and so was able to keep it until there was a dogmatic gathering in the neighborhood, then she would get it off, and surprise and distress them all, from pocket-pup to mastiff, which rewarded her for all her trouble. If there was a stranger he was nearly sure to be suspicious, and when he got his breath again he would ask her what it meant. And she always told him. He was never expecting this, but thought he would catch her; so when she told him, he was the one that looked ashamed, whereas he had thought it was going to be she. The others were always waiting for this, and glad of it and proud of her, for they knew what was going to happen, because they had had experience. When she told the meaning of a big word they were all so taken up with admiration that it never occurred to any dog to doubt if it was the right one; and that was natural, because, for one thing, she answered up so promptly that it seemed like a dictionary speaking, and for another thing, where could they find out whether it was right or not? for she was the only cultivated dog there was. By-and-by, when I was older, she brought home the word Unintellectual, one time, and worked it pretty hard all the week at different gatherings, making much unhappiness and despondency; and it was at this time that I noticed that during that week she was asked for the meaning at eight different assemblages, and flashed out a fresh definition every time, which showed me that she had more presence of mind than culture, though I said nothing, of course. She had one word which she

---

always kept on hand, and ready, like a life-preserver, a kind of emergency word to strap on when she was likely to get washed overboard in a sudden way—that was the word Synonymous. When she happened to fetch out a long word which had had its day weeks before and its prepared meanings gone to her dump-pile, if there was a stranger there of course it knocked him groggy for a couple of minutes, then he would come to, and by that time she would be away down the wind on another tack, and not expecting anything; so when he'd hail and ask her to cash in, I (the only dog on the inside of her game) could see her canvas flicker a moment,—but only just a moment,—then it would belly out taut and full, and she would say, as calm as a summer's day, "It's synonymous with supererogation," or some godless long reptile of a word like that, and go placidly about and skim away on the next tack, perfectly comfortable, you know, and leave that stranger looking profane and embarrassed, and the initiated slatting the floor with their tails in unison and their faces transfigured with a holy joy.

And it was the same with phrases. She would drag home a whole phrase, if it had a grand sound, and play it six nights and two matinees, and explain it a new way every time,—which she had to, for all she cared for was the phrase; she wasn't interested in what it meant, and knew those dogs hadn't wit enough to catch her, anyway. Yes, she was a daisy! She got so she wasn't afraid of anything, she had such confidence in the ignorance of those creatures. She even brought anecdotes that she had heard the family and the dinner guests laugh and shout over; and as a rule she got the nub of one chestnut hitched onto another chestnut, where, of course, it didn't fit and hadn't any point; and when she delivered the nub she fell over and rolled on the floor and laughed and barked in the most insane way, while I could see that she was wondering to herself why it didn't seem as funny as it did when she first heard it. But no harm was done; the others rolled and barked too, privately ashamed of themselves for not seeing the point, and never suspecting that the fault was not with them and there wasn't any to see.

You can see by these things that she was of a rather vain and frivolous character; still, she had virtues, and enough to make up, I think. She had a kind heart and gentle ways, and never harbored resentments for injuries done her, but put them easily out of her mind and forgot them; and she taught her children her kindly way, and from her we learned also to be brave and prompt in time of danger, and not to run away, but face the peril that threatened friend or stranger, and help him the best we could without stopping to think what the cost might be to us. And she taught us, not by words only, but by example, and that is the best way and the surest and the most lasting. Why, the brave things she did, the splendid things! she was just a soldier; and so modest about it—well, you couldn't help admiring her, and you couldn't help imitating her; not even a King Charles spaniel could remain entirely despicable in her society. So, as you see, there was more to her than her education.

II

When I was well grown, at last, I was sold and taken away, and I never saw her again. She was broken-hearted, and so was I, and we cried; but she comforted me as well as she could, and said we were sent into this world for a wise and good purpose, and must do our duties without repining, take our life as we might find it, live it for the best good of others, and never mind about the results; they were not our affair. She said men who did like this would have a noble and beautiful reward by-and-by in another world, and although we animals would not go there, to do well and right without reward would give to our brief lives a worthiness and dignity which in itself would be a reward. She had gathered these things from time to time when she had gone to the Sunday-school with the children, and had laid them up in her memory more carefully than she had done with those other words and phrases; and she had studied them deeply, for her good and ours. One may see by this that she had a wise and thoughtful head, for all there was so much lightness and vanity in it.

So we said our farewells, and looked our last upon each other through our tears; and the last thing she said—keeping it for the last to make me remember it the better, I think—was, "In memory of me, when there is a time of danger to another do not think of yourself, think of your mother, and do as she would do."

Do you think I could forget that? No.

III

It was such a charming home!—my new one; a fine great house, with pictures, and delicate decorations, and rich furniture, and no gloom anywhere, but all the wilderness of dainty colors lit up with flooding sunshine; and the spacious grounds around it, and the great garden—oh, greensward, and noble trees, and flowers, no end! And I was the same as a member of the family; and they loved me, and petted me, and did not give me a new name, but called me by my old one that was dear to me because my mother had given it me—Aileen Mavourneen. She got it out of a song; and the Grays knew that song, and said it was a beautiful name.

Mrs. Gray was thirty, and so sweet and so lovely, you cannot imagine it; and Sadie was ten, and just like her mother, just a darling slender little copy of her, with auburn tails down her back, and short frocks; and the baby was a year old, and plump and dimpled, and fond of me, and never could get enough of hauling on my tail, and hugging me, and laughing out its innocent happiness; and Mr. Gray was thirty-eight, and tall and slender and handsome, a little bald in front, alert, quick in his movements, businesslike, prompt, decided, unsentimental, and with that kind of trim-chiselled face that just seems to glint and sparkle with frosty intellectuality! He was a renowned scientist. I do not know what the word means, but my mother would know how to use it and get effects. She would know how to depress a rat-terrier with it and make a lap-dog look sorry he came. But that is not the best one; the best one was Laboratory. My mother could organize a Trust on that one that would skin the tax-collars off the whole herd. The laboratory was not a book, or a picture, or a place to wash your hands in, as the college president's dog said—no, that is the lavatory; the laboratory is quite different, and is filled with jars, and bottles, and electrics, and wires, and strange machines; and every week other scientists came there and sat in the place, and used the machines, and discussed, and made what they called experiments and discoveries; and often I came, too, and stood around and listened, and tried to learn, for the sake of my mother, and in loving memory of her, although it was a pain to me, as realizing what she was losing out of her life and I gaining nothing at all; for try as I might, I was never able to make anything out of it at all.

Other times I lay on the floor in the mistress's workroom and slept, she gently using me for a footstool, knowing it pleased me, for it was a caress; other times I spent an hour in the nursery, and got well tousled and made happy; other times I watched by the crib there, when the baby was asleep and the nurse out for a few minutes on the baby's affairs; other times I romped and raced through the grounds and the garden with Sadie till we were tired out, then slumbered on the grass in the shade of a tree while she read her book; other times I went visiting among the neighbor dogs,—for there were some most pleasant ones not far away, and one very handsome and courteous and graceful one, a curly haired Irish setter by the name of Robin Adair, who was a Presbyterian like me, and belonged to the Scotch minister.

The servants in our house were all kind to me and were fond of me, and so, as you see, mine was a pleasant life. There could not be a happier dog than I was, nor a gratefuller one. I will say this for myself, for it is only the truth: I tried in all ways to do well and right, and honor my mother's memory and her teachings, and earn the happiness that had come to me, as best I could.

By-and-by came my little puppy, and then my cup was full, my happiness was perfect. It was the dearest little waddling thing, and so smooth and soft and velvety, and had such cunning little awkward paws, and such affectionate eyes, and such a sweet and innocent face; and it made me so proud to see how the children and their mother adored it, and fondled it, and exclaimed over every little wonderful thing it did. It did seem to me that life was just too lovely to—

Then came the winter. One day I was standing a watch in the nursery. That is to say, I was asleep on the bed. The baby was asleep in the crib, which was alongside the bed, on the side next the fireplace. It was the kind of crib that has a lofty tent over it made of a gauzy stuff that you can see through. The nurse was out, and we two sleepers were alone. A spark from the wood-fire was shot out, and it lit on the slope of the tent. I suppose a quiet interval followed, then a scream from the baby woke me, and there was that tent flaming up toward the ceiling! Before I could think, I sprang to the floor in my fright, and in a second was half-way to the door; but in the next half-second my mother's farewell was sounding in my ears, and I was back on the bed again. I reached my head through the flames and dragged the baby out by the waistband, and tugged it along, and we fell to the floor together in a cloud of smoke; I snatched a new hold, and dragged the screaming little creature along and out at the door and around the bend of the hall, and was still tugging away, all excited and happy and proud, when the master's voice shouted:

"Begone, you cursed beast!" and I jumped to save myself; but he was wonderfully quick, and chased me up, striking furiously at me with his cane, I dodging this way and that, in terror, and at last a strong blow fell upon my left fore-leg, which made me shriek and fall, for the moment, helpless; the cane went up for another blow, but never descended, for the nurse's voice rang wildly out, "The nursery's on fire!" and the master rushed away in that direction, and my other bones were saved.

The pain was cruel, but, no matter, I must not lose any time; he might come back at any moment; so I limped on three legs to the other end of the hall, where there was a dark little stairway leading up into a garret where old boxes and such things were kept, as I had heard say, and where people seldom went. I managed to climb up there, then I searched my way through the dark among the piles of things, and hid in the secretest place I could find. It was foolish to be afraid there, yet still I was; so afraid that I held in and hardly even whimpered, though it would have been such a comfort to whimper, because that eases the pain, you know. But I could lick my leg, and that did me some good.

For half an hour there was a commotion down-stairs, and shoutings, and rushing footsteps, and then there was quiet again. Quiet for some minutes, and that was grateful to my spirit, for then my fears began to go down; and fears are worse than pains,—oh, much worse. Then came a sound that froze me! They were calling me—calling me by name—hunting for me!

It was muffled by distance, but that could not take the terror out of it, and it was the most dreadful sound to me that I had ever heard. It went all about, everywhere, down there: along the halls, through all the rooms, in both stories, and in the basement and the cellar; then outside, and further and further away—then back, and all about the house again, and I thought it would never, never stop. But at last it did, hours and hours after the vague twilight of the garret had long ago been blotted out by black darkness.

Then in that blessed stillness my terror fell little by little away, and I was at peace and slept. It was a good rest I had, but I woke before the twilight had come again. I was feeling fairly comfortable, and I could think out a plan now. I made a very good one; which was, to creep down, all the way down the back stairs, and hide behind the cellar door, and slip out and escape when the iceman came at dawn, while he was inside filling the refrigerator; then I would hide all day, and start on my journey when night came; my journey to—well, anywhere where they would not know me and betray me to the master. I was feeling almost cheerful now; then suddenly I thought, Why, what would life be without my puppy!

That was despair. There was no plan for me; I saw that; I must stay where I was; stay, and wait, and take what might come—it was not my affair; that was what life is—my mother had said it. Then— well, then the calling began again! All my sorrows came back. I said to myself, the master will never forgive. I did not know what I had done to make him so bitter and so unforgiving, yet I judged it was something a dog could not understand, but which was clear to a man and dreadful.

They called and called—days and nights, it seemed to me. So

long that the hunger and thirst near drove me mad, and I recognized that I was getting very weak. When you are this way you sleep a great deal, and I did. Once I woke in an awful fright—it seemed to me that the calling was right there in the garret! And so it was: it was Sadie's voice, and she was crying; my name was falling from her lips all broken, poor thing, and I could not believe my ears for the joy of it when I heard her say,

"Come back to us—oh, come back to us, and forgive—it is all so sad without our—"

I broke in with such a grateful little yelp, and the next moment Sadie was plunging and stumbling through the darkness and the lumber and shouting for the family to hear, "She's found! she's found!"

The days that followed—well, they were wonderful. The mother and Sadie and the servants—why, they just seemed to worship me. They couldn't seem to make me a bed that was fine enough; and as for food, they couldn't be satisfied with anything but game and delicacies that were out of season; and every day the friends and neighbors flocked in to hear about my heroism—that was the name they called it by, and it means agriculture. I remember my mother pulling it on a kennel once, and explaining it that way, but didn't say what agriculture was, except that it was synonymous with intramural incandescence; and a dozen times a day Mrs. Gray and Sadie would tell the tale to new-comers, and say I risked my life to save the baby's, and both of us had burns to prove it, and then the company would pass me around and pet me and exclaim about me, and you could see the pride in the eyes of Sadie and her mother; and when the people wanted to know what made me limp, they looked ashamed and changed the subject, and sometimes when people hunted them this way and that way with questions about it, it looked to me as if they were going to cry.

And this was not all the glory; no, the master's friends came, a whole twenty of the most distinguished people, and had me in the laboratory, and discussed me as if I was a kind of discovery; and some of them said it was wonderful in a dumb beast, the finest exhibition of instinct they could call to mind; but the master said, with vehemence, "It's far above instinct; it's reason, and many a man, privileged to be saved and go with you and me to a better world by right of its possession, has less of it than this poor silly quadruped that's foreordained to perish"; and then he laughed, and said, "Why, look at me—I'm a sarcasm! Bless you, with all my grand intelligence, the only thing I inferred was that the dog had gone mad and was destroying the child, whereas but for the beast's intelligence—it's reason, I tell you!—the child would have perished!"

They disputed and disputed, and I was the very centre and subject of it all, and I wished my mother could know that this grand honor had come to me; it would have made her proud.

Then they discussed optics, as they called it, and whether a certain injury to the brain would produce blindness or not, but they could not agree about it, and said they must test it by experiment by-and-by; and next they discussed plants, and that interested me, because in the summer Sadie and I had planted seeds—I helped her dig the holes, you know,—and after days and days a little shrub or a flower came up there, and it was a wonder how that could happen; but it did, and I wished I could talk,—I would have told those people about it and shown them how much I knew, and been all alive with the subject; but I didn't care for the optics; it was dull, and when they came back to it again it bored me, and I went to sleep.

Pretty soon it was spring, and sunny and pleasant and lovely, and the sweet mother and the children patted me and the puppy good-bye, and went away on a journey and a visit to their kin, and the master wasn't any company for us, but we played together and had good times, and the servants were kind and friendly, so we got along quite happily and counted the days and waited for the family.

And one day those men came again, and said now for the test, and they took the puppy to the laboratory, and I limped three-leggedly along, too, feeling proud, for any attention shown the puppy was a pleasure to me, of course. They discussed and experimented, and then suddenly the puppy shrieked, and they set him on the floor, and he went staggering around, with his head all bloody, and the master clapped his hands, and shouted:

"There, I've won—confess it! He's as blind as a bat!"

And they all said,

"It's so—you've proved your theory, and suffering humanity owes you a great debt from henceforth," and they crowded around him, and wrung his hand cordially and thankfully, and praised him.

But I hardly saw or heard these things, for I ran at once to my little darling, and snuggled close to it where it lay, and licked the blood, and it put its head against mine, whimpering softly, and I knew in my heart it was a comfort to it in its pain and trouble to feel its mother's touch, though it could not see me. Then it drooped down, presently, and its little velvet nose rested upon the floor, and it was still, and did not move any more.

Soon the master stopped discussing a moment, and rang in the footman, and said, "Bury it in the far corner of the garden," and then went on with the discussion, and I trotted after the footman, very happy and grateful, for I knew the puppy was out of its pain now, because it was asleep. We went far down the garden to the furthest end, where the children and the nurse and the puppy and I used to play in the summer in the shade of a great elm, and there the footman dug a hole, and I saw he was going to plant the puppy, and I was glad, because it would grow and come up a fine handsome dog, like Robin Adair, and be a beautiful surprise for the family when they came home; so I tried to help him dig, but my lame leg was no good, being stiff, you know, and you have to have two, or it is no use. When the footman had finished and covered little Robin up, he patted my head, and there were tears in his eyes, and he said, "Poor little doggie, you SAVED his child."

I have watched two whole weeks, and he doesn't come up! This last week a fright has been stealing upon me. I think there is something terrible about this. I do not know what it is, but the fear makes me sick, and I cannot eat, though the servants bring me the best of food; and they pet me so, and even come in the night, and cry, and say, "Poor doggie—do give it up and come home; don't break our hearts!" and all this terrifies me the more, and makes me sure something has happened. And I am so weak; since yesterday I cannot stand on my feet any more. And within this hour the servants, looking toward the sun where it was sinking out of sight and the night chill coming on, said things I could not understand, but they carried something cold to my heart.

"Those poor creatures! They do not suspect. They will come home in the morning, and eagerly ask for the little doggie that did the brave deed, and who of us will be strong enough to say the truth to them: 'The humble little friend is gone where go the beasts that perish.'"

THE OUTCASTS OF POKER FLAT[22]

Bret Harte (1839-1902)

As Mr. John Oakhurst, gambler, stepped into the main street of Poker Flat on the morning of the 23d of November, 1850, he was conscious of a change in its moral atmosphere since the preceding night. Two or three men, conversing earnestly together, ceased as he approached, and exchanged significant glances. There was a Sabbath lull in the air, which, in a settlement unused to Sabbath influences, looked ominous.

Mr. Oakhurst's calm, handsome face betrayed small concern in these indications. Whether he was conscious of any predisposing cause was another question. "I reckon they're after somebody," he reflected; "likely it's me." He returned to his pocket the handkerchief with which he had been whipping away the red dust of Poker Flat from his neat boots, and quietly discharged his mind of any further conjecture.

In point of fact, Poker Flat was "after somebody." It had lately suffered the loss of several thousand dollars, two valuable horses, and a prominent citizen. It was experiencing a spasm of virtuous reaction, quite as lawless and ungovernable as any of the acts that had provoked it. A secret committee had determined to rid the town of all improper persons. This was done permanently in regard of two men who were then hanging from the boughs of a sycamore in the gulch, and temporarily in the banishment of certain other objectionable characters. I regret to say that some of these were ladies. It is but due to the sex, however, to state that their impropriety was professional, and it was only in such easily established standards of evil that Poker Flat ventured to sit in judgment.

Mr. Oakhurst was right in supposing that he was included in this category. A few of the committee had urged hanging him as a possible example, and a sure method of reimbursing themselves from his pockets of the sums he had won from them. "It's agin justice," said Jim Wheeler, "to let this yer young man from Roaring Camp—an entire stranger—carry away our money." But a crude sentiment of equity residing in the breasts of those who had been fortunate enough to win from Mr. Oakhurst overruled this narrower local prejudice.

---

[22] From The Luck of Roaring Camp. 1871.

Mr. Oakhurst received his sentence with philosophic calmness, none the less coolly that he was aware of the hesitation of his judges. He was too much of a gambler not to accept fate. With him life was at best an uncertain game, and he recognized the usual percentage in favor of the dealer.

A body of armed men accompanied the deported wickedness of Poker Flat to the outskirts of the settlement. Besides Mr. Oakhurst, who was known to be a coolly desperate man, and for whose intimidation the armed escort was intended, the expatriated party consisted of a young woman familiarly known as the "Duchess"; another who had won the title of "Mother Shipton"; and "Uncle Billy," a suspected sluice-robber and confirmed drunkard. The cavalcade provoked no comments from the spectators, nor was any word uttered by the escort. Only when the gulch which marked the uttermost limit of Poker Flat was reached, the leader spoke briefly and to the point. The exiles were forbidden to return at the peril of their lives.

As the escort disappeared, their pent-up feelings found vent in a few hysterical tears from the Duchess, some bad language from Mother Shipton, and a Parthian volley of expletives from Uncle Billy. The philosophic Oakhurst alone remained silent. He listened calmly to Mother Shipton's desire to cut somebody's heart out, to the repeated statements of the Duchess that she would die in the road, and to the alarming oaths that seemed to be bumped out of Uncle Billy as he rode forward. With the easy good-humor characteristic of his class, he insisted upon exchanging his own riding-horse, "Five Spot," for the sorry mule which the Duchess rode. But even this act did not draw the party into any closer sympathy. The young woman readjusted her somewhat draggled plumes with a feeble, faded coquetry; Mother Shipton eyed the possessor of "Five Spot" with malevolence, and Uncle Billy included the whole party in one sweeping anathema.

The road to Sandy Bar—a camp that, not having as yet experienced the regenerating influences of Poker Flat, consequently seemed to offer some invitation to the emigrants—lay over a steep mountain range. It was distant a day's severe travel. In that advanced season, the party soon passed out of the moist, temperate regions of the foot-hills into the dry, cold, bracing air of the Sierras. The trail was narrow and difficult. At noon the Duchess, rolling out of her saddle upon the ground, declared her intention of going no farther, and the party halted.

The spot was singularly wild and impressive. A wooded amphitheatre, surrounded on three sides by precipitous cliffs of naked granite, sloped gently toward the crest of another precipice that overlooked the valley. It was, undoubtedly, the most suitable spot for a camp, had camping been advisable. But Mr. Oakhurst knew that scarcely half the journey to Sandy Bar was accomplished; and the party were not equipped or provisioned for delay. This fact he pointed out to his companions curtly, with a philosophic commentary on the folly of "throwing up their hand before the game was played out." But they were furnished with liquor, which in this emergency stood them in place of food, fuel, rest, and prescience. In spite of his remonstrances, it was not long before they were more or less under its influence. Uncle Billy passed rapidly from a bellicose state into one of stupor, the Duchess became maudlin, and Mother Shipton snored. Mr. Oakhurst alone remained erect, leaning against a rock, calmly surveying them.

Mr. Oakhurst did not drink. It interfered with a profession which required coolness, impassiveness, and presence of mind, and, in his own language, he "couldn't afford it." As he gazed at his recumbent fellow-exiles, the loneliness begotten of his pariah-trade, his habits of life, his very vices, for the first time seriously oppressed him. He bestirred himself in dusting his black clothes, washing his hands and face, and other acts characteristic of his studiously neat habits, and for a moment forgot his annoyance. The thought of deserting his weaker and more pitiable companions never perhaps occurred to him. Yet he could not help feeling the want of that excitement which, singularly enough, was most conducive to that calm equanimity for which he was notorious. He looked at the gloomy walls that rose a thousand feet sheer above the circling pines around him; at the sky, ominously clouded; at the valley below, already deepening into shadow. And, doing so, suddenly he heard his own name called.

A horseman slowly ascended the trail. In the fresh, open face of the new-comer Mr. Oakhurst recognized Tom Simson, otherwise known as the "Innocent," of Sandy Bar. He had met him some months before over a "little game," and had, with perfect equanimity, won the entire fortune—amounting to some forty dollars—of that guileless youth. After the game was finished, Mr. Oakhurst drew the youthful speculator behind the door and thus addressed him: "Tommy, you're a good little man, but you can't gamble worth a cent. Don't try it over again." He then handed him his money back, pushed him gently from the room, and so made a devoted slave of Tom Simson.

There was a remembrance of this in his boyish and enthusiastic greeting of Mr. Oakhurst. He had started, he said, to go to Poker Flat to seek his fortune. "Alone?" No, not exactly alone; in fact (a giggle), he had run away with Piney Woods. Didn't Mr. Oakhurst remember Piney? She that used to wait on the table at the Temperance House? They had been engaged a long time, but old Jake Woods had objected, and so they had run away, and were going to Poker Flat to be married, and here they were. And they were tired out, and how lucky it was they had found a place to camp, and company. All this the Innocent delivered rapidly, while Piney, a stout, comely damsel of fifteen, emerged from behind the pine-tree where she had been blushing unseen, and rode to the side of her lover.

Mr. Oakhurst seldom troubled himself with sentiment, still less with propriety; but he had a vague idea that the situation was not fortunate. He retained, however, his presence of mind sufficiently to kick Uncle Billy, who was about to say something, and Uncle Billy was sober enough to recognize in Mr. Oakhurst's kick a superior power that would not bear trifling. He then endeavored to dissuade Tom Simson from delaying further, but in vain. He even pointed out the fact that there was no provision, nor means of making a camp. But, unluckily, the Innocent met this objection by assuring the party that he was provided with an extra mule loaded with provisions, and by the discovery of a rude attempt at a log-house near the trail. "Piney can stay with Mrs. Oakhurst," said the Innocent, pointing to the Duchess, "and I can shift for myself."

Nothing but Mr. Oakhurst's admonishing foot saved Uncle Billy from bursting into a roar of laughter. As it was, he felt compelled to retire up the cañon until he could recover his gravity. There he confided the joke to the tall pine-trees, with many slaps of his leg, contortions of his face, and the usual profanity. But when he returned to the party, he found them seated by a fire—for the air had grown strangely chill and the sky overcast—in apparently amicable conversation. Piney was actually talking in an impulsive, girlish fashion to the Duchess, who was listening with an interest and animation she had not shown for many days. The Innocent was holding forth, apparently with equal effect, to Mr. Oakhurst and Mother Shipton, who was actually relaxing into amiability. "Is this yer a d—-d picnic?" said Uncle Billy, with inward scorn, as he surveyed the sylvan group, the glancing firelight, and the tethered animals in the foreground. Suddenly an idea mingled with the alcoholic fumes that disturbed his brain. It was apparently of a jocular nature, for he felt impelled to slap his leg again and cram his fist into his mouth.

As the shadows crept slowly up the mountain, a slight breeze rocked the tops of the pine-trees, and moaned through their long and gloomy aisles. The ruined cabin, patched and covered with pine-boughs, was set apart for the ladies. As the lovers parted they unaffectedly exchanged a kiss, so honest and sincere that it might have been heard above the swaying pines. The frail Duchess and the malevolent Mother Shipton were probably too stunned to remark upon this last evidence of simplicity, and so turned without a word to the hut. The fire was replenished, the men lay down before the door, and in a few minutes were asleep.

Mr. Oakhurst was a light sleeper. Toward morning he awoke benumbed and cold. As he stirred the dying fire, the wind, which was now blowing strongly, brought to his cheek that which caused the blood to leave it—snow!

He started to his feet with the intention of awakening the sleepers, for there was no time to lose. But turning to where Uncle Billy had been lying, he found him gone. A suspicion leaped to his brain and a curse to his lips. He ran to the spot where the mules had been tethered; they were no longer there. The tracks were already rapidly disappearing in the snow.

The momentary excitement brought Mr. Oakhurst back to the fire with his usual calm. He did not waken the sleepers. The Innocent slumbered peacefully, with a smile on his good-humored, freckled face; the virgin Piney slept beside her frailer sisters as sweetly as though attended by celestial guardians, and Mr. Oakhurst, drawing his blanket over his shoulders, stroked his mustaches and waited for the dawn. It came slowly in a whirling mist of snowflakes, that dazzled and confused the eye. What could be seen of the landscape appeared magically changed. He looked over the valley, and summed up the present and future in two words—"Snowed in!"

A careful inventory of the provisions, which, fortunately for the party, had been stored within the hut, and so escaped the felonious fingers of Uncle Billy, disclosed the fact that with care and prudence they might last ten days longer. "That is," said Mr. Oakhurst, sotto voce to the Innocent, "if you're willing to board us. If you ain't—and perhaps you'd better not—you can wait till Uncle Billy gets back with provisions." For some occult reason, Mr. Oakhurst could not bring himself to disclose Uncle Billy's rascality, and so offered the hypothesis that he had wandered from the camp and had accidentally stampeded the animals. He dropped a warning to the Duchess and Mother Shipton, who of course knew the facts of their associate's defection. "They'll find out the truth about us all when they find out anything," he added, significantly, "and there's no good frightening them now."

Tom Simson not only put all his worldly store at the disposal of Mr. Oakhurst, but seemed to enjoy the prospect of their enforced seclusion. "We'll have a good camp for a week, and then the snow'll melt, and we'll all go back together." The cheerful gayety of the young man and Mr. Oakhurst's calm infected the others. The Innocent, with the aid of pine-boughs, extemporized a thatch for the roofless cabin, and the Duchess directed Piney in the rearrangement of the interior with a taste and tact that opened the blue eyes of that provincial maiden to their fullest extent. "I reckon now you're used to fine things at Poker Flat," said Piney. The Duchess turned away sharply to conceal something that reddened her cheeks through their professional tint, and Mother Shipton requested Piney not to "chatter." But when Mr. Oakhurst returned from a weary search for the trail, he heard the sound of happy laughter echoed from the rocks. He stopped in some alarm, and his thoughts first naturally reverted to the whiskey, which he had prudently cachéd. "And yet it don't somehow sound like whiskey," said the gambler. It was not until he caught sight of the blazing fire through the still blinding storm and the group around it that he settled to the conviction that it was "square fun."

Whether Mr. Oakhurst had cachéd his cards with the whiskey as something debarred the free access of the community, I cannot say. It was certain that, in Mother Shipton's words, he "didn't say cards once," during that evening. Haply the time was beguiled by an accordion, produced somewhat ostentatiously by Tom Simson from his pack. Notwithstanding some difficulties attending the manipulation of this instrument, Piney Woods managed to pluck several reluctant melodies from its keys, to an accompaniment by the Innocent on a pair of bone castanets. But the crowning festivity of the evening was reached in a rude camp-meeting hymn, which the lovers, joining hands, sang with great earnestness and vociferation. I fear that a certain defiant tone and Covenanter's swing to its chorus, rather than any devotional quality, caused it speedily to infect the others, who at last joined in the refrain:

"I'm proud to live in the service of the Lord,
And I'm bound to die in His army."

The pines rocked, the storm eddied and whirled above the miserable group, and the flames of their altar leaped heavenward, as if in token of the vow.

At midnight the storm abated, the rolling clouds parted, and the stars glittered keenly above the sleeping camp. Mr. Oakhurst, whose professional habits had enabled him to live on the smallest possible amount of sleep, in dividing the watch with Tom Simson, somehow managed to take upon himself the greater part of that duty. He excused himself to the Innocent by saying that he had "often been a week without sleep." "Doing what?" asked Tom. "Poker!" replied Oakhurst, sententiously; "when a man gets a streak of luck—nigger-luck—he don't get tired. The luck gives in first. Luck," continued the gambler, reflectively, "is a mighty queer thing. All you know about it for certain is that it's bound to change. And it's finding out when it's going to change that makes you. We've had a streak of bad luck since we left Poker Flat—you come along, and slap you get into it, too. If you can hold your cards right along, you're all right. For," added the gambler, with cheerful irrelevance—

> "'I'm proud to live in the service of the Lord,
> And I'm bound to die in His army,'"

The third day came, and the sun, looking through the white-curtained valley, saw the outcasts divide their slowly decreasing store of provisions for the morning meal. It was one of the peculiarities of that mountain climate that its rays diffused a kindly warmth over the wintry landscape, as if in regretful commiseration of the past. But it revealed drift on drift of snow piled high around the hut—a hopeless, uncharted, trackless sea of white lying below the rocky shores to which the castaways still clung. Through the marvellously clear air the smoke of the pastoral village of Poker Flat rose miles away. Mother Shipton saw it, and from a remote pinnacle of her rocky fastness hurled in that direction a final malediction. It was her last vituperative attempt, and perhaps for that reason was invested with a certain degree of sublimity. It did her good, she privately informed the Duchess. "Just you go out there and cuss, and see." She then set herself to the task of amusing "the child," as she and the Duchess were pleased to call Piney. Piney was no chicken, but it was a soothing and original theory of the pair thus to account for the fact that she didn't swear and wasn't improper.

When night crept up again through the gorges, the reedy notes of the accordion rose and fell in fitful spasms and long-drawn gasps by the flickering camp-fire. But music failed to fill entirely the aching void left by insufficient food, and a new diversion was proposed by Piney—story-telling. Neither Mr., Oakhurst nor his female companions caring to relate their personal experiences, this plan would have failed, too, but for the Innocent. Some months before he had chanced upon a stray copy of Mr. Pope's ingenious translation of the Iliad. He now proposed to narrate the principal incidents of that poem—having thoroughly mastered the argument and fairly forgotten the words—in the current vernacular of Sandy Bar. And so for the rest of that night the Homeric demigods again walked the earth. Trojan bully and wily Greek wrestled in the winds, and the great pines in the cañon seemed to bow to the wrath of the son of Peleus. Mr. Oakhurst listened with quiet satisfaction. Most especially was he interested in the fate of "Ash-heels," as the Innocent persisted in denominating the "swift-footed Achilles."

So with small food and much of Homer and the accordion, a week passed over the heads of the outcasts. The sun again forsook them, and again from leaden skies the snowflakes were sifted over the land. Day by day closer around them drew the snowy circle, until at last they looked from their prison over drifted walls of dazzling white, that towered twenty feet above their heads. It became more and more difficult to replenish their fires, even from the fallen trees beside them, now half hidden in the drifts. And yet no one complained. The lovers turned from the dreary prospect and looked into each other's eyes, and were happy. Mr. Oakhurst settled himself coolly to the losing game before him. The Duchess, more cheerful than she had been, assumed the care of Piney. Only Mother Shipton—once the strongest of the party—seemed to sicken and fade. At midnight on the tenth day she called Oakhurst to her side. "I'm going," she said, in a voice of querulous weakness, "but don't say anything about it. Don't waken the kids. Take the bundle from under my head and open it." Mr. Oakhurst did so. It contained Mother Shipton's rations for the last week, untouched. "Give 'em to the child," she said, pointing to the sleeping Piney. "You've starved yourself," said the gambler. "That's what they call it," said the woman, querulously, as she lay down again, and, turning her face to the wall, passed quietly away.

The accordion and the bones were put aside that day, and Homer was forgotten. When the body of Mother Shipton had been committed to the snow, Mr. Oakhurst took the Innocent aside and showed him a pair of snow-shoes, which he had fashioned from the old pack-saddle. "There's one chance in a hundred to save her yet," he said, pointing to Piney; "but it's there," he added, pointing toward Poker Flat. "If you can reach there in two days she's safe." "And you?" asked Tom Simson. "I'll stay here," was the curt reply.

The lovers parted with a long embrace. "You are not going, too?" said the Duchess, as she saw Mr. Oakhurst apparently waiting to accompany him. "As far as the cañon," he replied. He turned suddenly and kissed the Duchess, leaving her pallid face aflame and her trembling limbs rigid with amazement.

Night came, but not Mr. Oakhurst. It brought the storm again and the whirling snow. Then the Duchess, feeding the fire, found that some one had quietly piled beside the hut enough fuel to last a few days longer. The tears rose to her eyes, but she hid them from Piney.

The women slept but little. In the morning, looking into each other's faces, they read their fate. Neither spoke; but Piney, accepting the position of the stronger, drew near and placed her arm around the Duchess's waist. They kept this attitude for the rest of the day. That night the storm reached its greatest fury, and, rending asunder the protecting pines, invaded the very hut.

Toward morning they found themselves unable to feed the fire, which gradually died away. As the embers slowly blackened, the Duchess crept closer to Piney, and broke the silence of many hours: "Piney, can you pray?" "No, dear," said Piney, simply. The Duchess, without knowing exactly why, felt relieved, and, putting her head upon Piney's shoulder, spoke no more. And so reclining, the younger and purer pillowing the head of her soiled sister upon her virgin breast, they fell asleep.

The wind lulled as if it feared to waken them. Feathery drifts of snow, shaken from the long pine-boughs, flew like white-winged birds, and settled about them as they slept. The moon through the rifted clouds looked down upon what had been the camp. But all human stain, all trace of earthly travail, was hidden beneath the spotless mantle mercifully flung from above.

They slept all that day and the next, nor did they waken when voices and footsteps broke the silence of the camp. And when pitying fingers brushed the snow from their wan faces, you could scarcely have told, from the equal peace that dwelt upon them, which was she that had sinned. Even the law of Poker Flat recognized this, and turned away, leaving them still locked in each other's arms.

But at the head of the gulch, on one of the largest pine-trees, they found the deuce of clubs pinned to the bark with a bowie-knife. It bore the following, written in pencil, in a firm hand:

    +

    BENEATH THIS TREE
    LIES THE BODY
    OF
    JOHN OAKHURST,
    WHO STRUCK A STREAK OF BAD LUCK
    ON THE 23D OF NOVEMBER, 1850,
    AND
    HANDED IN HIS CHECKS
    ON THE 7TH DECEMBER, 1850.
    +

And pulseless and cold, with a derringer by his side and a bullet in his heart, though still calm as in life, beneath the snow lay he who was at once the strongest and yet the weakest of the outcasts of Poker Flat.

THE THREE STRANGERS[23]

Thomas Hardy (1840)

Among the few features of agricultural England which retain an appearance but little modified by the lapse of centuries, may be reckoned the high, grassy and furzy downs, coombs, or ewe-leases, as they are indifferently called, that fill a large area of certain counties in the south and southwest. If any mark of human occupation is met with hereon, it usually takes the form of the solitary cottage of some shepherd.

Fifty years ago such a lonely cottage stood on such a down, and may possibly be standing there now. In spite of its loneliness, however, the spot, by actual measurement, was not more than five miles from a county-town. Yet that affected it little. Five miles of irregular upland, during the long inimical seasons, with their sleets, snows, rains, and mists, afford withdrawing space enough to isolate a Timon or a Nebuchadnezzar; much less, in fair weather, to please that less repellent tribe, the poets, philosophers, artists, and others who "conceive and meditate of pleasant things."

Some old earthen camp or barrow, some clump of trees, at least some starved fragment of ancient hedge is usually taken advantage of in the erection of these forlorn dwellings. But, in the present case, such a kind of shelter had been disregarded. Higher Crowstairs, as the house was called, stood quite detached and undefended. The only reason for its precise situation seemed to be the crossing of two footpaths at right angles hard by, which may have crossed there and thus for a good five hundred years. Hence the house was exposed to the elements on all sides. But, though the wind up here blew unmistakably when it did blow, and the rain hit hard whenever it fell, the various weathers of the winter season were not quite so formidable on the coomb as they were imagined to be by dwellers on low ground. The raw rimes were not so pernicious as in the hollows, and the frosts were scarcely so severe. When the shepherd and his family who tenanted the house were pitied for their sufferings from the exposure, they said that upon the whole they were less inconvenienced by "wuzzes and flames" (hoarses and phlegms) than when they had lived by the stream of a snug neighboring valley.

The night of March 28, 182-, was precisely one of the nights

---

that were wont to call forth these expressions of commiseration. The level rainstorm smote walls, slopes, and hedges like the clothyard shafts of Senlac and Crecy. Such sheep and outdoor animals as had no shelter stood with their buttocks to the winds; while the tails of little birds trying to roost on some scraggy thorn were blown inside-out like umbrellas. The gable-end of the cottage was stained with wet, and the eavesdroppings flapped against the wall. Yet never was commiseration for the shepherd more misplaced. For that cheerful rustic was entertaining a large party in glorification of the christening of his second girl.

The guests had arrived before the rain began to fall, and they were all now assembled in the chief or living room of the dwelling. A glance into the apartment at eight o'clock on this eventful evening would have resulted in the opinion that it was as cosy and comfortable a nook as could be wished for in boisterous weather. The calling of its inhabitant was proclaimed by a number of highly-polished sheep crooks without stems that were hung ornamentally over the fireplace, the curl of each shining crook varying from the antiquated type engraved in the patriarchal pictures of old family Bibles to the most approved fashion of the last local sheep-fair. The room was lighted by half-a-dozen candles, having wicks only a trifle smaller than the grease which enveloped them, in candlesticks that were never used but at high-days, holy-days, and family feasts. The lights were scattered about the room, two of them standing on the chimney-piece. This position of candles was in itself significant. Candles on the chimney-piece always meant a party.

On the hearth, in front of a back-brand to give substance, blazed a fire of thorns, that crackled "like the laughter of the fool."

Nineteen persons were gathered here. Of these, five women, wearing gowns of various bright hues, sat in chairs along the wall; girls shy and not shy filled the window-bench; four men, including Charley Jake the hedge-carpenter, Elijah New the parish-clerk, and John Pitcher, a neighboring dairyman, the shepherd's father-in-law, lolled in the settle; a young man and maid, who were blushing over tentative pourparlers on a life-companionship, sat beneath the corner-cupboard; and an elderly engaged man of fifty or upward moved restlessly about from spots where his betrothed was not to the spot where she was. Enjoyment was pretty general, and so much the more prevailed in being unhampered by conventional restrictions. Absolute confidence in each other's good opinion begat perfect ease, while the finishing stroke of manner, amounting to a truly princely serenity, was lent to the majority by the absence of any expression or trait denoting that they wished to get on in the world, enlarge their minds, or do any eclipsing thing whatever—

which nowadays so generally nips the bloom and bonhomie of all except the two extremes of the social scale.

Shepherd Fennel had married well, his wife being a dairyman's daughter from a vale at a distance, who brought fifty guineas in her pocket—and kept them there, till they should be required for ministering to the needs of a coming family. This frugal woman had been somewhat exercised as to the character that should be given to the gathering. A sit-still party had its advantages; but an undisturbed position of ease in chairs and settles was apt to lead on the men to such an unconscionable deal of toping that they would sometimes fairly drink the house dry. A dancing-party was the alternative; but this, while avoiding the foregoing objection on the score of good drink, had a counterbalancing disadvantage in the matter of good victuals, the ravenous appetites engendered by the exercise causing immense havoc in the buttery. Shepherdess Fennel fell back upon the intermediate plan of mingling short dances with short periods of talk and singing, so as to hinder any ungovernable rage in either. But this scheme was entirely confined to her own gentle mind: the shepherd himself was in the mood to exhibit the most reckless phases of hospitality.

The fiddler was a boy of those parts, about twelve years of age, who had a wonderful dexterity in jigs and reels, though his fingers were so small and short as to necessitate a constant shifting for the high notes, from which he scrambled back to the first position with sounds not of unmixed purity of tone. At seven the shrill tweedle-dee of this youngster had begun, accompanied by a booming ground-bass from Elijah New, the parish-clerk, who had thoughtfully brought with him his favorite musical instrument, the serpent. Dancing was instantaneous, Mrs. Fennel privately enjoining the players on no account to let the dance exceed the length of a quarter of an hour.

But Elijah and the boy, in the excitement of their position, quite forgot the injunction. Moreover, Oliver Giles, a man of seventeen, one of the dancers, who was enamoured of his partner, a fair girl of thirty-three rolling years, had recklessly handed a new crown-piece to the musicians, as a bribe to keep going as long as they had muscle and wind. Mrs. Fennel, seeing the steam begin to generate on the countenances of her guests, crossed over and touched the fiddler's elbow and put her hand on the serpent's mouth. But they took no notice, and fearing she might lose her character of genial hostess if she were to interfere too markedly, she retired and sat down helpless. And so the dance whizzed on with cumulative fury, the performers moving in their planet-like courses, direct and retrograde, from apogee to perigee, till the hand of the well-kicked clock at the bottom of the room had travelled over the circumference of an hour.

While these cheerful events were in course of enactment within Fennel's pastoral dwelling, an incident having considerable bearing on the party had occurred in the gloomy night without. Mrs. Fennel's concern about the growing fierceness of the dance corresponded in point of time with the ascent of a human figure to the solitary hill of Higher Crowstairs from the direction of the distant town. This personage strode on through the rain without a pause, following the little-worn path which, further on in its course, skirted the shepherd's cottage.

It was nearly the time of full moon, and on this account, though the sky was lined with a uniform sheet of dripping cloud, ordinary objects out of doors were readily visible. The sad wan light revealed the lonely pedestrian to be a man of supple frame; his gait suggested that he had somewhat passed the period of perfect and instinctive agility, though not so far as to be otherwise than rapid of motion when occasion required. At a rough guess, he might have been about forty years of age. He appeared tall, but a recruiting sergeant, or other person accustomed to the judging of men's heights by the eye, would have discerned that this was chiefly owing to his gauntness, and that he was not more than five-feet-eight or nine.

Notwithstanding the regularity of his tread, there was caution in it, as in that of one who mentally feels his way; and despite the fact that it was not a black coat nor a dark garment of any sort that he wore, there was something about him which suggested that he naturally belonged to the black-coated tribes of men. His clothes were of fustian, and his boots hobnailed, yet in his progress he showed not the mud-accustomed bearing of hobnailed and fustianed peasantry.

By the time that he had arrived abreast of the shepherd's premises the rain came down, or rather came along, with yet more determined violence. The outskirts of the little settlement partially broke the force of wind and rain, and this induced him to stand still. The most salient of the shepherd's domestic erections was an empty sty at the forward corner of his hedgeless garden, for in these latitudes the principle of masking the homelier features of your establishment by a conventional frontage was unknown. The traveller's eye was attracted to this small building by the pallid shine of the wet slates that covered it. He turned aside, and, finding it empty, stood under the pent-roof for shelter.

While he stood, the boom of the serpent within the adjacent house, and the lesser strains of the fiddler, reached the spot as an accompaniment to the surging hiss of the flying rain on the sod, its louder beating on the cabbage-leaves of the garden, on the eight or ten beehives just discernible by the path, and its dripping from the eaves into a row of buckets and pans that had been placed under the walls of the cottage. For at Higher Crowstairs, as at all such elevated domiciles, the grand difficulty of housekeeping was an insufficiency of water; and a casual rainfall was utilized by turning out, as catchers, every utensil that the house contained. Some queer stories might be told of the contrivances for economy in suds and dishwaters that are absolutely necessitated in upland habitations during the droughts of summer. But at this season there were no such exigencies; a mere acceptance of what the skies bestowed was sufficient for an abundant store.

At last the notes of the serpent ceased and the house was silent. This cessation of activity aroused the solitary pedestrian from the reverie into which he had elapsed, and, emerging from the shed, with an apparently new intention, he walked up the path to the house-door. Arrived here, his first act was to kneel down on a large stone beside the row of vessels, and to drink a copious draught from one of them. Having quenched his thirst, he rose and lifted his hand to knock, but paused with his eye upon the panel. Since the dark surface of the wood revealed absolutely nothing, it was evident that he must be mentally looking through the door, as if he wished to measure thereby all the possibilities that a house of this sort might include, and how they might bear upon the question of his entry.

In his indecision he turned and surveyed the scene around. Not a soul was anywhere visible. The garden-path stretched downward from his feet, gleaming like the track of a snail; the roof of the little well (mostly dry), the well-cover, the top rail of the garden-gate, were varnished with the same dull liquid glaze; while, far away in the vale, a faint whiteness of more than usual extent showed that the rivers were high in the meads. Beyond all this winked a few bleared lamplights through the beating drops—lights that denoted the situation of the county-town from which he had appeared to come. The absence of all notes of life in that direction seemed to clinch his intentions, and he knocked at the door.

Within, a desultory chat had taken the place of movement and musical sound. The hedge-carpenter was suggesting a song to the company, which nobody just then was inclined to undertake, so that the knock afforded a not unwelcome diversion.

"Walk in!" said the shepherd, promptly.

The latch clicked upward, and out of the night our pedestrian appeared upon the door-mat. The shepherd arose, snuffed two of the nearest candles, and turned to look at him.

Their light disclosed that the stranger was dark in complexion and not unprepossessing as to feature. His hat, which for a moment he did not remove, hung low over his eyes, without concealing that they were large, open, and determined, moving with a flash rather than a glance round the room. He seemed pleased with his survey, and, baring his shaggy head, said, in a rich, deep voice: "The rain is so heavy, friends, that I ask leave to come in and rest awhile."

"To be sure, stranger," said the shepherd. "And faith, you've been lucky in choosing your time, for we are having a bit of a fling for a glad cause—though, to be sure, a man could hardly wish that glad cause to happen more than once a year."

"Nor less," spoke up a woman. "For 'tis best to get your family over and done with, as soon as you can, so as to be all the earlier out of the fag o't."

"And what may be this glad cause?" asked the stranger.

"A birth and christening," said the shepherd.

The stranger hoped his host might not be made unhappy either by too many or two few of such episodes, and being invited by a gesture to a pull at the mug, he readily acquiesced. His manner, which, before entering, had been so dubious, was now altogether that of a careless and candid man.

"Late to be traipsing athwart this coomb—hey?" said the engaged man of fifty.

"Late it is, master, as you say.—I'll take a seat in the chimney-corner, if you have nothing to urge against it, ma'am; for I am a little moist on the side that was next the rain."

Mrs. Shepherd Fennel assented, and made room for the self-invited comer, who, having got completely inside the chimney-corner, stretched out his legs and arms with the expansiveness of a person quite at home.

"Yes, I am rather cracked in the vamp," he said freely, seeing that the eyes of the shepherd's wife fell upon his boots, "and I am not well fitted either. I have had some rough times lately, and have been forced to pick up what I can get in the way of wearing, but I must find a suit better fit for working-days when I reach home."

"One of hereabouts?" she inquired.

"Not quite that—further up the country."

"I thought so. And so be I; and by your tongue you come from my neighborhood."

"But you would hardly have heard of me," he said quickly. "My time would be long before yours, ma'am, you see."

This testimony to the youthfulness of his hostess had the effect of stopping her cross-examination.

"There is only one thing more wanted to make me happy,"

continued the new-comer, "and that is a little baccy, which I am sorry to say I am out of."

"I'll fill your pipe," said the shepherd.

"I must ask you to lend me a pipe likewise."

"A smoker, and no pipe about 'ee?"

"I have dropped it somewhere on the road."

The shepherd filled and handed him a new clay pipe, saying, as he did so, "Hand me your baccy-box—I'll fill that too, now I am about it."

The man went through the movement of searching his pockets.

"Lost that too?" said his entertainer, with some surprise.

"I am afraid so," said the man with some confusion. "Give it to me in a screw of paper." Lighting his pipe at the candle with a suction that drew the whole flame into the bowl, he resettled himself in the corner and bent his looks upon the faint steam from his damp legs, as if he wished to say no more.

Meanwhile the general body of guests had been taking little notice of this visitor by reason of an absorbing discussion in which they were engaged with the band about a tune for the next dance. The matter being settled, they were about to stand up when an interruption came in the shape of another knock at the door.

At sound of the same the man in the chimney-corner took up the poker and began stirring the brands as if doing it thoroughly were the one aim of his existence; and a second time the shepherd said, "Walk in!" In a moment another man stood upon the straw-woven door-mat. He too was a stranger.

This individual was one of a type radically different from the first. There was more of the commonplace in his manner, and a certain jovial cosmopolitanism sat upon his features. He was several years older than the first arrival, his hair being slightly frosted, his eyebrows bristly, and his whiskers cut back from his cheeks. His face was rather full and flabby, and yet it was not altogether a face without power. A few grog-blossoms marked the neighborhood of his nose. He flung back his long drab greatcoat, revealing that beneath it he wore a suit of cinder-gray shade throughout, large heavy seals, of some metal or other that would take a polish, dangling from his fob as his only personal ornament. Shaking the water-drops from his low-crowned glazed hat, he said, "I must ask for a few minutes' shelter, comrades, or I shall be wetted to my skin before I get to Casterbridge."

"Make yourself at home, master," said the shepherd, perhaps a trifle less heartily than on the first occasion. Not that Fennel had the least tinge of niggardliness in his composition; but the room was far from large, spare chairs were not numerous, and damp companions

were not altogether desirable at close quarters for the women and
girls in their bright-colored gowns.

However, the second comer, after taking off his greatcoat, and
hanging his hat on a nail in one of the ceiling-beams as if he had
been specially invited to put it there, advanced and sat down at the
table. This had been pushed so closely into the chimney-corner, to
give all available room to the dancers, that its inner edge grazed the
elbow of the man who had ensconced himself by the fire; and thus
the two strangers were brought into close companionship. They
nodded to each other by way of breaking the ice of unacquaintance,
and the first stranger handed his neighbor the family mug—a huge
vessel of brown ware, having its upper edge worn away like a
threshold by the rub of whole generations of thirsty lips that had
gone the way of all flesh, and bearing the following inscription burnt
upon its rotund side in yellow letters:

THERE IS NO FUN UNTILL I CUM

The other man, nothing loth, raised the mug to his lips, and
drank on, and on, and on—till a curious blueness overspread the
countenance of the shepherd's wife, who had regarded with no little
surprise the first stranger's free offer to the second of what did not
belong to him to dispense.

"I knew it!" said the toper to the shepherd with much
satisfaction. "When I walked up your garden before coming in, and
saw the hives all of a row, I said to myself, 'Where there's bees
there's honey, and where there's honey there's mead,' But mead of
such a truly comfortable sort as this I really didn't expect to meet in
my older days." He took yet another pull at the mug, till it assumed
an ominous elevation.

"Glad you enjoy it!" said the shepherd warmly.

"It is goodish mead," assented Mrs. Fennel, with an absence of
enthusiasm which seemed to say that it was possible to buy praise
for one's cellar at too heavy a price. "It is trouble enough to make—
and really I hardly think we shall make any more. For honey sells
well, and we ourselves can make shift with a drop o' small mead and
metheglin for common use from the comb-washings."

"O, but you'll never have the heart!" reproachfully cried the
stranger in cinder-gray, after taking up the mug a third time and
setting it down empty. "I love mead, when 'tis old like this, as I love
to go to church o' Sundays, or to relieve the needy any day of the
week."

"Ha, ha, ha!" said the man in the chimney-corner, who, in spite of the taciturnity induced by the pipe of tobacco, could not or would not refrain from this slight testimony to his comrade's humor.

Now the old mead of those days, brewed of the purest first-year or maiden honey, four pounds to the gallon—with its due complement of white of eggs, cinnamon, ginger, cloves, mace, rosemary, yeast, and processes of working, bottling, and cellaring—tasted remarkably strong; but it did not taste so strong as it actually was. Hence, presently, the stranger in cinder-gray at the table, moved by its creeping influence, unbuttoned his waistcoat, threw himself back in his chair, spread his legs, and made his presence felt in various ways.

"Well, well, as I say," he resumed, "I am going to Casterbridge, and to Casterbridge I must go. I should have been almost there by this time; but the rain drove me into your dwelling, and I'm not sorry for it."

"You don't live in Casterbridge?" said the shepherd.

"Not as yet; though I shortly mean to move there."

"Going to set up in trade, perhaps?"

"No, no," said the shepherd's wife. "It is easy to see that the gentleman is rich, and don't want to work at anything."

The cinder-gray stranger paused, as if to consider whether he would accept that definition of himself. He presently rejected it by answering, "Rich is not quite the word for me, dame. I do work, and I must work. And even if I only get to Casterbridge by midnight I must begin work there at eight to-morrow morning. Yes, het or wet, blow or snow, famine or sword, my day's work to-morrow must be done."

"Poor man! Then, in spite o' seeming, you be off than we." replied the shepherd's wife.

"'Tis the nature of my trade, men and maidens. Tis the nature of my trade more than my poverty.... But really and truly I must up and off, or I shan't get a lodging in the town." However, the speaker did not move, and directly added, "There's time for one more draught of friendship before I go; and I'd perform it at once if the mug were not dry."

"Here's a mug o' small," said Mrs. Fennel. "Small, we call it, though to be sure 'tis only the first wash o' the combs."

"No," said the stranger, disdainfully. "I won't spoil your first kindness by partaking o' your second."

"Certainly not," broke in Fennel. "We don't increase and multiply every day, and I'll fill the mug again." He went away to the dark place under the stairs where the barrel stood. The shepherdess followed him.

"Why should you do this?" she said, reproachfully, as soon as they were alone. "He's emptied it once, though it held enough for ten people; and now he's not contented wi' the small, but must needs call for more o' the strong! And a stranger unbeknown to any of us. For my part, I don't like the look o' the man at all."

"But he's in the house, my honey; and 'tis a wet night, and a christening. Daze it, what's a cup of mead more or less? There'll be plenty more next bee-burning."

"Very well—this time, then," she answered, looking wistfully at the barrel. "But what is the man's calling, and where is he one of, that he should come in and join us like this?"

"I don't know. I'll ask him again."

The catastrophe of having the mug drained dry at one pull by the stranger in cinder-gray was effectually guarded against this time by Mrs. Fennel. She poured out his allowance in a small cup, keeping the large one at a discreet distance from him. When he had tossed off his portion the shepherd renewed his inquiry about the stranger's occupation.

The latter did not immediately reply, and the man in the chimney-corner, with sudden demonstrativeness, said, "Anybody may know my trade—I'm a wheelwright."

"A very good trade for these parts," said the shepherd.

"And anybody may know mine—if they've the sense to find it out," said the stranger in cinder-gray.

"You may generally tell what a man is by his claws," observed the hedge-carpenter, looking at his own hands. "My fingers be as full of thorns as an old pin-cushion is of pins."

The hands of the man in the chimney-corner instinctively sought the shade, and he gazed into the fire as he resumed his pipe. The man at the table took up the hedge-carpenter's remark, and added smartly, "True; but the oddity of my trade is that, instead of setting a mark upon me, it sets a mark upon my customers."

No observation being offered by anybody in elucidation of this enigma, the shepherd's wife once more called for a song. The same obstacles presented themselves as at the former time—one had no voice, another had forgotten the first verse. The stranger at the table, whose soul had now risen to a good working temperature, relieved the difficulty by exclaiming that, to start the company, he would sing himself. Thrusting one thumb into the arm-hole of his waistcoat, he waved the other hand in the air, and, with an extemporizing gaze at the shining sheep-crooks above the mantelpiece, began:

"O my trade it is the rarest one,
Simple shepherds all—

My trade is a sight to see;
For my customers I tie, and take them up on high,
And waft 'em to a far countree!"

The room was silent when he had finished the verse—with one exception, that of the man in the chimney-corner, who, at the singer's word, "Chorus!" joined him in a deep bass voice of musical relish:
"And waft 'em to a far countree!"
Oliver Giles, John Pitcher the dairyman, the parish-clerk, the engaged man of fifty, the row of young women against the wall, seemed lost in thought not of the gayest kind. The shepherd looked meditatively on the ground, the shepherdess gazed keenly at the singer, and with some suspicion; she was doubting whether this stranger were merely singing an old song from recollection, or was composing one there and then for the occasion. All were as perplexed at the obscure revelation as the guests at Belshazzar's Feast, except the man in the chimney-corner, who quietly said, "Second verse, stranger," and smoked on.
The singer thoroughly moistened himself from his lips inward, and went on with the next stanza as requested:

"My tools are but common ones,
 Simple shepherds all—
My tools are no sight to see:
A little hempen string, and a post whereon to swing,
Are implements enough for me!"

Shepherd Fennel glanced round. There was no longer any doubt that the stranger was answering his question rhythmically. The guests one and all started back with suppressed exclamations. The young woman engaged to the man of fifty fainted half-way, and would have proceeded, but finding him wanting in alacrity for catching her she sat down trembling.
"O, he's the—!" whispered the people in the background, mentioning the name of an ominous public officer. "He's come to do it! 'Tis to be at Casterbridge jail to-morrow—the man for sheep-stealing—the poor clock-maker we heard of, who used to live away at Shottsford and had no work to do—Timothy Summers, whose family were a-starving, and so he went out of Shottsford by the high-road, and took a sheep in open daylight, defying the farmer and the farmer's wife and the farmer's lad, and every man jack among 'em. He" (and they nodded toward the stranger of the deadly trade) "is come from up the country to do it because there's not

enough to do in his own county-town, and he's got the place here now our own county man's dead; he's going to live in the same cottage under the prison wall."

The stranger in cinder-gray took no notice of this whispered string of observations, but again wetted his lips. Seeing that his friend in the chimney-corner was the only one who reciprocated his joviality in any way, he held out his cup toward that appreciative comrade, who also held out his own. They clinked together, the eyes of the rest of the room hanging upon the singer's actions. He parted his lips for the third verse; but at that moment another knock was audible upon the door. This time the knock was faint and hesitating.

The company seemed scared; the shepherd looked with consternation toward the entrance, and it was with some effort that he resisted his alarmed wife's deprecatory glance, and uttered for the third time the welcoming words, "Walk in!"

The door was gently opened, and another man stood upon the mat. He, like those who had preceded him, was a stranger. This time it was a short, small personage, of fair complexion, and dressed in a decent suit of dark clothes.

"Can you tell me the way to—?" he began: when, gazing round the room to observe the nature of the company among whom he had fallen, his eyes lighted on the stranger in cinder-gray. It was just at the instant when the latter, who had thrown his mind into his song with such a will that he scarcely heeded the interruption, silenced all whispers and inquiries by bursting into his third verse:

> "To-morrow is my working day,
> Simple shepherds all—
> To-morrow is a working day for me:
> For the farmer's sheep is slain, and the lad who did it ta'en,
> And on his soul may God ha' merc-y!"

The stranger in the chimney-corner, waving cups with the singer so heartily that his mead splashed over on the hearth, repeated in his bass voice as before:

"And on his soul may God ha' merc-y!"

All this time the third stranger had been standing in the doorway. Finding now that he did not come forward or go on speaking, the guests particularly regarded him. They noticed to their surprise that he stood before them the picture of abject terror—his knees trembling, his hand shaking so violently that the door-latch by which he supported himself rattled audibly: his white lips were parted, and his eyes fixed on the merry officer of justice in the middle of the room. A moment more and he had turned, closed the door, and fled.

"What a man can it be?" said the shepherd.

The rest, between the awfulness of their late discovery and the odd conduct of this third visitor, looked as if they knew not what to think, and said nothing. Instinctively they withdrew further and further from the grim gentleman in their midst, whom some of them seemed to take for the Prince of Darkness himself, till they formed a remote circle, an empty space of floor being left between them and him—

"... circulus, cujus centrum diabolus."

The room was so silent—though there were more than twenty people in it—that nothing could be heard but the patter of the rain against the window-shutters, accompanied by the occasional hiss of a stray drop that fell down the chimney into the fire, and the steady puffing of the man in the corner, who had now resumed his pipe of long clay.

The stillness was unexpectedly broken. The distant sound of a gun reverberated through the air—apparently from the direction of the county-town.

"Be jiggered!" cried the stranger who had sung the song, jumping up.

"What does that mean?" asked several.

"A prisoner escaped from the jail—that's what it means."

All listened. The sound was repeated, and none of them spoke but the man in the chimney-corner, who said quietly, "I've often been told that in this county they fire a gun at such times; but I never heard it till now."

"I wonder if it is my man?" murmured the personage in cinder-gray.

"Surely it is!" said the shepherd involuntarily. "And surely we've zeed him! That little man who looked in at the door by now, and quivered like a leaf when he zeed ye and heard your song!"

"His teeth chattered, and the breath went out of his body," said the dairyman.

"And his heart seemed to sink within him like a stone," said Oliver Giles.

"And he bolted as if he'd been shot at," said the hedge-carpenter.

"True—his teeth chattered, and his heart seemed to sink; and he bolted as if he'd been shot at," slowly summed up the man in the chimney-corner.

"I didn't notice it," remarked the hangman.

"We were all a-wondering what made him run off in such a

fright," faltered one of the women against the wall, "and now 'tis explained!"

The firing of the alarm-gun went on at intervals, low and sullenly, and their suspicions became a certainty. The sinister gentleman in cinder-gray roused himself. "Is there a constable here?" he asked, in thick tones. "If so, let him step forward."

The engaged man of fifty stepped quavering out from the wall, his betrothed beginning to sob on the back of the chair.

"You are a sworn constable?"

"I be, sir."

"Then pursue the criminal at once, with assistance, and bring him back here. He can't have gone far."

"I will, sir, I will—when I've got my staff. I'll go home and get it, and come sharp here, and start in a body."

"Staff!—never mind your staff; the man'll be gone!"

"But I can't do nothing without my staff—can I, William, and John, and Charles Jake? No; for there's the king's royal crown a-painted on en in yaller and gold, and the lion and the unicorn, so as when I raise en up and hit my prisoner, 'tis made a lawful blow thereby. I wouldn't 'tempt to take up a man without my staff—no, not I. If I hadn't the law to gie me courage, why, instead o' my taking up him he might take up me!"

"Now, I'm a king's man myself, and can give you authority enough for this," said the formidable officer in gray. "Now then, all of ye, be ready. Have ye any lanterns?"

"Yes—have ye any lanterns?—I demand it!" said the constable.

"And the rest of you able-bodied—"

"Able-bodied men—yes—the rest of ye!" said the constable.

"Have you some good stout staves and pitchforks—"

"Staves and pitchforks—in the name o' the law! And take 'em in yer hands and go in quest, and do as we in authority tell ye!"

Thus aroused, the men prepared to give chase. The evidence was, indeed, though circumstantial, so convincing, that but little argument was needed to show the shepherd's guests that after what they had seen it would look very much like connivance if they did not instantly pursue the unhappy third stranger, who could not as yet have gone more than a few hundred yards over such uneven country.

A shepherd is always well provided with lanterns; and, lighting these hastily, and with hurdle-staves in their hands, they poured out of the door, taking a direction along the crest of the hill, away from the town, the rain having fortunately a little abated.

Disturbed by the noise, or possibly by unpleasant dreams of her baptism, the child who had been christened began to cry heartbrokenly in the room overhead. These notes of grief came down through the chinks of the floor to the ears of the women below, who jumped up one by one, and seemed glad of the excuse to ascend and comfort the baby, for the incidents of the last half-hour greatly oppressed them. Thus in the space of two or three minutes the room on the ground-floor was deserted quite.

But it was not for long. Hardly had the sound of footsteps died away when a man returned round the corner of the house from the direction the pursuers had taken. Peeping in at the door, and seeing nobody there, he entered leisurely. It was the stranger of the chimney-corner, who had gone out with the rest. The motive of his return was shown by his helping himself to a cut piece of skimmer-cake that lay on a ledge beside where he had sat, and which he had apparently forgotten to take with him. He also poured out half a cup more mead from the quantity that remained, ravenously eating and drinking these as he stood. He had not finished when another figure came in just as quietly—his friend in cinder-gray.

"O—you here?" said the latter, smiling. "I thought you had gone to help in the capture." And this speaker also revealed the object of his return by looking solicitously round for the fascinating mug of old mead.

"And I thought you had gone," said the other, continuing his skimmer-cake with some effort.

"Well, on second thoughts, I felt there were enough without me," said the first confidentially, "and such a night as it is, too. Besides, 'tis the business o' the Government to take care of its criminals—not mine."

"True; so it is. And I felt as you did, that there were enough without me."

"I don't want to break my limbs running over the humps and hollows of this wild country."

"Nor I neither, between you and me."

"These shepherd-people are used to it—simple-minded souls, you know, stirred up to anything in a moment. They'll have him ready for me before the morning, and no trouble to me at all."

"They'll have him, and we shall have saved ourselves all labor in the matter."

"True, true. Well, my way is to Casterbridge; and 'tis as much as my legs will do to take me that far. Going the same way?"

"No, I am sorry to say! I have to get home over there" (he nodded indefinitely to the right), "and I feel as you do, that it is quite enough for my legs to do before bedtime."

The other had by this time finished the mead in the mug, after which, shaking hands heartily at the door, and wishing each other well, they went their several ways.

In the meantime the company of pursuers had reached the end of the hog's-back elevation which dominated this part of the down. They had decided on no particular plan of action; and, finding that the man of the baleful trade was no longer in their company, they seemed quite unable to form any such plan now. They descended in all directions down the hill, and straightway several of the party fell into the snare set by Nature for all misguided midnight ramblers over this part of the cretaceous formation. The "lanchets," or flint slopes, which belted the escarpment at intervals of a dozen yards, took the less cautious ones unawares, and losing their footing on the rubbly steep they slid sharply downward, the lanterns rolling from their hands to the bottom, and there lying on their sides till the horn was scorched through.

When they had again gathered themselves together, the shepherd, as the man who knew the country best, took the lead, and guided them round these treacherous inclines. The lanterns, which seemed rather to dazzle their eyes and warn the fugitive than to assist them in the exploration, were extinguished, due silence was observed; and in this more rational order they plunged into the vale. It was a grassy, briery, moist defile, affording some shelter to any person who had sought it; but the party perambulated it in vain, and ascended on the other side. Here they wandered apart, and after an interval closed together again to report progress. At the second time of closing in they found themselves near a lonely ash, the single tree on this part of the coomb, probably sown there by a passing bird some fifty years before. And here, standing a little to one side of the trunk, as motionless as the trunk itself, appeared the man they were in quest of, his outline being well defined against the sky beyond. The band noiselessly drew up and faced him.

"Your money or your life!" said the constable sternly to the still figure.

"No, no," whispered John Pitcher. "'Tisn't our side ought to say that. That's the doctrine of vagabonds like him, and we be on the side of the law."

"Well, well," replied the constable, impatiently; "I must say something, mustn't I? and if you had all the weight o' this undertaking upon your mind, perhaps you'd say the wrong thing, too!—Prisoner at the bar, surrender, in the name of the Father—the Crown, I mane!"

The man under the tree seemed now to notice them for the first time, and, giving them no opportunity whatever for exhibiting their courage, he strolled slowly toward them. He was, indeed, the little man, the third stranger; but his trepidation had in a great measure gone.

"Well, travellers," he said, "did I hear you speak to me?"

"You did; you've got to come and be our prisoner at once!" said the constable. "We arrest 'ee on the charge of not biding in Casterbridge jail in a decent proper manner to be hung to-morrow morning. Neighbors, do your duty, and seize the culpet!"

On hearing the charge, the man seemed enlightened, and, saying not another word, resigned himself with preternatural civility to the search-party, who, with their staves in their hands, surrounded him on all sides, and marched him back toward the shepherd's cottage.

It was eleven o'clock by the time they arrived. The light shining from the open door, a sound of men's voices within, proclaimed to them as they approached the house that some new events had arisen in their absence. On entering they discovered the shepherd's living-room to be invaded by two officers from Casterbridge jail, and a well-known magistrate who lived at the nearest country-seat, intelligence of the escape having become generally circulated.

"Gentlemen," said the constable, "I have brought back your man—not without risk and danger; but every one must do his duty! He is inside this circle of able-bodied persons, who have lent me useful aid, considering their ignorance of Crown work. Men, bring forward your prisoner!" And the third stranger was led to the light.

"Who is this?" said one of the officials.

"The man," said the constable.

"Certainly not," said the turnkey; and the first corroborated his statement.

"But how can it be otherwise?" asked the constable. "Or why was he so terrified at sight o' the singing instrument of the law who sat there?" Here he related the strange behavior of the third stranger on entering the house during the hangman's song.

"Can't understand it," said the officer coolly. "All I know is that it is not the condemned man. He's quite a different character from this one; a gauntish fellow, with dark hair and eyes, rather good-looking, and with a musical bass voice that if you heard it once you'd never mistake as long as you lived."

"Why, souls—'twas the man in the chimney-corner!"

"Hey—what?" said the magistrate, coming forward after inquiring particulars from the shepherd in the background. "Haven't you got the man after all?"

"Well, sir," said the constable, "he's the man we were in search of, that's true; and yet he's not the man we were in search of. For the man we were in search of was not the man we wanted, sir, if you understand my every-day way; for 'twas the man in the chimney-corner!"

"A pretty kettle of fish altogether!" said the magistrate. "You had better start for the other man at once."

The prisoner now spoke for the first time. The mention of the man in the chimney-corner seemed to have moved him as nothing else could do. "Sir," he said, stepping forward to the magistrate, "take no more trouble about me. The time is come when I may as well speak. I have done nothing; my crime is that the condemned man is my brother. Early this afternoon I left home at Shottsford to tramp it all the way to Casterbridge jail to bid him farewell. I was benighted, and called here to rest and ask the way. When I opened the door I saw before me the very man, my brother, that I thought to see in the condemned cell at Casterbridge. He was in this chimney-corner; and jammed close to him, so that he could not have got out if he had tried, was the executioner who'd come to take his life, singing a song about it and not knowing that it was his victim who was close by, joining in to save appearances. My brother looked a glance of agony at me, and I know he meant, 'Don't reveal what you see; my life depends on it.' I was so terror-struck that I could hardly stand, and, not knowing what I did, I turned and hurried away."

The narrator's manner and tone had the stamp of truth, and his story made a great impression on all around.

"And do you know where your brother is at the present time?" asked the magistrate.

"I do not. I have never seen him since I closed this door."

"I can testify to that, for we've been between ye ever since." said the constable.

"Where does he think to fly to?—what is his occupation?"

"He's a watch-and-clock-maker, sir."

"'A said 'a was a wheelwright—a wicked rogue," said the constable.

"The wheels of clocks and watches he meant, no doubt," said Shepherd Fennel. "I thought his hands were palish for's trade."

"Well, it appears to me that nothing can be gained by retaining this poor man in custody," said the magistrate; "your business lies with the other, unquestionably."

And so the little man was released off-hand; but he looked nothing the less sad on that account, it being beyond the power of magistrate or constable to raze out the written troubles in his brain, for they concerned another whom he regarded with more solicitude than himself. When this was done, and the man had gone his way, the night was found to be so far advanced that it was deemed useless to renew the search before the next morning.

Next day, accordingly, the quest for the clever sheep-stealer became general and keen, to all appearance at least. But the intended punishment was cruelly disproportioned to the transgression, and the sympathy of a great many country-folk in that district was strongly on the side of the fugitive. Moreover, his marvellous coolness and daring in hob-and-nobbing with the hangman, under the unprecedented circumstances of the shepherd's party, won their admiration. So that it may be questioned if all those who ostensibly made themselves so busy in exploring woods and fields and lanes were quite so thorough when it came to the private examination of their own lofts and outhouses. Stories were afloat of a mysterious figure being occasionally seen in some old overgrown trackway or other, remote from turnpike roads; but when a search was instituted in any of these suspected quarters nobody was found. Thus the days and weeks passed without tidings.

In brief, the bass-voiced man of the chimney-corner was never recaptured. Some said that he went across the sea, others that he did not, but buried himself in the depths of a populous city. At any rate, the gentleman in cinder-gray never did his morning's work at Casterbridge, nor met anywhere at all, for business purposes, the genial comrade with whom he had passed an hour of relaxation in the lonely house on the coomb.

The grass has long been green on the graves of Shepherd Fennel and his frugal wife; the guests who made up the christening party have mainly followed their entertainers to the tomb; the baby in whose honor they all had met is a matron in the sere and yellow leaf. But the arrival of the three strangers at the shepherd's that night, and the details connected therewith, is a story as well-known as ever in the country about Higher Crowstairs.

March, 1883.

JULIA BRIDE[24]

Henry James (1843)

I

She had walked with her friend to the top of the wide steps of the Museum, those that descended from the galleries of painting, and then, after the young man had left her, smiling, looking back, waving all gayly and expressively his hat and stick, had watched him, smiling too, but with a different intensity—had kept him in sight till he passed out of the great door. She might have been waiting to see if he would turn there for a last demonstration; which was exactly what he did, renewing his cordial gesture and with his look of glad devotion, the radiance of his young face, reaching her across the great space, as she felt, in undiminished truth. Yes, so she could feel, and she remained a minute even after he was gone; she gazed at the empty air as if he had filled it still, asking herself what more she wanted and what, if it didn't signify glad devotion, his whole air could have represented.

She was at present so anxious that she could wonder if he stepped and smiled like that for mere relief at separation; yet if he desired in that degree to break the spell and escape the danger why did he keep coming back to her, and why, for that matter, had she felt safe a moment before in letting him go? She felt safe, felt almost reckless—that was the proof—so long as he was with her; but the chill came as soon as he had gone, when she took the measure, instantly, of all she yet missed. She might now have been taking it afresh, by the testimony of her charming clouded eyes and of the rigor that had already replaced her beautiful play of expression. Her radiance, for the minute, had "carried" as far as his, travelling on the light wings of her brilliant prettiness—he, on his side, not being facially handsome, but only sensitive, clean and eager. Then, with its extinction, the sustaining wings dropped and hung.

She wheeled about, however, full of a purpose; she passed back through the pictured rooms, for it pleased her, this idea of a talk with Mr. Pitman—as much, that is, as anything could please a young person so troubled. It happened indeed that when she saw him rise at sight of her from the settee where he had told her five minutes before that she would find him, it was just with her nervousness

---

that his presence seemed, as through an odd suggestion of help, to connect itself. Nothing truly would be quite so odd for her case as aid proceeding from Mr. Pitman; unless perhaps the oddity would be even greater for himself—the oddity of her having taken into her head an appeal to him.

She had had to feel alone with a vengeance—inwardly alone and miserably alarmed—to be ready to "meet," that way, at the first sign from him, the successor to her dim father in her dim father's lifetime, the second of her mother's two divorced husbands. It made a queer relation for her; a relation that struck her at this moment as less edifying, less natural and graceful than it would have been even for her remarkable mother—and still in spite of this parent's third marriage, her union with Mr. Connery, from whom she was informally separated. It was at the back of Julia's head as she approached Mr. Pitman, or it was at least somewhere deep within her soul, that if this last of Mrs. Connery's withdrawals from the matrimonial yoke had received the sanction of the court (Julia had always heard, from far back, so much about the "Court") she herself, as after a fashion, in that event, a party to it, would not have had the cheek to make up—which was how she inwardly phrased what she was doing—to the long, lean, loose, slightly cadaverous gentleman who was a memory, for her, of the period from her twelfth to her seventeenth year. She had got on with him, perversely, much better than her mother had, and the bulging misfit of his duck waistcoat, with his trick of swinging his eye-glass, at the end of an extraordinarily long string, far over the scene, came back to her as positive features of the image of her remoter youth. Her present age—for her later time had seen so many things happen—gave her a perspective.

Fifty things came up as she stood there before him, some of them floating in from the past, others hovering with freshness: how she used to dodge the rotary movement made by his pince-nez while he always awkwardly, and kindly, and often funnily, talked—it had once hit her rather badly in the eye; how she used to pull down and straighten his waistcoat, making it set a little better, a thing of a sort her mother never did; how friendly and familiar she must have been with him for that, or else a forward little minx; how she felt almost capable of doing it again now, just to sound the right note, and how sure she was of the way he would take it if she did; how much nicer he had clearly been, all the while, poor dear man, than his wife and the court had made it possible for him publicly to appear; how much younger, too, he now looked, in spite of his rather melancholy, his mildly jaundiced, humorously determined sallowness and his careless assumption, everywhere, from his forehead to his exposed and relaxed blue socks, almost sky-blue, as in past days, of creases and folds and furrows that would have been perhaps tragic if they hadn't seemed rather to show, like his whimsical black eyebrows, the vague, interrogative arch.

Of course he wasn't wretched if he wasn't more sure of his wretchedness than that! Julia Bride would have been sure—had she been through what she supposed he had! With his thick, loose black hair, in any case, untouched by a thread of gray, and his kept gift of a certain big-boyish awkwardness—that of his taking their encounter, for instance, so amusedly, so crudely, though, as she was not unaware, so eagerly too—he could by no means have been so little his wife's junior as it had been that lady's habit, after the divorce, to represent him. Julia had remembered him as old, since she had so constantly thought of her mother as old; which Mrs. Connery was indeed now—for her daughter—with her dozen years of actual seniority to Mr. Pitman and her exquisite hair, the densest, the finest tangle of arranged silver tendrils that had ever enhanced the effect of a preserved complexion.

Something in the girl's vision of her quondam stepfather as still comparatively young—with the confusion, the immense element of rectification, not to say of rank disproof, that it introduced into Mrs. Connery's favorite picture of her own injured past—all this worked, even at the moment, to quicken once more the clearness and harshness of judgment, the retrospective disgust, as she might have called it, that had of late grown up in her, the sense of all the folly and vanity and vulgarity, the lies, the perversities, the falsification of all life in the interest of who could say what wretched frivolity, what preposterous policy; amid which she had been condemned so ignorantly, so pitifully to sit, to walk, to grope, to flounder, from the very dawn of her consciousness. Didn't poor Mr. Pitman just touch the sensitive nerve of it when, taking her in with his facetious, cautious eyes, he spoke to her, right out, of the old, old story, the everlasting little wonder of her beauty?

"Why, you know, you've grown up so lovely—you're the prettiest girl I've ever seen!" Of course she was the prettiest girl he had ever seen; she was the prettiest girl people much more privileged than he had ever seen; since when hadn't she been passing for the prettiest girl any one had ever seen? She had lived in that, from far back, from year to year, from day to day and from hour to hour—she had lived for it and literally by it, as who should say; but Mr. Pitman was somehow more illuminating than he knew, with the present lurid light that he cast upon old dates, old pleas, old values, and old mysteries, not to call them old abysses: it had rolled over her in a swift wave, with the very sight of him, that her mother couldn't possibly have been right about him—as about what in the world had she ever been right?—so that in fact he was simply offered her there as one more of Mrs. Connery's lies. She might have thought she knew them all by this time; but he represented for her, coming in just as he did, a fresh discovery, and it was this contribution of freshness that made her somehow feel she liked him. It was she herself who, for so long, with her retained impression, had been right about him; and the rectification he represented had all shone out of him, ten minutes before, on his catching her eye while she moved through the room with Mr. French. She had never doubted of his probable faults—which her mother had vividly depicted as the basest of vices; since some of them, and the most obvious (not the vices, but the faults) were written on him as he stood there: notably, for instance, the exasperating "business slackness" of which Mrs. Connery had, before the tribunal, made so pathetically much. It might have been, for that matter, the very business slackness that affected Julia as presenting its friendly breast, in the form of a cool loose sociability, to her own actual tension; though it was also true for her, after they had exchanged fifty words, that he had as well his inward fever and that, if he was perhaps wondering what was so particularly the matter with her, she could make out not less that something was the matter with him. It had been vague, yet it had been intense, the mute reflection, "Yes, I'm going to like him, and he's going somehow to help me!" that had directed her steps so straight to him. She was sure even then of this, that he wouldn't put to her a query about his former wife, that he took to-day no grain of interest in Mrs. Connery; that his interest, such as it was—and he couldn't look quite like that, to Julia Bride's expert perception, without something in the nature of a new one—would be a thousand times different.

It was as a value of disproof that his worth meanwhile so rapidly grew: the good sight of him, the good sound and sense of him, such as they were, demolished at a stroke so blessedly much of the horrid inconvenience of the past that she thought of him; she clutched at him, for a general saving use, an application as sanative, as redemptive as some universal healing wash, precious even to the point of perjury if perjury should be required. That was the terrible thing, that had been the inward pang with which she watched Basil French recede: perjury would have to come in somehow and somewhere—oh so quite certainly!—before the so strange, so rare young man, truly smitten though she believed him, could be made to rise to the occasion, before her measureless prize could be assured. It was present to her, it had been present a hundred times, that if there had only been some one to (as it were) "deny

145

everything" the situation might yet be saved. She so needed some one to lie for her—ah, she so need some one to lie! Her mother's version of everything, her mother's version of anything, had been at the best, as they said, discounted; and she herself could but show, of course, for an interested party, however much she might claim to be none the less a decent girl—to whatever point, that is, after all that had both remotely and recently happened, presumptions of anything to be called decency could come in.

After what had recently happened—the two or three indirect but so worrying questions Mr. French had put to her—it would only be some thoroughly detached friend or witness who might effectively testify. An odd form of detachment certainly would reside, for Mr. Pitman's evidential character, in her mother's having so publicly and so brilliantly—though, thank the powers, all off in North Dakota!—severed their connection with him; and yet mightn't it do her some good, even if the harm it might do her mother were so little ambiguous? The more her mother had got divorced—with her dreadful cheap-and-easy second performance in that line and her present extremity of alienation from Mr. Connery, which enfolded beyond doubt the germ of a third petition on one side or the other—the more her mother had distinguished herself in the field of folly the worse for her own prospect with the Frenches, whose minds she had guessed to be accessible, and with such an effect of dissimulated suddenness, to some insidious poison.

It was very unmistakable, in other words, that the more dismissed and detached Mr. Pitman should have come to appear, the more as divorced, or at least as divorcing, his before-time wife would by the same stroke figure—so that it was here poor Julia could but lose herself. The crazy divorces only, or the half-dozen successive and still crazier engagements only—gathered fruit, bitter fruit, of her own incredibly allowed, her own insanely fostered frivolity—either of these two groups of skeletons at the banquet might singly be dealt with; but the combination, the fact of each party's having been so mixed-up with whatever was least presentable for the other, the fact of their having so shockingly amused themselves together, made all present steering resemble the classic middle course between Scylla and Charybdis.

It was not, however, that she felt wholly a fool in having obeyed this impulse to pick up again her kind old friend. She at least had never divorced him, and her horrid little filial evidence in court had been but the chatter of a parrakeet, of precocious plumage and croak, repeating words earnestly taught her, and that she could scarce even pronounce. Therefore, as far as steering went, he must for the hour take a hand. She might actually have wished in fact that he shouldn't now have seemed so tremendously struck with her; since it was an extraordinary situation for a girl, this crisis of her fortune, this positive wrong that the flagrancy, what she would have been ready to call the very vulgarity, of her good looks might do her at a moment when it was vital she should hang as straight as a picture on the wall. Had it ever yet befallen any young woman in the world to wish with secret intensity that she might have been, for her convenience, a shade less inordinately pretty? She had come to that, to this view of the bane, the primal curse, of their lavish physical outfit, which had included everything and as to which she lumped herself resentfully with her mother. The only thing was that her mother was, thank goodness, still so much prettier, still so assertively, so publicly, so trashily, so ruinously pretty. Wonderful the small grimness with which Julia Bride put off on this parent the middle-aged maximum of their case and the responsibility of their defect. It cost her so little to recognize in Mrs. Connery at forty-seven, and in spite, or perhaps indeed just by reason, of the arranged silver tendrils which were so like some rare bird's-nest in a morning frost, a facile supremacy for the dazzling effect—it cost her so little that her view even rather exaggerated the lustre of the different maternal items. She would have put it all off if possible, all off on other shoulders and on other graces and other morals than her own, the burden of physical charm that had made so easy a ground, such a native favoring air, for the aberrations which, apparently inevitable and without far consequences at the time, had yet at this juncture so much better not have been.

She could have worked it out at her leisure, to the last link of the chain, the way their prettiness had set them trap after trap, all along—had foredoomed them to awful ineptitude. When you were as pretty as that you could, by the whole idiotic consensus, be nothing but pretty; and when you were nothing "but" pretty you could get into nothing but tight places, out of which you could then scramble by nothing but masses of fibs. And there was no one, all the while, who wasn't eager to egg you on, eager to make you pay to the last cent the price of your beauty. What creature would ever for a moment help you to behave as if something that dragged in its wake a bit less of a lumbering train would, on the whole, have been better for you? The consequences of being plain were only negative—you failed of this and that; but the consequences of being as they were, what were these but endless? though indeed, as far as failing went, your beauty too could let you in for enough of it. Who, at all events, would ever for a moment credit you, in the luxuriance of that beauty, with the study, on your own side, of such truths as these? Julia Bride could, at the point she had reached, positively ask herself this even while lucidly conscious of the inimitable, the triumphant and attested projection, all round her, of her exquisite image. It was only Basil French who had at last, in his doubtless dry, but all distinguished way—the way surely, as it was borne in upon her, of all the blood of all the Frenches—stepped out of the vulgar rank. It was only he who, by the trouble she discerned in him, had made her see certain things. It was only for him—and not a bit ridiculously, but just beautifully, almost sublimely—that their being "nice," her mother and she between them, had not seemed to profit by their being so furiously handsome.

This had, ever so grossly and ever so tiresomely, satisfied every one else; since every one had thrust upon them, had imposed upon them, as by a great cruel conspiracy, their silliest possibilities; fencing them in to these, and so not only shutting them out from others, but mounting guard at the fence, walking round and round outside it, to see they didn't escape, and admiring them, talking to them, through the rails, in mere terms of chaff, terms of chucked cakes and apples—as if they had been antelopes or zebras, or even some superior sort of performing, of dancing, bear. It had been reserved for Basil French to strike her as willing to let go, so to speak, a pound or two of this fatal treasure if he might only have got in exchange for it an ounce or so more of their so much less obvious and Jess published personal history. Yes, it described him to say that, in addition to all the rest of him, and of his personal history, and of his family, and of theirs, in addition to their social posture, as that of a serried phalanx, and to their notoriously enormous wealth and crushing respectability, she might have been ever so much less lovely for him if she had been only—well, a little prepared to answer questions. And it wasn't as if quiet, cultivated, earnest, public-spirited, brought up in Germany, infinitely travelled, awfully like a high-caste Englishman, and all the other pleasant things, it wasn't as if he didn't love to be with her, to look at her, just as she was; for he loved it exactly as much, so far as that footing simply went, as any free and foolish youth who had ever made the last demonstration of it. It was that marriage was, for him—and for them all, the serried Frenches—a great matter, a goal to which a man of intelligence, a real shy, beautiful man of the world, didn't hop on one foot, didn't skip and jump, as if he were playing an urchins' game, but toward which he proceeded with a deep and anxious, a noble and highly just deliberation.

For it was one thing to stare at a girl till she was bored with it, it was one thing to take her to the Horse Show and the Opera, and to send her flowers by the stack, and chocolates by the ton, and "great" novels, the very latest and greatest, by the dozen; but something

148

quite other to hold open for her, with eyes attached to eyes, the gate, moving on such stiff silver hinges, of the grand square forecourt of the palace of wedlock. The state of being "engaged" represented to him the introduction to this precinct of some young woman with whom his outside parley would have had the duration, distinctly, of his own convenience. That might be cold-blooded if one chose to think so; but nothing of another sort would equal the high ceremony and dignity and decency, above all the grand gallantry and finality, of their then passing in. Poor Julia could have blushed red, before that view, with the memory of the way the forecourt, as she now imagined it, had been dishonored by her younger romps. She had tumbled over the wall with this, that, and the other raw playmate, and had played "tag" and leap-frog, as she might say, from corner to corner. That would be the "history" with which, in case of definite demand, she should be able to supply Mr. French: that she had already, again and again, any occasion offering, chattered and scuffled over ground provided, according to his idea, for walking the gravest of minuets. If that then had been all their kind of history, hers and her mother's, at least there was plenty of it: it was the superstructure raised on the other group of facts, those of the order of their having been always so perfectly pink and white, so perfectly possessed of clothes, so perfectly splendid, so perfectly idiotic. These things had been the "points" of antelope and zebra; putting Mrs. Connery for the zebra, as the more remarkably striped or spotted. Such were the data Basil French's inquiry would elicit: her own six engagements and her mother's three nullified marriages—nine nice distinct little horrors in all. What on earth was to be done about them?

It was notable, she was afterward to recognize, that there had been nothing of the famous business slackness in the positive pounce with which Mr. Pitman put it to her that, as soon as he had made her out "for sure," identified her there as old Julia grown-up and gallivanting with a new admirer, a smarter young fellow than ever yet, he had had the inspiration of her being exactly the good girl to help him. She certainly found him strike the hour again, with these vulgarities of tone—forms of speech that her mother had anciently described as by themselves, once he had opened the whole battery, sufficient ground for putting him away. Full, however, of the use she should have for him, she wasn't going to mind trifles. What she really gasped at was that, so oddly, he was ahead of her at the start. "Yes, I want something of you, Julia, and I want it right now: you can do me a turn, and I'm blest if my luck—which has once or twice been pretty good, you know—hasn't sent you to me." She knew the luck he meant—that of her mother's having so enabled him to get rid of her; but it was the nearest allusion of the merely invidious kind that he would make. It had thus come to our young woman on the spot and by divination: the service he desired of her matched with remarkable closeness what she had so promptly taken into her head to name to himself—to name in her own interest, though deterred as yet from having brought it right out. She had been prevented by his speaking, the first thing, in that way, as if he had known Mr. French—which surprised her till he explained that every one in New York knew by appearance a young man of his so-quoted wealth ("What did she take them all in New York then for?") and of whose marked attention to her he had moreover, for himself, round at clubs and places, lately heard. This had accompanied the inevitable free question "Was she engaged to him now?"—which she had in fact almost welcomed as holding out to her the perch of opportunity. She was waiting to deal with it properly, but meanwhile he had gone on, and to such effect that it took them but three minutes to turn out, on either side, like a pair of pickpockets comparing, under shelter, their day's booty, the treasures of design concealed about their persons.

"I want you to tell the truth for me—as you only can. I want you to say that I was really all right—as right as you know; and that I simply acted like an angel in a story-book, gave myself away to have it over."

"Why, my dear man," Julia cried, "you take the wind straight out of my sails! What I'm here to ask of you is that you'll confess to having been even a worse fiend than you were shown up for; to having made it impossible mother should not take proceedings." There!—she had brought it out, and with the sense of their situation turning to high excitement for her in the teeth of his droll stare, his strange grin, his characteristic "Lordy, lordy! What good will that do you?" She was prepared with her clear statement of reasons for her appeal, and feared so he might have better ones for his own that all her story came in a flash. "Well, Mr. Pitman, I want to get married this time, by way of a change; but you see we've been such fools that, when something really good at last comes up, it's too dreadfully awkward. The fools we were capable of being—well, you know better than any one: unless perhaps not quite so well as Mr. Connery. It has got to be denied," said Julia ardently—"it has got to be denied flat. But I can't get hold of Mr. Connery—Mr. Connery has gone to China. Besides, if he were here," she had ruefully to confess, "he'd be no good—on the contrary. He wouldn't deny anything—he'd only tell more. So thank heaven he's away—there's that amount of good! I'm not engaged yet," she went on—but he had already taken her up.

"You're not engaged to Mr. French?" It was all, clearly, a wondrous show for him, but his immediate surprise, oddly, might have been greatest for that.

"No, not to any one—for the seventh time!" She spoke as with her head held well up both over the shame and the pride. "Yes, the next time I'm engaged I want something to happen. But he's afraid; he's afraid of what may be told him. He's dying to find out, and yet he'd die if he did! He wants to be talked to, but he has got to be talked to right. You could talk to him right, Mr. Pitman—if you only would! He can't get over mother—that I feel: he loathes and scorns divorces, and we've had first and last too many. So if he could hear from you that you just made her life a hell—why," Julia concluded, "it would be too lovely. If she had to go in for another—after having already, when I was little, divorced father—it would 'sort of' make, don't you see? one less. You'd do the high-toned thing by her: you'd say what a wretch you then were, and that she had had to save her life. In that way he mayn't mind it. Don't you see, you sweet man?" poor Julia pleaded. "Oh," she wound up as if his fancy lagged or his scruple looked out, "of course I want you to lie for me!"

It did indeed sufficiently stagger him. "It's a lovely idea for the moment when I was just saying to myself—as soon as I saw you— that you'd speak the truth for me!"

"Ah, what's the matter with 'you'?" Julia sighed with an impatience not sensibly less sharp for her having so quickly scented some lion in her path.

"Why, do you think there's no one in the world but you who has seen the cup of promised affection, of something really to be depended on, only, at the last moment, by the horrid jostle of your elbow, spilled all over you? I want to provide for my future too as it happens; and my good friend who's to help me to that—the most charming of women this time—disapproves of divorce quite as much as Mr. French. Don't you see," Mr. Pitman candidly asked, "what that by itself must have done toward attaching me to her? She has got to be talked to—to be told how little I could help it."

"Oh, lordy, lordy!" the girl emulously groaned. It was such a relieving cry. "Well, I won't talk to her!" she declared.

"You won't, Julia?" he pitifully echoed. "And yet you ask of me—!"

His pang, she felt, was sincere; and even more than she had guessed, for the previous quarter of an hour he had been building up his hope, building it with her aid for a foundation. Yet was he going to see how their testimony, on each side, would, if offered, have to conflict? If he was to prove himself for her sake—or, more queerly still, for that of Basil French's high conservatism—a person whom there had been no other way of dealing with, how could she prove him, in this other and so different interest, a mere gentle sacrifice to his wife's perversity? She had, before him there, on the instant, all acutely, a sense of rising sickness—a wan glimmer of foresight as to the end of the fond dream. Everything else was against her, everything in her dreadful past—just as if she had been a person represented by some "emotional actress," some desperate erring lady "hunted down" in a play; but was that going to be the case too with her own very decency, the fierce little residuum deep within her, for which she was counting, when she came to think, on so little glory or even credit? Was this also going to turn against her and trip her up—just to show she was really, under the touch and the test, as decent as any one; and with no one but herself the wiser for it meanwhile, and no proof to show but that, as a consequence, she should be unmarried to the end? She put it to Mr. Pitman quite with resentment: "Do you mean to say you're going to be married-?"

"Oh, my dear, I too must get engaged first!"—he spoke with his inimitable grin. "But that, you see, is where you come in. I've told her about you. She wants awfully to meet you. The way it happens is too lovely—that I find you just in this place. She's coming," said Mr. Pitman—and as in all the good faith of his eagerness now; "she's coming in about three minutes."

"Coming here?"

"Yes, Julia—right here. It's where we usually meet"; and he was wreathed again, this time as if for life, in his large slow smile. "She loves this place—she's awfully keen on art. Like you, Julia, if you haven't changed—I remember how you did love art." He looked at her quite tenderly, as to keep her up to it. "You must still of course— from the way you're here. Just let her feel that," the poor man fantastically urged. And then with his kind eyes on her and his good ugly mouth stretched as for delicate emphasis from ear to ear: "Every little helps!"

He made her wonder for him, ask herself, and with a certain intensity, questions she yet hated the trouble of; as whether he were still as moneyless as in the other time—which was certain indeed, for any fortune he ever would have made. His slackness, on that ground, stuck out of him almost as much as if he had been of rusty or "seedy" aspect—which, luckily for him, he wasn't at all: he looked, in his way, like some pleasant eccentric, ridiculous, but real gentleman, whose taste might be of the queerest, but his credit with his tailor none the less of the best. She wouldn't have been the least ashamed, had their connection lasted, of going about with him: so that what a fool, again, her mother had been—since Mr. Connery, sorry as one might be for him, was irrepressibly vulgar. Julia's quickness was, for the minute, charged with all this; but she had none the less her feeling of the right thing to say and the right way to say it. If he was after a future financially assured, even as she herself so frantically was, she wouldn't cast the stone. But if he had talked about her to strange women she couldn't be less than a little majestic. "Who then is the person in question for you—?"

"Why, such a dear thing, Julia—Mrs. David E. Drack. Have you heard of her?" he almost fluted.

New York was vast, and she had not had that advantage. "She's a widow—?"

"Oh yes: she's not—" He caught himself up in time. "She's a real one." It was as near as he came. But it was as if he had been looking at her now so pathetically hard. "Julia, she has millions."

Hard, at any rate—whether pathetic or not—was the look she gave him back. "Well, so has—or so will have—Basil French. And more of them than Mrs. Drack, I guess," Julia quavered.

"Oh, I know what they've got!" He took it from her—with the effect of a vague stir, in his long person, of unwelcome embarrassment. But was she going to give up because he was embarrassed? He should know at least what he was costing her. It came home to her own spirit more than ever, but meanwhile he had found his footing. "I don't see how your mother matters. It isn't a question of his marrying her."

"No; but, constantly together as we've always been, it's a question of there being so disgustingly much to get over. If we had, for people like them, but the one ugly spot and the one weak side; if we had made, between us, but the one vulgar kind of mistake: well, I don't say!" She reflected with a wistfulness of note that was in itself a touching eloquence. "To have our reward in this world we've had too sweet a time. We've had it all right down here!" said Julia Bride. "I should have taken the precaution to have about a dozen fewer lovers."

"Ah, my dear, 'lovers'—!" He ever so comically attenuated.

"Well they were!" She quite flared up. "When you've had a ring from each (three diamonds, two pearls, and a rather bad sapphire: I've kept them all, and they tell my story!) what are you to call them?"

"Oh, rings—!" Mr. Pitman didn't call rings anything. "I've given Mrs. Drack a ring."

Julia stared. "Then aren't you her lover?"

"That, dear child," he humorously wailed, "is what I want you to find out! But I'll handle your rings all right," he more lucidly added.

"You'll 'handle' them?"

"I'll fix your lovers. I'll lie about them, if that's all you want."

"Oh, about 'them'—!" She turned away with a sombre drop, seeing so little in it. "That wouldn't count—from you!" She saw the great shining room, with its mockery of art and "style" and security, all the things she was vainly after, and its few scattered visitors who had left them, Mr. Pitman and herself, in their ample corner, so conveniently at ease. There was only a lady in one of the far doorways, of whom she took vague note and who seemed to be looking at them. "They'd have to lie for themselves!"

"Do you mean he's capable of putting it to them?"

Mr. Pitman's tone threw discredit on that possibility, but she knew perfectly well what she meant. "Not of getting at them directly, not, as mother says, of nosing round himself; but of listening—and small blame to him!—to the horrible things other people say of me."

"But what other people?"

"Why, Mrs. George Maule, to begin with—who intensely loathes us, and who talks to his sisters, so that they may talk to him: which they do, all the while, I'm morally sure (hating me as they also must). But it's she who's the real reason—I mean of his holding off. She poisons the air he breathes."

"Oh well," said Mr. Pitman, with easy optimism, "if Mrs. George Maule's a cat—!"

"If she's a cat she has kittens—four little spotlessly white ones, among whom she'd give her head that Mr. French should make his pick. He could do it with his eyes shut—you can't tell them apart. But she has every name, every date, as you may say, for my dark 'record'—as of course they all call it: she'll be able to give him, if he brings himself to ask her, every fact in its order. And all the while, don't you see? there's no one to speak for me."

It would have touched a harder heart than her loose friend's to note the final flush of clairvoyance witnessing this assertion and under which her eyes shone as with the rush of quick tears. He stared at her, and at what this did for the deep charm of her prettiness, as in almost witless admiration. "But can't you—lovely as you are, you beautiful thing!—speak for yourself?"

"Do you mean can't I tell the lies? No, then, I can't—and I wouldn't if I could. I don't lie myself, you know—as it happens; and it could represent to him then about the only thing, the only bad one, I don't do. I did—'lovely as I am'!—have my regular time; I wasn't so hideous that I couldn't! Besides, do you imagine he'd come and ask me?"

"Gad, I wish he would, Julia!" said Mr. Pitman, with his kind eyes on her.

"Well then, I'd tell him!" And she held her head again high. "But he won't."

It fairly distressed her companion. "Doesn't he want, then, to know—?"

"He wants not to know. He wants to be told without asking—told, I mean, that each of the stories, those that have come to him, is a fraud and a libel. Qui s'excuse s'accuse, don't they say?—so that do you see me breaking out to him, unprovoked, with four or five what-do-you-call-'ems, the things mother used to have to prove in court, a set of neat little 'alibis' in a row? How can I get hold of so many precious gentlemen, to turn them on? How can they want everything fished up?"

She paused for her climax, in the intensity of these considerations; which gave Mr. Pitman a chance to express his honest faith. "Why, my sweet child, they'd be just glad—!"

It determined in her loveliness almost a sudden glare. "Glad to swear they never had anything to do with such a creature? Then I'd be glad to swear they had lots!"

His persuasive smile, though confessing to bewilderment, insisted. "Why, my love, they've got to swear either one thing or the other."

"They've got to keep out of the way—that's their view of it, I guess," said Julia. "Where are they, please—now that they may be wanted? If you'd like to hunt them up for me you're very welcome." With which, for the moment, over the difficult case, they faced each other helplessly enough. And she added to it now the sharpest ache of her despair. "He knows about Murray Brush. The others"—and her pretty white-gloved hands and charming pink shoulders gave them up—"may go hang!"

"Murray Brush—?" It had opened Mr. Pitman's eyes.

"Yes—yes; I do mind him."

"Then what's the matter with his at least rallying—?"

"The matter is that, being ashamed of himself, as he well might, he left the country as soon as he could and has stayed away. The matter is that he's in Paris or somewhere, and that if you expect him to come home for me—!" She had already dropped, however, as at Mr. Pitman's look.

"Why, you foolish thing, Murray Brush is in New York!" It had quite brightened him up.

"He has come back—?"

"Why, sure! I saw him—when was it? Tuesday!—on the Jersey boat." Mr. Pitman rejoiced in his news. "He's your man!"

Julia too had been affected by it; it had brought, in a rich wave, her hot color back. But she gave the strangest dim smile. "He was!"

"Then get hold of him, and—if he's a gentleman—he'll prove for you, to the hilt, that he wasn't."

It lighted in her face, the kindled train of this particular sudden suggestion, a glow, a sharpness of interest, that had deepened the next moment, while she gave a slow and sad head-shake, to a greater strangeness yet. "He isn't a gentleman."

"Ah, lordy, lordy!" Mr. Pitman again sighed. He struggled out of it but only into the vague. "Oh, then, if he's a pig—!"

"You see there are only a few gentlemen—not enough to go round—and that makes them count so!" It had thrust the girl herself, for that matter, into depths; but whether most of memory or of roused purpose he had no time to judge—aware as he suddenly was of a shadow (since he mightn't perhaps too quickly call it a light) across the heaving surface of their question. It fell upon Julia's face, fell with the sound of the voice he so well knew, but which could only be odd to her for all it immediately assumed.

"There are indeed very few—and one mustn't try them too much!" Mrs. Drack, who had supervened while they talked, stood, in monstrous magnitude—at least to Julia's reimpressed eyes—between them: she was the lady our young woman had descried across the room, and she had drawn near while the interest of their issue so held them. We have seen the act of observation and that of reflection alike swift in Julia—once her subject was within range—and she had now, with all her perceptions at the acutest, taken in, by a single stare, the strange presence to a happy connection with which Mr. Pitman aspired and which had thus sailed, with placid majesty, into their troubled waters. She was clearly not shy, Mrs. David E. Drack, yet neither was she ominously bold; she was bland and "good," Julia made sure at a glance, and of a large complacency, as the good and the bland are apt to be—a large complacency, a large sentimentality, a large innocent, elephantine archness: she fairly rioted in that dimension of size. Habited in an extraordinary quantity of stiff and lustrous black brocade, with enhancements, of every description, that twinkled and tinkled, that rustled and rumbled with her least movement, she presented a huge, hideous, pleasant face, a featureless desert in a remote quarter of which the disproportionately small eyes might have figured a pair of rash adventurers all but buried in the sand. They reduced themselves when she smiled to barely discernible points—a couple of mere tiny emergent heads—though the foreground of the scene, as if to make up for it, gaped with a vast benevolence. In a word Julia saw—and as if she had needed nothing more; saw Mr. Pitman's opportunity, saw her own, saw the exact nature both of Mrs. Drack's circumspection and of Mrs. Drack's sensibility, saw even, glittering there in letters of gold and as a part of the whole metallic coruscation, the large figure of her income, largest of all her attributes, and (though perhaps a little more as a luminous blur beside all this) the mingled ecstasy and agony of Mr. Pitman's hope and Mr. Pitman's fear.

He was introducing them, with his pathetic belief in the virtue for every occasion, in the solvent for every trouble, of an extravagant, genial, professional humor; he was naming her to Mrs. Drack as the charming young friend he had told her so much about and who had been as an angel to him in a weary time; he was saying that the loveliest chance in the world, this accident of a meeting in those promiscuous halls, had placed within his reach the pleasure of bringing them together. It didn't indeed matter, Julia felt, what he was saying: he conveyed everything, as far as she was concerned, by a moral pressure as unmistakable as if, for a symbol of it, he had thrown himself on her neck. Above all, meanwhile, this high consciousness prevailed—that the good lady herself, however huge she loomed, had entered, by the end of a minute, into a condition as of suspended weight and arrested mass, stilled to artless awe by the fact of her vision. Julia had practised almost to lassitude the art of tracing in the people who looked at her the impression promptly sequent; but it was a striking point that if, in irritation, in depression, she felt that the lightest eyes of men, stupid at their clearest, had given her pretty well all she should ever care for, she could still gather a freshness from the tribute of her own sex, still care to see her reflection in the faces of women. Never, probably, never would that sweet be tasteless—with such a straight grim spoon was it mostly administered, and so flavored and strengthened by the competence of their eyes. Women knew so much best how a woman surpassed—how and where and why, with no touch or torment of it lost on them; so that as it produced mainly and primarily the instinct of aversion, the sense of extracting the recognition, of gouging out the homage, was on the whole the highest crown one's felicity could wear. Once in a way, however, the grimness beautifully dropped, the jealousy failed: the admiration was all there and the poor plain sister handsomely paid it. It had never been so paid, she was presently certain, as by this great generous object of Mr., Pitman's flame, who without optical aid, it well might have seemed, nevertheless entirely grasped her—might in fact, all benevolently, have been groping her over as by some huge mild proboscis. She gave Mrs. Brack pleasure in short; and who could say of what other pleasures the poor lady hadn't been cheated?

It was somehow a muddled world in which one of her conceivable joys, at this time of day, would be to marry Mr. Pitman—to say nothing of a state of things in which this gentleman's own fancy could invest such a union with rapture. That, however, was their own mystery, and Julia, with each instant, was more and more clear about hers: so remarkably primed in fact, at the end of three minutes, that though her friend, and though his friend, were both saying things, many things and perhaps quite wonderful things, she had no free attention for them and was only rising and soaring. She was rising to her value, she was soaring with it—the value Mr. Pitman almost convulsively imputed to her, the value that consisted for her of being so unmistakably the most dazzling image Mrs. Brack had ever beheld. These were the uses, for Julia, in fine, of adversity; the range of Mrs. Brack's experience might have been as small as the measure of her presence was large: Julia was at any rate herself in face of the occasion of her life, and, after all her late repudiations and reactions, had perhaps never yet known the quality of this moment's success. She hadn't an idea of what, on either side, had been uttered—beyond Mr. Pitman's allusion to her having befriended him of old: she simply held his companion with her radiance and knew she might be, for her effect, as irrelevant as she chose. It was relevant to do what he wanted—it was relevant to dish herself. She did it now with a kind of passion, to say nothing of her knowing, with it, that every word of it added to her beauty. She gave him away in short, up to the hilt, for any use of her own, and should have nothing to clutch at now but the possibility of Murray Brush.

"He says I was good to him, Mrs. Drack; and I'm sure I hope I was, since I should be ashamed to be anything else. If I could be good to him now I should be glad—that's just what, a while ago, I rushed up to him here, after so long, to give myself the pleasure of saying. I saw him years ago very particularly, very miserably tried—and I saw the way he took it. I did see it, you dear man," she sublimely went on—"I saw it for all you may protest, for all you may hate me to talk about you! I saw you behave like a gentleman—since Mrs. Drack agrees with me, so charmingly, that there are not many to be met. I don't know whether you care, Mrs. Drack"—she abounded, she revelled in the name—"but I've always remembered it of him: that under the most extraordinary provocation he was decent and patient and brave. No appearance of anything different matters, for I speak of what I know. Of course I'm nothing and nobody; I'm only a poor frivolous girl, but I was very close to him at the time. That's all my little story—if it should interest you at all." She measured every beat of her wing, she knew how high she was going and paused only when it was quite vertiginous. Here she hung a moment as in the glare of the upper blue; which was but the glare—what else could it be?—of the vast and magnificent attention of both her auditors, hushed, on their side, in the splendor she emitted. She had at last to steady herself, and she scarce knew afterward at what rate or in what way she had still inimitably come down—her own eyes fixed all the while on the very figure of her achievement. She had sacrificed her mother on the altar—proclaimed her as false and cruel: and if that didn't "fix" Mr. Pitman, as he would have said—well, it was all she could do. But the cost of her action already somehow came back to her with increase; the dear gaunt man fairly wavered, to her sight, in the glory of it, as if signalling at her, with wild gleeful arms, from some mount of safety, while the massive lady just spread and spread like a rich fluid a bit helplessly spilt. It was really the outflow of the poor woman's honest response, into which she seemed to melt, and Julia scarce distinguished the two apart even for her taking gracious leave of each. "Good-bye, Mrs. Drack; I'm awfully happy to have met you"—like as not it was for this she had grasped Mr. Pitman's hand. And then to him or to her, it didn't matter which, "Good-bye, dear good Mr. Pitman—hasn't it been nice after so long?"

II

Julia floated even to her own sense swan-like away—she left in her wake their fairly stupefied submission: it was as if she had, by an exquisite authority, now placed them, each for each, and they would have nothing to do but be happy together. Never had she so exulted as on this ridiculous occasion in the noted items of her beauty. Le compte y était, as they used to say in Paris—every one of them, for her immediate employment, was there; and there was something in it after all. It didn't necessarily, this sum of thumping little figures, imply charm—especially for "refined" people: nobody knew better than Julia that inexpressible charm and quotable "charms" (quotable like prices, rates, shares, or whatever, the things they dealt in down-town) are two distinct categories; the safest thing for the latter being, on the whole, that it might include the former, and the great strength of the former being that it might perfectly dispense with the latter. Mrs. Drack was not refined, not the least little bit; but what would be the case with Murray Brush now—after his three years of Europe? He had done so what he liked

159

with her—which had seemed so then just the meaning, hadn't it? of their being "engaged"—that he had made her not see, while the absurdity lasted (the absurdity of their pretending to believe they could marry without a cent), how little he was of metal without alloy: this had come up for her, remarkably, but afterward—come up for her as she looked back. Then she had drawn her conclusion, which was one of the many that Basil French had made her draw. It was a queer service Basil was going to have rendered her, this having made everything she had ever done impossible, if he wasn't going to give her a new chance. If he was it was doubtless right enough. On the other hand, Murray might have improved, if such a quantity of alloy, as she called it, were, in any man, reducible, and if Paris were the place all happily to reduce it. She had her doubts—anxious and aching on the spot, and had expressed them to Mr. Pitman: certainly, of old, he had been more open to the quotable than to the inexpressible, to charms than to charm. If she could try the quotable, however, and with such a grand result, on Mrs. Drack, she couldn't now on Murray—in respect to whom everything had changed. So that if he hadn't a sense for the subtler appeal, the appeal appreciable by people not vulgar, on which alone she could depend, what on earth would become of her? She could but yearningly hope, at any rate, as she made up her mind to write to him immediately at his club. It was a question of the right sensibility in him. Perhaps he would have acquired it in Europe.

Two days later indeed—for he had promptly and charmingly replied, keeping with alacrity the appointment she had judged best to propose for a morning hour in a sequestered alley of the Park—two days later she was to be struck well-nigh to alarm by everything he had acquired: so much it seemed to make that it threatened somehow a complication, and her plan, so far as she had arrived at one, dwelt in the desire above all to simplify. She wanted no grain more of extravagance or excess of anything—risking as she had done, none the less, a recall of ancient license in proposing to Murray such a place of meeting. She had her reasons—she wished intensely to discriminate: Basil French had several times waited on her at her mother's habitation, their horrible flat which was so much too far up and too near the East Side; he had dined there and lunched there and gone with her thence to other places, notably to see pictures, and had in particular adjourned with her twice to the Metropolitan Museum, in which he took a great interest, in which she professed a delight, and their second visit to which had wound up in her encounter with Mr. Pitman, after her companion had yielded, at her urgent instance, to an exceptional need of keeping a business engagement. She mightn't, in delicacy, in decency, entertain Murray Brush where she had entertained Mr. French—she was given over now to these exquisite perceptions and proprieties and bent on devoutly observing them; and Mr. French, by good-luck, had never been with her in the Park: partly because he had never pressed it, and partly because she would have held off if he had, so haunted were those devious paths and favoring shades by the general echo of her untrammelled past. If he had never suggested their taking a turn there this was because, quite divinably, he held it would commit him further than he had yet gone; and if she on her side had practised a like reserve it was because the place reeked for her, as she inwardly said, with old associations. It reeked with nothing so much perhaps as with the memories evoked by the young man who now awaited her in the nook she had been so competent to indicate; but in what corner of the town, should she look for them, wouldn't those footsteps creak back into muffled life, and to what expedient would she be reduced should she attempt to avoid all such tracks? The Museum was full of tracks, tracks by the hundred—the way really she had knocked about!—but she had to see people somewhere, and she couldn't pretend to dodge every ghost.

All she could do was not to make confusion, make mixtures, of the living; though she asked herself enough what mixture she mightn't find herself to have prepared if Mr. French should, not so very impossibly, for a restless, roaming man—her effect on him!—happen to pass while she sat there with the mustachioed personage round whose name Mrs. Maule would probably have caused detrimental anecdote most thickly to cluster. There existed, she was sure, a mass of luxuriant legend about the "lengths" her engagement with Murray Brush had gone; she could herself fairly feel them in the air, these streamers of evil, black flags flown as in warning, the vast redundancy of so cheap and so dingy social bunting, in fine, that flapped over the stations she had successively moved away from and which were empty now, for such an ado, even to grotesqueness. The vivacity of that conviction was what had at present determined her, while it was the way he listened after she had quickly broken ground, while it was the special character of the interested look in his handsome face, handsomer than ever yet, that represented for her the civilization he had somehow taken on. Just so it was the quantity of that gain, in its turn, that had at the end of ten minutes begun to affect her as holding up a light to the wide reach of her step. "There was never anything the least serious between us, not a sign or a scrap, do you mind? of anything beyond the merest pleasant friendly acquaintance; and if you're not ready to go to the stake on it for me you may as well know in time what it is you'll probably cost me."

She had immediately plunged, measuring her effect and having thought it well over; and what corresponded to her question of his having become a better person to appeal to was the appearance of interest she had so easily created in him. She felt on the spot the difference that made—it was indeed his form of being more civilized: it was the sense in which Europe in general and Paris in particular had made him develop. By every calculation—and her calculations, based on the intimacy of her knowledge, had been many and deep—he would help her the better the more intelligent he should have become; yet she was to recognize later on that the first chill of foreseen disaster had been caught by her as, at a given moment, this greater refinement of his attention seemed to exhale it. It was just what she had wanted—"if I can only get him interested—!" so that, this proving quite vividly possible, why did the light it lifted strike her as lurid? Was it partly by reason of his inordinate romantic good looks, those of a gallant, genial conqueror, but which, involving so glossy a brownness of eye, so manly a crispness of curl, so red-lipped a radiance of smile, so natural a bravery of port, prescribed to any response he might facially, might expressively, make a sort of florid, disproportionate amplitude? The explanation, in any case, didn't matter; he was going to mean well—that she could feel, and also that he had meant better in the past, presumably, than he had managed to convince her of his doing at the time: the oddity she hadn't now reckoned with was this fact that from the moment he did advertise an interest it should show almost as what she would have called weird. It made a change in him that didn't go with the rest—as if he had broken his nose or put on spectacles, lost his handsome hair or sacrificed his splendid mustache: her conception, her necessity, as she saw, had been that something should be added to him for her use, but nothing for his own alteration.

He had affirmed himself, and his character, and his temper, and his health, and his appetite, and his ignorance, and his obstinacy, and his whole charming, coarse, heartless personality, during their engagement, by twenty forms of natural emphasis, but never by emphasis of interest. How in fact could you feel interest unless you should know, within you, some dim stir of imagination? There was nothing in the world of which Murray Brush was less capable than of such a dim stir, because you only began to imagine when you felt some approach to a need to understand. He had never felt it; for hadn't he been born, to his personal vision, with that perfect intuition of everything which reduces all the suggested preliminaries of judgment to the impertinence—when it's a question of your entering your house—of a dumpage of bricks at your door? He had had, in short, neither to imagine nor to perceive, because he had, from the first pulse of his intelligence, simply and supremely known: so that, at this hour, face to face with him, it came over her that she had, in their old relation, dispensed with any such convenience of comprehension on his part even to a degree she had not measured at the time. What therefore must he not have seemed to her as a form of life, a form of avidity and activity, blatantly successful in its own conceit, that he could have dazzled her so against the interest of her very faculties and functions? Strangely and richly historic all that backward mystery, and only leaving for her mind the wonder of such a mixture of possession and detachment as they would clearly to-day both know. For each to be so little at last to the other when, during months together, the idea of all abundance, all quantity, had been, for each, drawn from the other and addressed to the other—what was it monstrously like but some fantastic act of getting rid of a person by going to lock yourself up in the sanctum sanctorum of that person's house, amid every evidence of that person's habits and nature? What was going to happen, at any rate, was that Murray would show himself as beautifully and consciously understanding—and it would be prodigious that Europe should have inoculated him with that delicacy. Yes, he wouldn't claim to know now till she had told him— an aid to performance he had surely never before waited for, or been indebted to, from any one; and then, so knowing, he would charmingly endeavor to "meet," to oblige and to gratify. He would find it, her case, ever so worthy of his benevolence, and would be literally inspired to reflect that he must hear about it first.

She let him hear then everything, in spite of feeling herself slip, while she did so, to some doom as yet incalculable; she went on very much as she had done for Mr. Pitman and Mrs. Drack, with the rage of desperation and, as she was afterward to call it to herself, the fascination of the abyss. She didn't know, couldn't have said at the time, why his projected benevolence should have had most so the virtue to scare her: he would patronize her, as an effect of her vividness, if not of her charm, and would do this with all high intention, finding her case, or rather their case, their funny old case, taking on of a sudden such refreshing and edifying life, to the last degree curious and even important; but there were gaps of connection between this and the intensity of the perception here overtaking her that she shouldn't be able to move in any direction without dishing herself. That she couldn't afford it where she had got to—couldn't afford the deplorable vulgarity of having been so many times informally affianced and contracted (putting it only at that, at its being by the new lights and fashions so unpardonably vulgar): he took this from her without turning, as she might have said, a hair; except just to indicate, with his new superiority, that he felt the distinguished appeal and notably the pathos of it. He still took it from her that she hoped nothing, as it were, from any other alibi—the people to drag into court being too many and too scattered; but that, as it was with him, Murray Brush, she had been most vulgar, most everything she had better not have been, so she depended on him for the innocence it was actually vital she should establish. He flushed or frowned or winced no more at that than he did when she once more fairly emptied her satchel and, quite as if they had been Nancy and the Artful Dodger, or some nefarious pair of that sort, talking things over in the manner of Oliver Twist, revealed to him the fondness of her view that, could she but have produced a cleaner slate, she might by this time have pulled it off with Mr. French. Yes, he let her in that way sacrifice her honorable connection with him—all the more honorable for being so completely at an end—to the crudity of her plan for not missing another connection, so much more brilliant than what he offered, and for bringing another man, with whom she so invidiously and unflatteringly compared him, into her greedy life.

There was only a moment during which, by a particular lustrous look she had never had from him before, he just made her wonder which turn he was going to take; she felt, however, as safe as was consistent with her sense of having probably but added to her danger, when he brought out, the next instant: "Don't you seem to take the ground that we were guilty—that you were ever guilty—of something we shouldn't have been? What did we ever do that was secret, or underhand, or any way not to be acknowledged? What did we do but exchange our young vows with the best faith in the world—publicly, rejoicingly, with the full assent of every one connected with us? I mean of course," he said with his grave kind smile, "till we broke off so completely because we found that— practically, financially, on the hard worldly basis—we couldn't work it. What harm, in the sight of God or man, Julia," he asked in his fine rich way, "did we ever do?"

She gave him back his look, turning pale. "Am I talking of that? Am I talking of what we know? I'm talking of what others feel—of what they have to feel; of what it's just enough for them to know not to be able to get over it, once they do really know it. How do they know what didn't pass between us, with all the opportunities we had? That's none of their business—if we were idiots enough, on the top of everything! What you may or mayn't have done doesn't count, for you; but there are people for whom it's loathsome that a girl should have gone on like that from one person to another and still pretend to be—well, all that a nice girl is supposed to be. It's as if we had but just waked up, mother and I, to such a remarkable prejudice; and now we have it—when we could do so well without it!—staring us in the face. That mother should have insanely let me, should so vulgarly have taken it for my natural, my social career—that's the disgusting, humiliating thing: with the lovely account it gives of both of us! But mother's view of a delicacy in things!" she went on with scathing grimness; "mother's measure of anything, with her grand 'gained cases' (there'll be another yet, she finds them so easy!) of which she's so publicly proud! You see I've no margin," said Julia; letting him take it from her flushed face as much as he would that her mother hadn't left her an inch. It was that he should make use of the spade with her for the restoration of a bit of a margin just wide enough to perch on till the tide of peril should have ebbed a little, it was that he should give her that lift—!

Well, it was all there from him after these last words; it was before her that he really took hold. "Oh, my dear child, I can see! Of course there are people—ideas change in our society so fast!—who are not in sympathy with the old American freedom and who read, I dare say, all sorts of uncanny things into it. Naturally you must take them as they are—from the moment," said Murray Brush, who had lighted, by her leave, a cigarette, "your life-path does, for weal or for woe, cross with theirs." He had every now and then such an elegant phrase. "Awfully interesting, certainly, your case. It's enough for me that it is yours—I make it my own. I put myself absolutely in your place; you'll understand from me, without professions, won't you? that I do. Command me in every way! What I do like is the sympathy with which you've inspired him. I don't, I'm sorry to say, happen to know him personally,"—he smoked away, looking off; "but of course one knows all about him generally, and I'm sure he's right for you, I'm sure it would be charming, if you yourself think so. Therefore trust me and even—what shall I say?—leave it to me a little, won't you?" He had been watching, as in his fumes, the fine growth of his possibilities; and with this he turned on her the large warmth of his charity. It was like a subscription of a half-a-million. "I'll take care of you."

She found herself for a moment looking up at him from as far below as the point from which the school-child, with round eyes raised to the wall, gazes at the parti-colored map of the world. Yes, it was a warmth, it was a special benignity, that had never yet dropped on her from any one; and she wouldn't for the first few moments have known how to describe it or even quite what to do with it.

Then, as it still rested, his fine improved expression aiding, the sense of what had happened came over her with a rush. She was being, yes, patronized; and that was really as new to her—the freeborn American girl who might, if she had wished, have got engaged and disengaged not six times but sixty—as it would have been to be crowned or crucified. The Frenches themselves didn't do it—the Frenches themselves didn't dare it. It was as strange as one would: she recognized it when it came, but anything might have come rather—and it was coming by (of all people in the world) Murray Brush! It overwhelmed her; still she could speak, with however faint a quaver and however sick a smile. "You'll lie for me like a gentleman?"

"As far as that goes till I'm black in the face!" And then while he glowed at her and she wondered if he would pointedly look his lies that way, and if, in fine, his florid, gallant, knowing, almost winking intelligence, common as she had never seen the common vivified, would represent his notion of "blackness": "See here, Julia; I'll do more."

"'More'—?"

"Everything. I'll take it right in hand. I'll fling over you—"

"Fling over me—?" she continued to echo as he fascinatingly fixed her.

"Well, the biggest kind of rose-colored mantle!" And this time, oh, he did wink: it would be the way he was going to wink (and in the grandest good faith in the world) when indignantly denying, under inquisition, that there had been "a sign or a scrap" between them. But there was more to come; he decided she should have it all. "Julia, you've got to know now." He hung fire but an instant more. "Julia, I'm going to be married." His "Julias" were somehow death to her; she could feel that even through all the rest. "Julia, I announce my engagement."

"Oh, lordy, lordy!" she wailed: it might have been addressed to Mr. Pitman.

The force of it had brought her to her feet, but he sat there smiling up as at the natural tribute of her interest. "I tell you before any one else; it's not to be 'out' for a day or two yet. But we want you to know; she said that as soon as I mentioned to her that I had heard from you. I mention to her everything, you see!"—and he almost simpered while, still in his seat, he held the end of his cigarette, all delicately and as for a form of gentle emphasis, with the tips of his fine fingers. "You've not met her, Mary Lindeck, I think: she tells me she hasn't the pleasure of knowing you, but she desires it so much—particularly longs for it. She'll take an interest too," he went on; "you must let me immediately bring her to you. She has heard so much about you and she really wants to see you."

"Oh mercy me!" poor Julia gasped again—so strangely did history repeat itself and so did this appear the echo, on Murray Brush's lips, and quite to drollery, of that sympathetic curiosity of Mrs. Drack's which Mr. Pitman had, as they said, voiced. Well, there had played before her the vision of a ledge of safety in face of a rising tide; but this deepened quickly to a sense more forlorn, the cold swish of waters already up to her waist and that would soon be up to her chin. It came really but from the air of her friend, from the perfect benevolence and high unconsciousness with which he kept his posture—as if to show he could patronize her from below upward quite as well as from above down. And as she took it all in, as it spread to a flood, with the great lumps and masses of truth it was floating, she knew inevitable submission, not to say submersion, as she had never known it in her life; going down and down before it, not even putting out her hands to resist or cling by the way, only reading into the young man's very face an immense fatality and, for all his bright nobleness his absence of rancor or of protesting pride, the great gray blankness of her doom. It was as if the earnest Miss Lindeck, tall and mild, high and lean, with eye-glasses and a big nose, but "marked" in a noticeable way, elegant and distinguished and refined, as you could see from a mile off, and as graceful, for common despair of imitation, as the curves of the "copy" set of old by one's writing-master—it was as if this stately well-wisher, whom indeed she had never exchanged a word with, but whom she had recognized and placed and winced at as soon as he spoke of her, figured there beside him now as also in portentous charge of her case.

He had ushered her into it in that way as if his mere right word sufficed; and Julia could see them throne together, beautifully at one in all the interests they now shared, and regard her as an object of almost tender solicitude. It was positively as if they had become engaged for her good—in such a happy light as it shed. That was the way people you had known, known a bit intimately, looked at you as soon as they took on the high matrimonial propriety that sponged over the more or less wild past to which you belonged, and of which, all of a sudden, they were aware only through some suggestion it made them for reminding you definitely that you still had a place. On her having had a day or two before to meet Mrs. Drack and to rise to her expectation she had seen and felt herself act, had above all admired herself, and had at any rate known what she said, even though losing, at her altitude, any distinctness in the others. She could have repeated later on the detail of her performance—if she hadn't preferred to keep it with her as a mere locked-up, a mere unhandled treasure. At present, however, as everything was for her at first deadened and vague, true to the general effect of sounds and motions in water, she couldn't have said afterward what words she spoke, what face she showed, what impression she made—at least till she had pulled herself round to precautions. She only knew she had turned away, and that this movement must have sooner or later determined his rising to join her, his deciding to accept it, gracefully and condoningly—condoningly in respect to her natural emotion, her inevitable little pang—for an intimation that they would be better on their feet.

They trod then afresh their ancient paths; and though it pressed upon her hatefully that he must have taken her abruptness for a smothered shock, the flare-up of her old feeling at the breath of his news, she had still to see herself condemned to allow him this, condemned really to encourage him in the mistake of believing her suspicious of feminine spite and doubtful of Miss Lindeck's zeal. She was so far from doubtful that she was but too appalled at it and at the officious mass in which it loomed, and this instinct of dread, before their walk was over, before she had guided him round to one of the smaller gates, there to slip off again by herself, was positively to find on the bosom of her flood a plank by the aid of which she kept in a manner and for the time afloat. She took ten minutes to pant, to blow gently, to paddle disguisedly, to accommodate herself, in a word, to the elements she had let loose; but as a reward of her effort at least she then saw how her determined vision accounted for everything. Beside her friend on the bench she had truly felt all his cables cut, truly swallowed down the fact that if he still perceived she was pretty—and how pretty!—it had ceased appreciably to matter to him. It had lighted the folly of her preliminary fear, the fear of his even yet to some effect of confusion or other inconvenience for her, proving more alive to the quotable in her, as she had called it, than to the inexpressible. She had reckoned with the awkwardness of that possible failure of his measure of her charm, by which his renewed apprehension of her grosser ornaments, those with which he had most affinity, might too much profit; but she need have concerned herself as little for his sensibility on one head as on the other. She had ceased personally, ceased materially—in respect, as who should say, to any optical or tactile advantage—to exist for him, and the whole office of his manner had been the more piously and gallantly to dress the dead presence with flowers. This was all to his credit and his honor, but what it clearly certified was that their case was at last not even one of spirit reaching out to spirit. He had plenty of spirit—had all the spirit required for his having engaged himself to Miss Lindeck, into which result, once she had got her head well up again, she read, as they proceeded, one sharp meaning after another. It was therefore toward the subtler essence of that mature young woman alone that he was occupied in stretching; what was definite to him about Julia Bride being merely, being entirely—which was indeed thereby quite enough—that she might end by scaling her worldly height. They would push, they would shove, they would "boost," they would arch both their straight backs as pedestals for her tiptoe; and at the same time, by some sweet prodigy of mechanics, she would pull them up and up with her.

Wondrous things hovered before her in the course of this walk; her consciousness had become, by an extraordinary turn, a music-box in which, its lid well down, the most remarkable tunes were sounding. It played for her ear alone, and the lid, as she might have figured, was her firm plan of holding out till she got home, of not betraying—to her companion at least—the extent to which she was demoralized. To see him think her demoralized by mistrust of the sincerity of the service to be meddlesomely rendered her by his future wife—she would have hurled herself publicly into the lake there at their side, would have splashed, in her beautiful clothes, among the frightened swans, rather than invite him to that ineptitude. Oh, her sincerity, Mary Lindeck's—she would be drenched with her sincerity, and she would be drenched, yes, with his; so that, from inward convulsion to convulsion, she had, before they reached their gate, pulled up in the path. There was something her head had been full of these three or four minutes, the intensest little tune of the music-box, and it made its way to her lips now; belonging—for all the good it could do her!—to the two or three sorts of solicitude she might properly express.

"I hope she has a fortune, if you don't mind my speaking of it: I mean some of the money we didn't in our time have—and that we missed, after all, in our poor way and for what we then wanted of it, so quite dreadfully."

She had been able to wreathe it in a grace quite equal to any he himself had employed; and it was to be said for him also that he kept up, on this, the standard. "Oh, she's not, thank goodness, at all badly off, poor dear. We shall do very well. How sweet of you to have thought of it! May I tell her that too?" he splendidly glared. Yes, he glared—how couldn't he, with what his mind was really full of? But, all the same, he came just here, by her vision, nearer than at any other point to being a gentleman. He came quite within an ace of it—with his taking from her thus the prescription of humility of service, his consenting to act in the interest of her avidity, his letting her mount that way, on his bowed shoulders, to the success in which he could suppose she still believed. He couldn't know, he would never know, that she had then and there ceased to believe in it—that she saw as clear as the sun in the sky the exact manner in which, between them, before they had done, the Murray Brushes, all zeal and sincerity, all interest in her interesting case, would dish, would ruin, would utterly destroy her. He wouldn't have needed to go on, for the force and truth of this; but he did go on—he was as crashingly consistent as a motorcar without a brake. He was visibly in love with the idea of what they might do for her and of the rare "social" opportunity that they would, by the same stroke, embrace. How he had been offhand with it, how he had made it parenthetic, that he didn't happen "personally" to know Basil French—as if it would have been at all likely he should know him, even im personally, and as if he could conceal from her the fact that, since she had made him her overture, this gentleman's name supremely baited her hook! Oh, they would help Julia Bride if they could—they would do their remarkable best; but they would at any rate have made his acquaintance over it, and she might indeed leave the rest to their thoroughness. He would already have known, he would already have heard; her appeal, she was more and more sure, wouldn't have come to him as a revelation. He had already talked it over with her, with Miss Lindeck, to whom the Frenches, in their fortress, had never been accessible, and his whole attitude bristled, to Julia's eyes, with the betrayal of her hand, her voice, her pressure, her calculation. His tone, in fact, as he talked, fairly thrust these things into her face. "But you must see her for yourself. You'll judge her. You'll love her. My dear child"—he brought it all out, and if he spoke of children he might, in his candor, have been himself infantine—"my dear child, she's the person to do it for you. Make it over to her; but," he laughed, "of course see her first! Couldn't you," he wound up—for they were now near their gate, where she was to leave him—"couldn't you just simply make us meet him, at tea say, informally; just us alone, as pleasant old friends of whom you'd have so naturally and frankly spoken to him: and then see what we'd make of that?"

It was all in his expression; he couldn't keep it out of that, and his shining good looks couldn't: ah, he was so fatally much too handsome for her! So the gap showed just there, in his admirable mask and his admirable eagerness; the yawning little chasm showed where the gentleman fell short. But she took this in, she took everything in, she felt herself do it, she heard herself say, while they paused before separation, that she quite saw the point of the meeting, as he suggested, at her tea. She would propose it to Mr.

French and would let them know; and he must assuredly bring Miss Lindeck, bring her "right away," bring her soon, bring them, his fiancée and her, together somehow, and as quickly as possible—so that they should be old friends before the tea. She would propose it to Mr. French, propose it to Mr. French: that hummed in her ears as she went—after she had really got away; hummed as if she were repeating it over, giving it out to the passers, to the pavement, to the sky, and all as in wild discord with the intense little concert of her music-box. The extraordinary thing too was that she quite believed she should do it, and fully meant to; desperately, fantastically passive—since she almost reeled with it as she proceeded—she was capable of proposing anything to any one: capable too of thinking it likely Mr. French would come, for he had never on her previous proposals declined anything. Yes, she would keep it up to the end, this pretence of owing them salvation, and might even live to take comfort in having done for them what they wanted. What they wanted couldn't but be to get at the Frenches, and what Miss Lindeck above all wanted, baffled of it otherwise, with so many others of the baffled, was to get at Mr. French—for all Mr. French would want of either of them!—still more than Murray did. It was not till after she had got home, got straight into her own room and flung herself on her face, that she yielded to the full taste of the bitterness of missing a connection, missing the man himself, with power to create such a social appetite, such a grab at what might be gained by them. He could make people, even people like these two and whom there were still other people to envy, he could make them push and snatch and scramble like that—and then remain as incapable of taking her from the hands of such patrons as of receiving her straight, say, from those of Mrs. Drack. It was a high note, too, of Julia's wonderful composition that, even in the long, lonely moan of her conviction of her now certain ruin, all this grim lucidity, the perfect clearance of passion, but made her supremely proud of him.

A LODGING FOR THE NIGHT

Robert Louis Stevenson (1850-1894)

It was late in November 1456. The snow fell over Paris with rigorous, relentless persistence; sometimes the wind made a sally and scattered it in flying vortices; sometimes there was a lull, and flake after flake descended out of the black night air, silent, circuitous, interminable. To poor people, looking up under moist eyebrows, it seemed a wonder where it all came from. Master Francis Villon had propounded an alternative that afternoon, at a tavern window: was it only Pagan Jupiter plucking geese upon Olympus, or were the holy angels moulting? He was only a poor Master of Arts, he went on; and as the question somewhat touched upon divinity, he durst not venture to conclude. A silly old priest from Montargis, who was among the company, treated the young rascal to a bottle of wine in honor of the jest and the grimaces with which it was accompanied, and swore on his own white beard that he had been just such another irreverent dog when he was Villon's age.

The air was raw and pointed, but not far below freezing; and the flakes were large, damp, and adhesive. The whole city was sheeted up. An army might have marched from end to end and not a footfall given the alarm. If there were any belated birds in heaven, they saw the island like a large white patch, and the bridges like slim white spars, on the black ground of the river. High up overhead the snow settled among the tracery of the cathedral towers. Many a niche was drifted full; many a statue wore a long white bonnet on its grotesque or sainted head. The gargoyles had been transformed into great false noses, drooping toward the point. The crockets were like upright pillows swollen on one side. In the intervals of the wind there was a dull sound of dripping about the precincts of the church.

The cemetery of St. John had taken its own share of the snow. All the graves were decently covered; tall, white housetops stood around in grave array; worthy burghers were long ago in bed, benightcapped like their domiciles; there was no light in all the neighborhood but a little peep from a lamp that hung swinging in the church choir, and tossed the shadows to and fro in time to its oscillations. The clock was hard on ten when the patrol went by with halberds and a lantern, beating their hands; and they saw nothing suspicious about the cemetery of St. John.

Yet there was a small house, backed up against the cemetery wall, which was still awake, and awake to evil purpose, in that snoring district. There was not much to betray it from without; only a stream of warm vapor from the chimney-top, a patch where the snow melted on the roof, and a few half-obliterated footprints at the door. But within, behind the shuttered windows, Master Francis Villon, the poet, and some of the thievish crew with whom he consorted, were keeping the night alive and passing round the bottle.

A great pile of living embers diffused a strong and ruddy glow from the arched chimney. Before this straddled Dom Nicolas, the Picardy monk, with his skirts picked up and his fat legs bared to the comfortable warmth. His dilated shadow cut the room in half; and the firelight only escaped on either side of his broad person, and in a little pool between his outspread feet. His face had the beery, bruised appearance of the continual drinker's; it was covered with a network of congested veins, purple in ordinary circumstances, but now pale violet, for even with his back to the fire the cold pinched him on the other side. His cowl had half fallen back, and made a strange excrescence on either side of his bull neck. So he straddled, grumbling, and cut the room in half with the shadow of his portly frame.

On the right, Villon and Guy Tabary were huddled together over a scrap of parchment; Villon making a ballade which he was to call the Ballade of Roast Fish, and Tabary spluttering admiration at his shoulder. The poet was a rag of a man, dark, little, and lean, with hollow cheeks and thin black locks. He carried his four-and-twenty years with feverish animation. Greed had made folds about his eyes, evil smiles had puckered his mouth. The wolf and pig struggled together in his face. It was an eloquent, sharp, ugly, earthly countenance. His hands were small and prehensile, with fingers knotted like a cord; and they were continually flickering in front of him in violent and expressive pantomime. As for Tabary, a broad, complacent, admiring imbecility breathed from his squash nose and slobbering lips: he had become a thief, just as he might have become the most decent of burgesses, by the imperious chance that rules the lives of human geese and human donkeys.

At the monk's other hand, Montigny and Thevenin Pensete played a game of chance. About the first there clung some flavor of good birth and training, as about a fallen angel; something long, lithe, and courtly in the person; something aquiline and darkling in the face. Thevenin, poor soul, was in great feather: he had done a good stroke of knavery that afternoon in the Faubourg St. Jacques, and all night he had been gaining from Montigny. A flat smile illuminated his face; his bald head shone rosily in a garland of red curls; his little protuberant stomach shook with silent chucklings as he swept in his gains.

"Doubles or quits?" said Thevenin.

Montigny nodded grimly.

"Some may prefer to dine in state" wrote Villon, "On bread and cheese on silver plate. Or—or—help me out, Guido!"

Tabary giggled.

"Or parsley on a silver dish" scribbled the poet.

The wind was freshening without; it drove the snow before it, and sometimes raised its voice in a victorious whoop, and made sepulchral grumblings in the chimney. The cold was growing sharper as the night went on. Villon, protruding his lips, imitated the gust with something between a whistle and a groan. It was an eerie, uncomfortable talent of the poet's, much detested by the Picardy monk.

"Can't you hear it rattle in the gibbet?" said Villon. "They are all dancing the devil's jig on nothing, up there. You may dance, my gallants, you'll be none the warmer! Whew, what a gust! Down went somebody just now! A medlar the fewer on the three-legged medlar-tree!—I say, Dom Nicolas, it'll be cold to-night on the St. Denis Road?" he asked.

Dom Nicolas winked both his big eyes, and seemed to choke upon his Adam's apple. Montfaucon, the great grisly Paris gibbet, stood hard by the St. Denis Road, and the pleasantry touched him on the raw. As for Tabary, he laughed immoderately over the medlars; he had never heard anything more light-hearted; and he held his sides and crowed. Villon fetched him a fillip on the nose, which turned his mirth into an attack of coughing.

"Oh, stop that row," said Villon, "and think of rhymes to 'fish.'"

"Doubles or quits," said Montigny doggedly.

"With all my heart," quoth Thevenin.

"Is there any more in that bottle?" asked the monk.

"Open another," said Villon. "How do you ever hope to fill that big hogshead, your body, with little things like bottles? And how do you expect to get to heaven? How many angels, do you fancy, can be spared to carry up a single monk from Picardy? Or do you think yourself another Elias—and they'll send the coach for you?"

"Hominibus impossibile" replied the monk, as he filled his glass.

Tabary was in ecstasies.

Villon filliped his nose again.

"Laugh at my jokes, if you like," he said.

"It was very good," objected Tabary.

Villon made a face at him. "Think of rhymes to 'fish,'" he said.

"What have you to do with Latin? You'll wish you knew none of it at the great assizes, when the devil calls for Guido Tabary, clericus— the devil with the humpback and red-hot finger-nails. Talking of the devil," he added, in a whisper, "look at Montigny!"

All three peered covertly at the gamester. He did not seem to be enjoying his luck. His mouth was a little to a side; one nostril nearly shut, and the other much inflated. The black dog was on his back, as people say, in terrifying nursery metaphor; and he breathed hard under the gruesome burden.

"He looks as if he could knife him," whispered Tabary, with round eyes.

The monk shuddered, and turned his face and spread his open hands to the red embers. It was the cold that thus affected Dom Nicolas, and not any excess of moral sensibility.

"Come now," said Villon—"about this ballade. How does it run so far?" And beating time with his hand, he read it aloud to Tabary.

They were interrupted at the fourth rhyme by a brief and fatal movement among the gamesters. The round was completed, and Thevenin was just opening his mouth to claim another victory, when Montigny leaped up, swift as an adder, and stabbed him to the heart. The blow took effect before he had time to utter a cry, before he had time to move. A tremor or two convulsed his frame; his hands opened and shut, his heels rattled on the floor; then his head rolled backward over one shoulder with the eyes open, and Thevenin Pensete's spirit had returned to Him who made it.

Everyone sprang to his feet; but the business was over in two twos. The four living fellows looked at each other in rather a ghastly fashion; the dead man contemplating a corner of the roof with a singular and ugly leer.

"My God!" said Tabary, and he began to pray in Latin.

Villon broke out into hysterical laughter. He came a step forward and clucked a ridiculous bow at Thevenin, and laughed still louder. Then he sat down suddenly, all of a heap, upon a stool, and continued laughing bitterly as though he would shake himself to pieces.

Montigny recovered his composure first.

"Let's see what he has about him," he remarked; and he picked the dead man's pockets with a practised hand, and divided the money into four equal portions on the table. "There's for you," he said.

The monk received his share with a deep sigh, and a single stealthy glance at the dead Thevenin, who was beginning to sink into himself and topple sideways off the chair.

"We're all in for it," cried Villon, swallowing his mirth. "It's a hanging job for every man jack of us that's here—not to speak of those who aren't." He made a shocking gesture in the air with his raised right hand, and put out his tongue and threw his head on one side, so as to counterfeit the appearance of one who has been hanged. Then he pocketed his share of the spoil, and executed a shuffle with his feet as if to restore the circulation.

Tabary was the last to help himself; he made a dash at the money, and retired to the other end of the apartment.

Montigny stuck Thevenin upright in the chair, and drew out the dagger, which was followed by a jet of blood.

"You fellows had better be moving," he said, as he wiped the blade on his victim's doublet.

"I think we had," returned Villon with a gulp. "Damn his fat head!" he broke out. "It sticks in my throat like phlegm. What right has a man to have red hair when he is dead?" And he fell all of a heap again upon the stool, and fairly covered his face with his hands.

Montigny and Dom Nicolas laughed aloud, even Tabary feebly chiming in.

"Cry baby," said the monk.

"I always said he was a woman," added Montigny with a sneer. "Sit up, can't you?" he went on, giving another shake to the murdered body. "Tread out that fire, Nick." But Nick was better employed; he was quietly taking Villon's purse, as the poet sat, limp and trembling, on the stool where he had been making a ballade not three minutes before. Montigny and Tabary dumbly demanded a share of the booty, which the monk silently promised as he passed the little bag into the bosom of his gown. In many ways an artistic nature unfits a man for practical existence.

No sooner had the theft been accomplished than Villon shook himself, jumped to his feet, and began helping to scatter and extinguish the embers. Meanwhile Montigny opened the door and cautiously peered into the street. The coast was clear; there was no meddlesome patrol in sight. Still it was judged wiser to slip out severally; and as Villon was himself in a hurry to escape from the neighborhood of the dead Thevenin, and the rest were in a still greater hurry to get rid of him before he should discover the loss of his money, he was the first by general consent to issue forth into the street.

The wind had triumphed and swept all the clouds from heaven. Only a few vapors, as thin as moonlight, fleeted rapidly across the stars. It was bitter cold; and by a common optical effect, things seemed almost more definite than in the broadest daylight. The sleeping city was absolutely still: a company of white hoods, a field full of little Alps, below the twinkling stars. Villon cursed his fortune. Would it were still snowing! Now, wherever he went he left an indelible trail behind him on the glittering streets; wherever he went he was still tethered to the house by the cemetery of St. John; wherever he went he must weave, with his own plodding feet, the rope that bound him to the crime and would bind him to the gallows. The leer of the dead man came back to him with a new significance. He snapped his fingers as if to pluck up his own spirits, and choosing a street at random, stepped boldly forward in the snow.

Two things preoccupied him as he went: the aspect of the gallows at Montfaucon in this bright windy phase of the night's existence, for one; and for another, the look of the dead man with his bald head and garland of red curls. Both struck cold upon his heart, and he kept quickening his pace as if he could escape from unpleasant thoughts by mere fleetness of foot. Sometimes he looked back over his shoulder with a sudden nervous jerk; but he was the only moving thing in the white streets, except when the wind swooped round a corner and threw up the snow, which was beginning to freeze, in spouts of glittering dust.

Suddenly he saw, a long way before him, a black clump and a couple of lanterns. The clump was in motion, and the lanterns swung as though carried by men walking. It was a patrol. And though it was merely crossing his line of march, he judged it wiser to get out of eyeshot as speedily as he could. He was not in the humor to be challenged, and he was conscious of making a very conspicuous mark upon the snow. Just on his left hand there stood a great hotel, with some turrets and a large porch before the door; it was half-ruinous, he remembered, and had long stood empty; and so he made three steps of it and jumped inside the shelter of the porch. It was pretty dark inside, after the glimmer of the snowy streets, and he was groping forward with outspread hands, when he stumbled over some substance which offered an indescribable mixture of resistances, hard and soft, firm and loose. His heart gave a leap, and he sprang two steps back and stared dreadfully at the obstacle. Then he gave a little laugh of relief. It was only a woman, and she dead. He knelt beside her to make sure upon this latter point. She was freezing cold, and rigid like a stick. A little ragged finery fluttered in the wind about her hair, and her cheeks had been heavily rouged that same afternoon. Her pockets were quite empty; but in her stocking, underneath the garter, Villon found two of the small coins that went by the name of whites. It was little enough; but it was always something; and the poet was moved with a deep sense of pathos that she should have died before she had spent her money. That seemed to him a dark and pitiable mystery; and he looked from the coins in his hand to the dead woman, and back again to the coins, shaking his head over the riddle of man's life. Henry V. of England, dying at Vincennes just after he had conquered France, and this poor jade cut off by a cold draught in a great man's doorway, before she had time to spend her couple of whites—it seemed a cruel way to carry on the world. Two whites would have taken such a little while to squander; and yet it would have been one more good taste in the mouth, one more smack of the lips, before the devil got the soul, and the body was left to birds and vermin. He would like to use all his tallow before the light was blown out and the lantern broken.

While these thoughts were passing through his mind, he was feeling, half-mechanically, for his purse. Suddenly his heart stopped beating; a feeling of cold scales passed up the back of his legs, and a cold blow seemed to fall upon his scalp. He stood petrified for a moment; then he felt again with one feverish movement; and then his loss burst upon him, and he was covered with perspiration. To spendthrifts money is so living and actual—it is such a thin veil between them and their pleasures! There is only one limit to their fortune—that of time; and a spendthrift with only a few crowns is the Emperor of Rome until they are spent. For such a person to lose his money is to suffer the most shocking reverse, and fall from heaven to hell, from all to nothing, in a breath. And all the more if he has put his head in the halter for it; if he may be hanged to-morrow for that same purse, so dearly earned, so foolishly departed. Villon stood and cursed; he threw the two whites into the street; he shook his fist at heaven; he stamped, and was not horrified to find himself trampling the poor corpse. Then he began rapidly to retrace his steps toward the house beside the cemetery. He had forgotten all fear of the patrol, which was long gone by at any rate, and had no idea but that of his lost purse. It was in vain that he looked right and left upon the snow; nothing was to be seen. He had not dropped it in the streets. Had it fallen in the house? He would have liked dearly to go in and see; but the idea of the grisly occupant unmanned him. And he saw besides, as he drew near, that their efforts to put out the fire had been unsuccessful; on the contrary, it had broken into a blaze, and a changeful light played in the chinks of the door and window, and revived his terror for the authorities and Paris gibbet.

He returned to the hotel with the porch, and groped about upon the snow for the money he had thrown away in his childish passion. But he could only find one white; the other had probably struck sideways and sunk deeply in. With a single white in his pocket, all his projects for a rousing night in some wild tavern vanished utterly away. And it was not only pleasure that fled laughing from his grasp; positive discomfort, positive pain, attacked him as he stood ruefully before the porch. His perspiration had dried upon him; and though the wind had now fallen, a binding frost was setting in stronger with every hour, and he felt benumbed and sick at heart. What was to be done? Late as was the hour, improbable as was success, he would try the house of his adopted father, the chaplain of St. Benoit.

He ran there all the way, and knocked timidly. There was no answer. He knocked again and again, taking heart with every stroke; and at last steps were heard approaching from within. A barred wicket fell open in the iron-studded door, and emitted a gush of yellow light.

"Hold up your face to the wicket," said the chaplain from within.

"It's only me," whimpered Villon.

"Oh, it's only you, is it?" returned the chaplain; and he cursed him with foul unpriestly oaths for disturbing him at such an hour, and bade him be off to hell, where he came from.

"My hands are blue to the wrists," pleaded Villon; "my feet are dead and full of twinges; my nose aches with the sharp air; the cold lies at my heart. I may be dead before morning. Only this once, father, and before God I will never ask again."

"You should have come earlier," said the ecclesiastic, coolly. "Young men require a lesson now and then." He shut the wicket and retired deliberately into the interior of the house.

Villon was beside himself; he beat upon the door with his hands and feet, and shouted hoarsely after the chaplain.

"Wormy old fox," he cried. "If I had my hand under your twist, I would send you flying headlong into the bottomless pit."

A door shut in the interior, faintly audible to the poet down long passages. He passed his hand over his mouth with an oath. And then the humor of the situation struck him, and he laughed and looked lightly up to heaven, where the stars seemed to be winking over his discomfiture.

What was to be done? It looked very like a night in the frosty streets. The idea of the dead woman popped into his imagination, and gave him a hearty fright; what had happened to her in the early night might very well happen to him before morning. And he so young! and with such immense possibilities of disorderly amusement before him! He felt quite pathetic over the notion of his own fate, as if it had been some one else's, and made a little imaginative vignette of the scene in the morning when they should find his body.

He passed all his chances under review, turning the white between his thumb and forefinger. Unfortunately he was on bad terms with some old friends who would once have taken pity on him in such a plight. He had lampooned them in verses, he had beaten and cheated them; and yet now, when he was in so close a pinch, he thought there was at least one who might perhaps relent. It was a chance. It was worth trying at least, and he would go and see.

On the way, two little accidents happened to him which colored his musings in a very different manner. For, first, he fell in with the track of a patrol, and walked in it for some yards, although it lay out of his direction. And this spirited him up; at least he had confused his trail; for he was still possessed with the idea of people tracking him all about Paris over the snow, and collaring him next morning before he was awake. The other matter affected him very differently. He passed a street corner, where, not so long before, a woman and her child had been devoured by wolves. This was just the kind of weather, he reflected, when wolves might take it into their heads to enter Paris again; and a lone man in these deserted streets would run the chance of something worse than a mere scare. He stopped and looked upon the place with unpleasant interest—it was a centre where several lanes intersected each other; and he looked down them all one after another, and held his breath to listen, lest he should detect some galloping black things on the snow or hear the sound of howling between him and the river. He remembered his mother telling him the story and pointing out the spot, while he was yet a child. His mother! If he only knew where she lived, he might make sure at least of shelter. He determined he would inquire upon the morrow: nay, he would go and see her, too, poor old girl! So thinking, he arrived at his destination—his last hope for the night.

The house was quite dark, like its neighbors, and yet after a few taps, he heard a movement overhead, a door opening, and a cautious voice asking who was there. The poet named himself in a loud whisper, and waited, not without some trepidation, the result. Nor had he to wait long. A window was suddenly opened, and a pailful of slops splashed down upon the doorstep. Villon had not been unprepared for something of the sort, and had put himself as much in shelter as the nature of the porch admitted; but for all that, he was deplorably drenched below the waist. His hose began to freeze almost at once. Death from cold and exposure stared him in the face; he remembered he was of phthisical tendency, and began coughing tentatively. But the gravity of the danger steadied his nerves. He stopped a few hundred yards from the door where he had been so rudely used, and reflected with his finger to his nose. He could only see one way of getting a lodging, and that was to take

it. He had noticed a house not far away which looked as if it might
be easily broken into, and thither he betook himself promptly,
entertaining himself on the way with the idea of a room still hot,
with a table still loaded with the remains of supper, where he might
pass the rest of the black hours, and whence he should issue, on the
morrow, with an armful of valuable plate. He even considered on
what viands and what wines he should prefer; and as he was calling
the roll of his favorite dainties, roast fish presented itself to his mind
with an odd mixture of amusement and horror.

"I shall never finish that ballade," he thought to himself; and
then, with another shudder at the recollection, "Oh, damn his fat
head!" he repeated fervently, and spat upon the snow.

The house in question looked dark at first sight; but as Villon
made a preliminary inspection in search of the handiest point of
attack, a little twinkle of light caught his eye from behind a
curtained window.

"The devil!" he thought. "People awake! Some student or some
saint, confound the crew! Can't they get drunk and lie in bed
snoring like their neighbors! What's the good of curfew, and poor
devils of bell-ringers jumping at a rope's-end in bell-towers? What's
the use of day, if people sit up all night? The gripes to them!" He
grinned as he saw where his logic was leading him. "Every man to
his business, after all," added he, "and if they're awake, by the Lord,
I may come by a supper honestly for this once, and cheat the devil."

He went boldly to the door, and knocked with an assured hand.
On both previous occasions he had knocked timidly and with some
dread of attracting notice; but now, when he had just discarded the
thought of a burglarious entry, knocking at a door seemed a mighty
simple and innocent proceeding. The sound of his blows echoed
through the house with thin, phantasmal reverberations, as though
it were quite empty; but these had scarcely died away before a
measured tread drew near, a couple of bolts were withdrawn, and
one wing was opened broadly, as though no guile or fear of guile
were known to those within. A tall figure of a man, muscular and
spare, but a little bent, confronted Villon. The head was massive in
bulk, but finely sculptured; the nose blunt at the bottom but refining
upward to where it joined a pair of strong and honest eyebrows; the
mouth and eyes surrounded with delicate markings, and the whole
face based upon a thick white beard, boldly and squarely trimmed.
Seen as it was by the light of a flickering hand-lamp, it looked
perhaps nobler than it had a right to do; but it was a fine face,
honorable rather than intelligent, strong, simple, and righteous.

"You knock late, sir," said the old man in resonant, courteous
tones.

Villon cringed, and brought up many servile words of apology; at a crisis of this sort, the beggar was uppermost in him, and the man of genius hid his head with confusion.

"You are cold," repeated the old man, "and hungry? Well, step in." And he ordered him into the house with a noble enough gesture.

"Some great seigneur," thought Villon, as his host, setting down the lamp on the flagged pavement of the entry, shot the bolts once more into their places.

"You will pardon me if I go in front," he said, when this was done; and he preceded the poet up-stairs into a large apartment, warmed with a pan of charcoal and lit by a great lamp hanging from the roof. It was very bare of furniture; only some gold plate on a sideboard; some folios; and a stand of armor between the windows. Some smart tapestry hung upon the walls, representing the crucifixion of our Lord in one piece, and in another a scene of shepherds and shepherdesses by a running stream. Over the chimney was a shield of arms.

"Will you seat yourself," said the old man, "and forgive me if I leave you? I am alone in my house to-night, and if you are to eat I must forage for you myself."

No sooner was his host gone than Villon leaped from the chair on which he just seated himself, and began examining the room, with the stealth and passion of a cat. He weighed the gold flagons in his hand, opened all the folios, and investigated the arms upon the shield, and the stuff with which the seats were lined. He raised the window-curtains, and saw that the windows were set with rich stained glass in figures, so far as he could see, of martial import. Then he stood in the middle of the room, drew a long breath, and retaining it with puffed cheeks, looked round and round him, turning on his heels, as if to impress every feature of the apartment on his memory.

"Seven pieces of plate," he said. "If there had been ten I would have risked it. A fine house, and a fine old master, so help me all the saints."

And just then, hearing the old man's tread returning along the corridor, he stole back to his chair, and began toasting his wet legs before the charcoal pan.

His entertainer had a plate of meat in one hand and a jug of wine in the other. He set down the plate upon the table, motioning Villon to draw in his chair, and going to the sideboard, brought back two goblets, which he filled.

"I drink to your better fortune," he said, gravely touching Villon's cup with his own.

"To our better acquaintance," said the poet, growing bold. A mere man of the people would have been awed by the courtesy of the old seigneur, but Villon was hardened in that matter; he had made mirth for great lords before now, and found them as black rascals as himself. And so he devoted himself to the viands with a ravenous gusto, while the old man, leaning backward, watched him with steady, curious eyes.

"You have blood on your shoulder, my man," he said.

Montigny must have laid his wet right hand upon him as he left the house. He cursed Montigny in his heart.

"It was none of my shedding," he stammered.

"I had not supposed so," returned his host quietly. "A brawl?"

"Well, something of that sort," Villon admitted with a quaver.

"Perhaps a fellow murdered?"

"Oh, no, not murdered," said the poet, more and more confused. "It was all fair play—murdered by accident. I had no hand in it, God strike me dead!" he added fervently.

"One rogue the fewer, I dare say," observed the master of the house.

"You may dare to say that," agreed Villon, infinitely relieved. "As big a rogue as there is between here and Jerusalem. He turned up his toes like a lamb. But it was a nasty thing to look at. I dare say you've seen dead men in your time, my lord?" he added, glancing at the armor.

"Many," said the old man. "I have followed the wars, as you imagine."

Villon laid down his knife and fork, which he had just taken up again.

"Were any of them bald?" he asked.

"Oh, yes, and with hair as white as mine."

"I don't think I would mind the white so much," said Villon. "His was red." And he had a return of his shuddering and tendency to laughter, which he drowned with a great draught of wine. "I'm a little put out when I think of it," he went on. "I knew him—damn him! And the cold gives a man fancies—or the fancies give a man cold, I don't know which."

"Have you any money?" asked the old man.

"I have one white," returned the poet, laughing. "I got it out of a dead jade's stocking in a porch. She was as dead as Caesar, poor wench, and as cold as a church, with bits of ribbon sticking in her hair. This is a hard world in winter for wolves and wenches and poor rogues like me."

"I," said the old man, "am Enguerrand de la Feuillee, seigneur de Brisetout, bailly du Patatrac. Who and what may you be?"

Villon rose and made a suitable reverence. "I am called Francis Villon," he said, "a poor Master of Arts of this university. I know some Latin, and a deal of vice. I can make chansons, ballades, lais, virelais, and roundels, and I am very fond of wine. I was born in a garret, and I shall not improbably die upon the gallows. I may add, my lord, that from this night forward I am your lordship's very obsequious servant to command."

"No servant of mine," said the knight; "my guest for this evening, and no more."

"A very grateful guest," said Villon, politely; and he drank in dumb show to his entertainer.

"You are shrewd," began the old man, tapping his forehead, "very shrewd; you have learning; you are a clerk; and yet you take a small piece of money off a dead woman in the street. Is it not a kind of theft?"

"It is a kind of theft much practised in the wars, my lord."

"The wars are the field of honor," returned the old man proudly. "There a man plays his life upon the cast; he fights in the name of his lord the king, his Lord God, and all their lordships the holy saints and angels."

"Put it," said Villon, "that I were really a thief, should I not play my life also, and against heavier odds?"

"For gain, and not for honor."

"Gain?" repeated Villon with a shrug. "Gain! The poor fellow wants supper, and takes it. So does the soldier in a campaign. Why, what are all these requisitions we hear so much about? If they are not gain to those who take them, they are loss enough to the others. The men-at-arms drink by a good fire, while the burgher bites his nails to buy them wine and wood. I have seen a good many ploughmen swinging on trees about the country; ay, I have seen thirty on one elm, and a very poor figure they made; and when I asked some one how all these came to be hanged, I was told it was because they could not scrape together enough crowns to satisfy the men-at-arms."

"These things are a necessity of war, which the low-born must endure with constancy. It is true that some captains drive overhard; there are spirits in every rank not easily moved by pity; and, indeed, many follow arms who are no better than brigands."

"You see," said the poet, "you cannot separate the soldier from the brigand; and what is a thief but an isolated brigand with circumspect manners? I steal a couple of mutton chops, without so much as disturbing the farmer's sheep; the farmer grumbles a bit, but sups none the less wholesomely on what remains. You come up blowing gloriously on a trumpet, take away the whole sheep, and beat the farmer pitifully into the bargain. I have no trumpet; I am only Tom, Dick, or Harry; I am a rogue and a dog, and hanging's too good for me—with all my heart—but just you ask the farmer which of us he prefers, just find out which of us he lies awake to curse on cold nights."

"Look at us two," said his lordship. "I am old, strong, and honored. If I were turned from my house to-morrow, hundreds would be proud to shelter me. Poor people would go out and pass the night in the streets with their children, if I merely hinted that I wished to be alone. And I find you up, wandering homeless, and picking farthings off dead women by the wayside! I fear no man and nothing; I have seen you tremble and lose countenance at a word. I wait God's summons contentedly in my own house, or, if it please the king to call me out again, upon the field of battle. You look for the gallows; a rough, swift death, without hope or honor. Is there no difference between these two?"

"As far as to the moon," Villon acquiesced. "But if I had been born lord of Brisetout, and you had been the poor scholar Francis, would the difference have been any the less? Should not I have been warming my knees at this charcoal pan, and would not you have been groping for farthings in the snow? Should not I have been the soldier, and you the thief?"

"A thief!" cried the old man. "I a thief! If you understood your words, you would repent them."

Villon turned out his hands with a gesture of inimitable impudence. "If your lordship had done me the honor to follow my argument!" he said.

"I do you too much honor in submitting to your presence," said the knight. "Learn to curb your tongue when you speak with old and honorable men, or some one hastier than I may reprove you in a sharper fashion." And he rose and paced the lower end of the apartment, struggling with anger and antipathy. Villon surreptitiously refilled his cup, and settled himself more comfortably in the chair, crossing his knees and leaning his head upon one hand and the elbow against the back of the chair. He was now replete and warm; and he was in nowise frightened for his host, having gauged him as justly as was possible between two such different characters. The night was far spent, and in a very comfortable fashion after all; and he felt morally certain of a safe departure on the morrow.

"Tell me one thing," said the old man, pausing in his walk. "Are you really a thief?"

"I claim the sacred rights of hospitality," returned the poet. "My lord, I am."

"You are very young," the knight continued.

"I should never have been so old," replied Villon; showing his fingers, "if I had not helped myself with these ten talents. They have been my nursing mothers and my nursing fathers."

"You may still repent and change."

"I repent daily," said the poet. "There are few people more given to repentance than poor Francis. As for change, let somebody change my circumstances. A man must continue to eat, if it were only that he may continue to repent."

"The change must begin in the heart," returned the old man solemnly.

"My dear lord," answered Villon, "do you really fancy that I steal for pleasure? I hate stealing, like any other piece of work or danger. My teeth chatter when I see a gallows. But I must eat, I must drink, I must mix in society of some sort. What the devil! Man is not a solitary animal—Cui Deus foeminam tradit. Make me king's pantler—make me abbot of St. Denis; make me bailly of the Patatrac; and then I shall be changed indeed. But as long as you leave me the poor scholar Francis Villon, without a farthing, why, of course, I remain the same."

"The grace of God is all-powerful."

"I should be a heretic to question it," said Francis. "It has made you lord of Brisetout, and bailly of the Patatrac; it has given me nothing but the quick wits under my hat and these ten toes upon my hands. May I help myself to wine? I thank you respectfully. By God's grace, you have a very superior vintage."

The lord of Brisetout walked to and fro with his hands behind his back. Perhaps he was not yet quite settled in his mind about the parallel between thieves and soldiers; perhaps Villon had interested him by some cross-thread of sympathy; perhaps his wits were simply muddled by so much unfamiliar reasoning; but whatever the cause, he somehow yearned to convert the young man to a better way of thinking, and could not make up his mind to drive him forth again into the street.

"There is something more than I can understand in this," he said, at length. "Your mouth is full of subtleties, and the devil has led you very far astray; but the devil is only a very weak spirit before God's truth, and all his subtleties vanish at a word of true honor, like darkness at morning. Listen to me once more. I learned long ago that a gentleman should live chivalrously and lovingly to God, and the king, and his lady; and though I have seen many strange things done, I have still striven to command my ways upon that rule. It is not only written in all noble histories, but in every man's heart, if he will take care to read. You speak of food and wine, and I know very well that hunger is a difficult trial to endure; but you do not speak of other wants; you say nothing of honor, of faith to God and other men, of courtesy, of love without reproach. It may be that I am not very wise—and yet I think I am—but you seem to me like one who has lost his way and made a great error in life. You are attending to the little wants, and you have totally forgotten the great and only real ones, like a man who should be doctoring a toothache on the Judgment Day. For such things as honor and love and faith are not only nobler than food and drink, but, indeed, I think that we desire them more, and suffer more sharply for their absence. I speak to you as I think you will most easily understand me. Are you not, while careful to fill your belly, disregarding another appetite in your heart, which spoils the pleasure of your life and keeps you continually wretched?"

Villon was sensibly nettled under all this sermonizing. "You think I have no sense of honor!" he cried. "I'm poor enough, God knows! It's hard to see rich people with their gloves, and you blowing your hands. An empty belly is a bitter thing, although you speak so lightly of it. If you had had as many as I, perhaps you would change your tune. Anyway, I'm a thief—make the most of that—but I'm not a devil from hell, God strike me dead. I would have you to know I've an honor of my own, as good as yours, though I don't prate about it all day long, as if it were a God's miracle to have any. It seems quite natural to me; I keep it in its box till it's wanted. Why now, look you here, how long have I been in this room with you? Did you not tell me you were alone in the house? Look at your gold plate! You're strong, if you like, but you're old and unarmed, and I have my knife. What did I want but a jerk of the elbow, and here would have been you with the cold steel in your bowels, and there would have been me, linking in the streets, with an armful of gold cups! Did you suppose I hadn't wit enough to see that? And I scorned the action. There are your damned goblets, as safe as in a church; there are you, with your heart ticking as good as new; and here am I, ready to go out again as poor as I came in, with my one white that you threw in my teeth! And you think I have no sense of honor—God strike me dead!"

The old man stretched out his right arm. "I will tell you what you are," he said. "You are a rogue, my man, an impudent and a black-hearted rogue and vagabond. I have passed an hour with you. Oh! believe me, I feel myself disgraced! And you have eaten and drank at my table. But now I am sick at your presence; the day has come, and the night-bird should be off to his roost. Will you go before, or after?"

"Which you please," returned the poet, rising. "I believe you to be strictly honorable." He thoughtfully emptied his cup. "I wish I could add you were intelligent," he went on, knocking on his head with his knuckles. "Age, age! the brains stiff and rheumatic."

The old man preceded him from a point of self-respect; Villon followed, whistling, with his thumbs in his girdle.

"God pity you," said the lord of Brisetout at the door.

"Good-bye, papa," returned Villon, with a yawn. "Many thanks for the cold mutton."

The door closed behind him. The dawn was breaking over the white roofs. A chill, uncomfortable morning ushered in the day. Villon stood and heartily stretched himself in the middle of the road.

"A very dull old gentleman," he thought. "I wonder what his goblets may be worth."